Microsoft® Excel 5 Projects for Windows™

Gary R. Brent
Scottsdale Community College

William J. Belisle

The Benjamin/Cummings Publishing Company, Inc.
Redwood City, California • Menlo Park, California
Reading, Massachusetts • New York • Don Mills, Ontario
Wokingham, U.K. • Amsterdam • Bonn • Sydney
Singapore • Tokyo • Madrid • San Juan

ISBN 0-8053-0804-0

Contents

PROJECT 3: MODIFYING AND ENHANCING A WORKSHEET   EX-60

PROJECT 4: USING FORMULAS IN A WORKSHEET   EX-92

Study Questions EX-205
Multiple Choice EX-205
Short Answer EX-206
For Discussion EX-206
Review Exercises EX-207
Personal Budget EX-207
Computing a Report of Accounts Past Due EX-207
Assignments EX-208
Creating a Spreadsheet of Birthdays and Ages EX-208
Computing Commercial Lease Payments EX-208
Balancing Your Own Checkbook EX-209

PROJECT 7: USING DATABASES AND MACROS EX-210

Objectives EX-210
Case Study: Automating a Checkbook Register EX-210
Recognizing Databases EX-210
Designing the Solution EX-211
Transforming the Check Register into a Database EX-212
Using the Clear Command EX-213
Using Tracer Arrows for Rapid Cell Movement EX-215
Designating the Database Range EX-215
Preventing the Database from Exceeding a Designated Size EX-216
Working with Data Forms and Filters EX-217
Using Selection Criteria with Data Forms EX-219
Using Complex Criteria EX-220
Using Data Filters EX-221
Sorting a Database EX-226
Using Command Macros EX-229
Examining a Recorded Macro EX-232
Running a Macro EX-233
Creating Other Sporting Macros EX-234
Creating Customized Buttons EX-236
The Next Step EX-240
Summary and Exercises EX-240
Summary EX-240
Key Terms and Operations EX-241
Multiple Choice EX-241
Short Answer EX-242
For Discussion EX-242
Review Exercises EX-243
Building a Macro to Sort by the Match Field EX-243
Building a Macro to Activate the Data Form EX-243
Assignments EX-243
Building Macros for Commonly Typed Text EX-243
Constructing a Movie Database EX-243
Constructing a Home Inventory EX-243

OPERATIONS REFERENCE EX-244

GLOSSARY EX-247

INDEX EX-249

Overview

Objectives

After completing this overview, you should be able to:

▶ Start Microsoft Excel

▶ Navigate workbooks and worksheets

▶ Identify common pointer shapes

▶ Change the active cell

▶ Select cells and ranges

▶ Manipulate toolbars

▶ Access Help

▶ Exit Excel

Among the many far-reaching developments of the Renaissance was the widespread application, in fourteenth-century Tuscany, of double-entry bookkeeping. Prior to this, the accounts of bankers and merchants were kept in a haphazard, loosely organized manner. The Tuscan innovation, made possible by the importation of Arabic and Hindu numbers, was to organize accounts into tables with rows and columns, thus making them much easier to maintain.

Now double-entry bookkeeping probably doesn't rank very highly on your list of exciting things, but it contributed to the advent of the commercial and industrial revolution that utterly transformed the Western world.

Until about 1980, most people who created tables of numbers and text worked in much the same way as the Tuscans. Electronic calculators made the job easier, but the use of larger computers was difficult and restricted to major projects.

Accounting tables are called *worksheets* or *spreadsheets,* and if you're creating one the traditional way, you will need some green ledger paper or a lab notebook, a pencil, and a calculator. You'll also need a big eraser, because one of the worst problems with manual worksheets is revision: if one number must change, then it will probably affect dozens of other numbers. The burden of recalculating parts of a traditional worksheet makes it difficult to experiment—to perform "what if" analysis. If you want to make a chart or graph presenting the information pictorially, you will have to get some help from a graphic artist or do your best with colored pens and a ruler.

The invention of personal computers and electronic spreadsheet programs changed this situation dramatically. An electronic spreadsheet presents the table, with its rows and columns, on a computer screen. It is much easier to make modifications, because recalculation happens automatically in response to changes.

The first electronic spreadsheet programs made the basic tasks of building and modifying a worksheet much easier. Contemporary programs, such as Microsoft Excel 5 for Windows, vastly extend these capabilities with such features as data analysis, charting, and typographical formatting. Erasers and green eye-visors are optional.

DESIGNING WORKSHEETS

An electronic spreadsheet program is a tool not only for accountants. Anyone who wants to organize information in tables can benefit from one. Financial analysts, biologists, engineers, attorneys, marketing specialists, physical scientists, managers, political analysts, health professionals, and many others routinely use electronic spreadsheets. Apart from being universally useful, spreadsheet programs are also fun, because building a worksheet is like creating your own little machine—a worksheet is dynamic: it does things and responds to changes.

If you heard about a car that required you to hoist out the engine to change the oil, you would probably think the machine was poorly designed and difficult to maintain. Because, like machines, worksheets should be functional, you must pay close attention to design principles when creating them. You will want to design worksheets that are efficient, easy to use, easy to change, and easy to understand.

The projects in this module use examples that highlight many common design issues. When you finish the module, you will be able to apply your knowledge of Excel commands and worksheet-design techniques to your own area of expertise.

A NOTE TO THE STUDENT

As in other programs, there is often more than one way to perform a particular command or action in Excel. Many commands can be accessed from a regular menu bar, a toolbar button, a shortcut mouse menu, and a keystroke shortcut. Though most mouse actions have keyboard equivalents, in general Excel works best with a mouse. Some powerful features of the program, such as toolbars, are accessible *only* with a mouse. This module presumes that you will be using a mouse with Excel.

If you want to review how to use the mouse, windows, menus, and dialog boxes, refer to the Introduction to Windows.

STARTING EXCEL

The standard name of the group window containing the Excel program icon is Microsoft Office, but on your system the group could have a different name, such as WinApps or Excel 5.

 To start Excel:

1 Open the group window containing the Microsoft Excel icon. Figure 0.1 shows an example of what you will see.

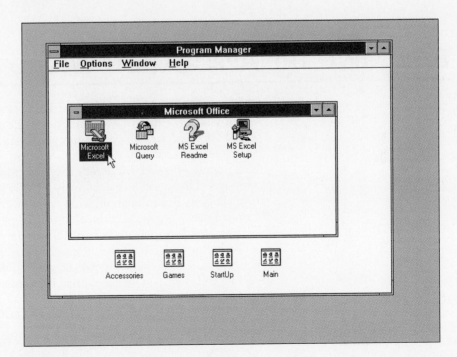

Figure 0.1

2 Double-click the Microsoft Excel icon.
The screen should now resemble Figure 0.2.

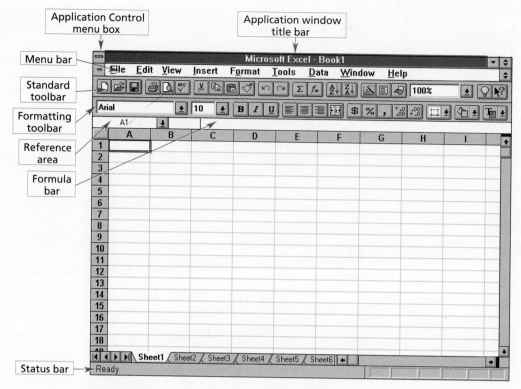

Figure 0.2

EXPLORING THE APPLICATION WINDOW

The two main types of windows in Excel are the *application window*, which you can think of as representing the Excel program itself, and *workbook windows*, which are composed of *sheets* that contain things you create using Excel. The application window, whose title bar when you start Excel reads *Microsoft Excel–Book1*, is a window that frames workbook windows. The workbook window is initially maximized within the application window. Both the application window and the workbook window have Control menu boxes, Minimize buttons, Restore buttons, and Maximize buttons, so it's important not to confuse the two types of windows.

To better understand the difference between these two kinds of windows, you will now reduce the size of the workbook window so its borders are visible, and then you will minimize it to an icon.

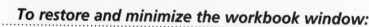

To restore and minimize the workbook window:

1 Click the workbook window's Restore button.
The screen should now resemble Figure 0.3. The workbook window is reduced in size so its borders are visible. Notice that the default name for the workbook, *Book1*, appears in its title bar.

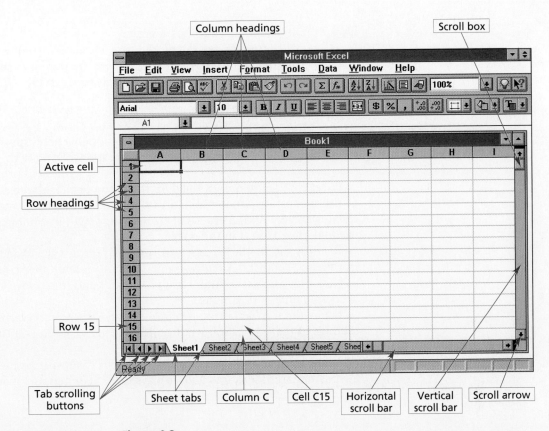

Figure 0.3

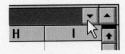

2 Click the *workbook* window's Minimize button.
The screen should now resemble Figure 0.4. The workbook window is reduced to an icon in the lower-left corner of the application window.

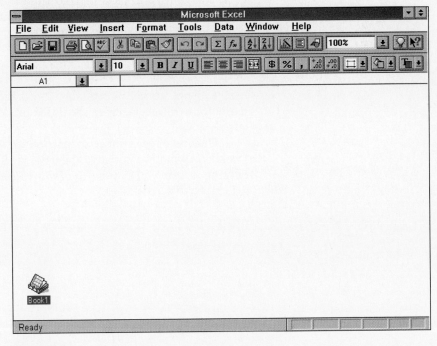

Figure 0.4

3 Double-click the workbook icon.

The screen now resembles Figure 0.3; the workbook window is again visible within the application window. Repeat the minimize-and-restore procedure, if necessary, to clearly distinguish between the application and document windows.

> *Tip* When you have multiple workbooks open, check the title bar of a window to ascertain which document you are working with.

Excel commands are grouped on the *menu bar* displayed across the top of the application window. You can select the options on a menu bar by clicking them with the mouse or by pressing (ALT) in combination with the underlined letter in the option.

Beneath the menu bar are two rows of buttons: the Standard and Formatting toolbars. A *toolbar* contains buttons and other controls that provide quick access to important commands and functions. Toolbars are accessible only with a mouse.

Below the toolbars is the *formula bar* and the *reference area.* These sections of the application window become active when you type or change information in a worksheet.

At the bottom of the application window is the *status bar,* which includes keyboard-status indicators and displays brief help messages when you use Excel commands.

NAVIGATING THE WORKBOOK

A workbook is composed of one or more sheets, each of which can be a worksheet, chart sheet, or module. A worksheet, designed to hold text and numbers and to perform calculations, is the most common type, and is what you will spend most of your time with when using Excel. A *chart sheet* is used to hold an Excel chart. A *module* or macro sheet is a sheet used to hold Excel macros (programs that you create).

Changing among Sheets

A new, blank workbook contains 16 worksheets. You can add any combination of worksheets, chart sheets, or modules to this. You can also delete any sheets.

The name of each sheet appears on its *sheet tab* near the bottom of the workbook window. Initially, Sheet1 is visible. You can view a sheet by clicking its tab; you can use the *tab scrolling buttons,* as shown in Figure 0.5, to see different tabs.

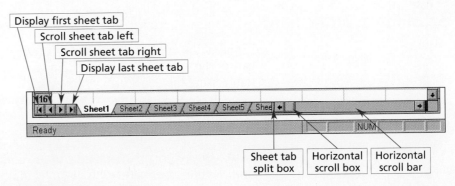

Figure 0.5

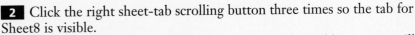

To activate a sheet:

1 Click the tab named Sheet2.
You are now viewing a different worksheet, Sheet2.

2 Click the right sheet-tab scrolling button three times so the tab for Sheet8 is visible.
Note that though the tab for Sheet2 is not currently visible, you are still looking at the Sheet2 worksheet.

3 Click the tab scrolling button to display the last sheet tab.

4 Click the tab for Sheet16.
Sheet16 now appears.

5 Click the tab scrolling button to display the first sheet tab.

6 Click the tab for Sheet1.
The screen should once again resemble Figure 0.3.

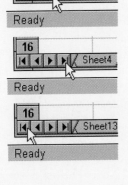

Much of your work in this module will be done with a single worksheet.

Tip

- You can use (CTRL) + (PGDN) to change to the next sheet and (CTRL) + (PGUP) to change to the previous sheet.
- If you hold down (SHFT) and click a sheet-tab scrolling button, you can scroll by several tabs at once.

Navigating within a Worksheet

Each Excel worksheet is composed of *columns* and *rows*. Columns are labeled with the letters of the alphabet, starting with A and continuing through Z, followed by AA, AB, and so forth, to IV for a maximum of 256 columns. Rows are labeled with numbers from 1 to 16,384. The worksheets you will build won't use nearly so large an area; the average worksheet size for this module is about 10 columns by 20 rows.

The basic building block of a worksheet, the intersection of a column and a row, is called a *cell,* and it is identified by its column letter and row number. For example, the *cell reference* C15 refers to the cell at the intersection of column C and row 15.

Scrolling a Worksheet

Think of the workbook window as a frame through which you can see only part of the total worksheet area. To view a different area, you can shift the frame using the scroll bars or arrow keys.

Because Book1 is the only workbook currently in use, you should first maximize its window to make best use of the screen.

> **Tip** Even if you plan primarily to use a mouse, in the steps that follow you should experiment with both the mouse and the keyboard actions.

To scroll the worksheet window:

1 Click the Maximize button in the upper-right corner of the Book1 workbook window.

The screen should appear similar to Figure 0.2.

2 Mouse: Click the down scroll arrow (at the bottom of the vertical scroll bar). Press and hold down the mouse button on a scroll arrow to repeat the scrolling action.

or Keys: Press and hold down ⊘ until the window begins to move. The window will shift down row by row. You can use the other scroll arrows (and the other arrow keys, ⊖ ⊖ ⊕) to move by single columns or rows in other directions. Experiment with the other scroll arrows or arrow keys.

3 Press CTRL + HOME to return to the upper-left corner of the worksheet, cell A1.

4 Mouse: Click in the middle of the vertical scroll bar. Notice that the scroll box moves to the bottom of the scroll bar. You can click in the vertical scroll bar to shift the window in the opposite direction.

or Keys: Press PGDN

If you pressed PGDN, the window shifts down by one window's height to show a different portion of the worksheet. Press PGUP to shift the window farther up; to shift the window farther down, press PGDN. Experiment with PGDN and PGUP.

5 Press CTRL + HOME to return to the upper-left corner of the worksheet, cell A1.

6 Click in the middle of the horizontal scroll bar to move the horizontal scroll box to the right edge of the horizontal scroll bar.

The window shifts right by one window's width to show a different portion of the worksheet. You can also click and drag the scroll boxes.

7 Press CTRL + HOME to return to the upper-left corner of the worksheet, cell A1.

Positioning the Active Cell

The cell appearing with a heavy border around it indicates the ***active cell*** rectangle. The active cell (also called the selected cell, current cell, or cell pointer) is where the action will take place if you type data or perform a command. When you first activate a new, empty worksheet, A1 is the active cell.

To position the active cell:

1 Mouse: Move the pointer to cell E2 and click the mouse button.
   or Keys: Use the arrow keys to move the active cell rectangle to E2. Notice that the cell reference of the active cell is displayed in the reference area.

2 Try scrolling the window (by clicking one of the scroll arrows).

> **Tip**   Notice that scrolling with the mouse does *not* change the active cell, whereas using the arrow keys does.

Changing Pointer Shapes

The shape of the pointer changes depending on where the pointer is positioned on-screen. In the steps that follow, you will carefully move the pointer to the locations described and observe the changes in its appearance. Notice that pointer shapes change in response to specific mouse movements and screen locations. Don't worry about memorizing the meanings of all the different pointer shapes at this time.

To change pointer shapes:

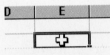

1 Position the pointer in the middle of the active cell or in any other cell.
The pointer appears as a hollow plus sign; this pointer is used to select a new active cell or a group of cells.

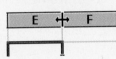

2 Position the pointer on a line separating two column letters.
The pointer appears as a double arrow, which you will use in later projects to change the width of a column.

3 Position the pointer on the line separating any two row headings.
This double arrow is similar to the column-width pointer and is used to change the height of a row.

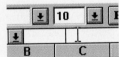

4 Position the pointer in the middle of the formula bar.
The pointer changes to an insertion symbol, called an *I-beam;* you will use this to edit text within the formula bar.

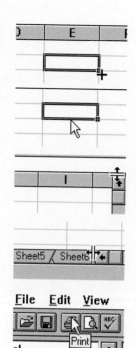

5 Position the pointer so it just touches the lower-right corner of the active cell.

This pointer is called the *fill handle* and is used to copy cell contents.

6 Position the pointer so it just touches any of the edges of the active cell.

The pointer turns into an arrow, which you can use to move the contents of a cell to a new location.

7 Position the pointer on the small black rectangle at the top of the vertical scroll bar.

This area is called the *split bar*, and it is used to split a window into two sections. A horizontal split bar is at the right of the horizontal scroll bar.

8 Position the pointer on the small rectangle just to the left of the left scroll arrow.

You can click and drag this split bar to control the relative width of the scroll bar and sheet-tab scroll areas.

9 Position the pointer on any button within a toolbar, such as the Print button. Do not click.

A small box appears, called a *ToolTip*, which identifies the function of the button that you position the pointer on.

MAKING SELECTIONS

As you use Excel, you will occasionally want to perform an action that affects an entire worksheet, but most of the time you will want to change only a portion of a worksheet. Before using most commands, you first indicate your *selection,* the part of the worksheet you want to change. Most Excel commands operate on a selection. You can select a single cell, a *range* (a rectangular block of cells), or a group of ranges. After you make a selection, you can choose a command to affect that selection.

Selecting a Single Cell

The active cell is the currently selected cell. You can select a single cell by positioning the active-cell rectangle. You can select a cell that is not currently visible by first scrolling the window and then clicking the cell to make a selection. Suppose you want to select cell B5.

To select cell B5:

1 Mouse: Position the pointer on cell B5 and click.
   or Keys: Use the arrow keys to position the active-cell rectangle on cell B5.

2 Scroll until cell J35 is visible and then select it.

Selecting a Range of Cells

A *range* is a *rectangular* block of cells referred to by its upper-left and lower-right diagonal corner cells. For example, the range whose upper-left corner is cell B2 and whose lower-right corner is cell C5 would be referred to as B2:C5. A range can be as small as a single cell or as large as the entire worksheet.

To select a range, you would first select any corner cell and then use the mouse to extend the selection to cover the entire range. Suppose you want to select the range B2:C5.

 ### To select the range B2:C5:

1 Select cell B2 by clicking in it, and ensure that the pointer forms a hollow plus sign positioned inside the active cell.

2 Hold down the mouse button and drag down to row 5 and across to column C to select the range, then release the mouse button. You could also extend the selection to the right first and then down; the order doesn't matter.

The range B2:C5 is selected, as shown in Figure 0.6.

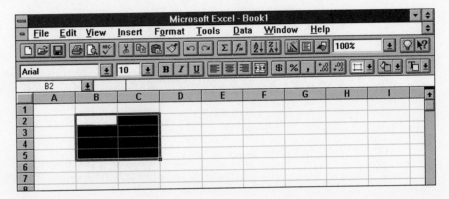

Figure 0.6

Tip   If you need to select a large range and don't want to hold down the mouse button for a long time, select a cell that is any corner of the range, use the scroll bars if necessary to shift the window, position the pointer on the cell that is the diagonally opposite corner, hold down (SHFT), and click.

Practice selecting other ranges. Notice that when you make a new selection, the previous selection markings disappear. You will also notice that there's always one cell in the selection that is not darkened, yet is still within the thick bordered area that defines the selection.

Selecting an Entire Column or Row

A complete column or row is just a large range. Selecting an entire column or row is easy: you click the column or row heading. You must be very careful to click directly on the heading letter or number, and not on a dividing line between headings (the dividing line is used to change column widths).

 ### To select an entire column or row:

1 Click the column heading (letter) G.
This selects all of column G (the range G1:G16384).
The screen should resemble Figure 0.7.

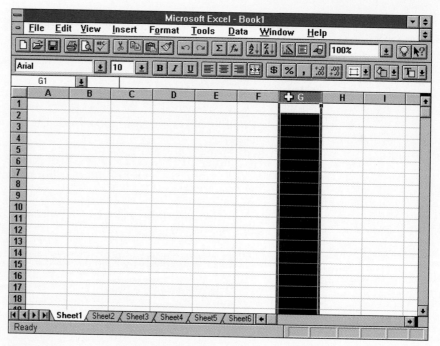

Figure 0.7

2 Click the row heading (number) 7.
This selects all of row 7 (the range A7:IV7). Practice selecting other columns and rows.

Selecting Adjacent Columns or Rows

To select a group of adjacent columns or rows, you first select one column or row and then extend the selection through the other columns or rows.

To select an adjacent group of columns or rows:

1 Select column C.

2 Hold down the mouse button, drag to column F, and then release the mouse button.
This extends the selection across column headings D, E, and F. The selected range is C1:F16384, which can be abbreviated to C:F.

3 Select row 7. (The previous selection of C:F will be canceled.)

4 Extend the selection down through row 10.
Practice with other column-and-row group selections.

Making Nonadjacent Selections

You will sometimes want to affect an area of the worksheet that is not rectangular and that cannot be selected as a single range. Excel allows you to compose a more complicated selection, called a ***nonadjacent selection,*** from a group of ranges.

You have noticed that if you move away from a selection and make another cell active, the previous selection is no longer marked. To make a composite selection out of a group of separate ranges, columns, or rows, you will hold down (CTRL) while making your selections with the mouse.

To make nonadjacent selections:

1 Select the range B3:D8. After making this selection, release the mouse button.

2 Position the mouse pointer on cell G10.

3 Hold down (CTRL) and then hold down the mouse button.

4 Drag the mouse to select the range G10:H15, and then release both the mouse button and (CTRL)

The screen should look similar to Figure 0.8. Using this method, practice making other nonadjacent selections.

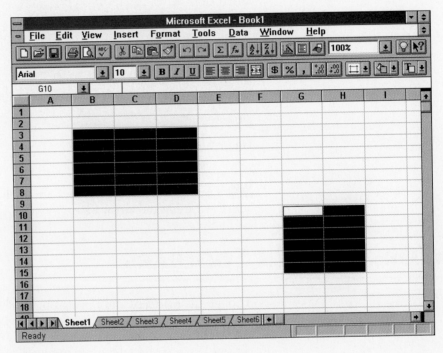

Figure 0.8

Selecting an Entire Sheet

Clicking the button above the heading for row 1 and to the left of the heading for column A selects the entire worksheet.

 To select the entire worksheet:

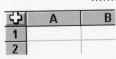

1 Click the Select All button.
The entire worksheet is selected, as shown in Figure 0.9.

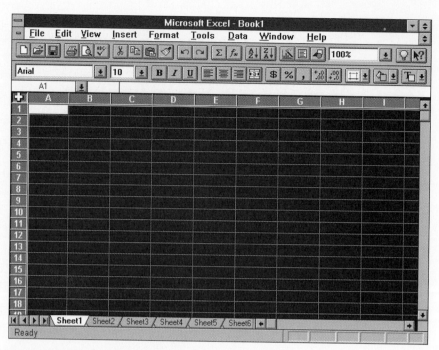

Figure 0.9

2 To cancel the selection, click any individual cell or reposition the active cell using the arrow keys.

WORKING WITH TOOLBARS

Though the Standard and Formatting toolbars appear by default on the screen, 11 other toolbars are available for various kinds of tasks. Any toolbar can be customized to contain tools—buttons and other controls—of your choice. You can also create new toolbars of your own design. More than 200 tools are available for placement in toolbars.

Sometimes a particular toolbar will display automatically, depending on the actions you are performing in Excel. At other times, you may want to hide, display, or rearrange toolbars as you work. You will occasionally want to hide a toolbar just to give yourself more screen space for other information.

Initially, the Standard and Formatting toolbars are ***docked*** (anchored) to the top section of the application window, but any toolbar can be made into a *floating toolbar*—a small window that can be positioned anywhere on-screen. Any toolbar can be docked to the top or bottom of the window, and most can also be docked to the left or right side of the window.

To hide a toolbar:

1 Open the **View** menu, and then choose **Toolbars.**
The Toolbars dialog box appears.

2 Select **Formatting** to clear its check box.
The screen should now resemble Figure 0.10.

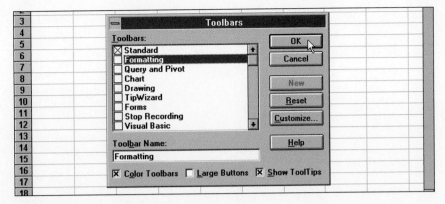

Figure 0.10

3 Select **OK.**
The Formatting toolbar no longer appears, allowing you to see a few more rows of the worksheet.

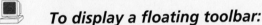

To display a floating toolbar:

1 Open the **View** menu, and then choose **Toolbars.**
The Toolbars dialog box appears.

2 Scroll down the list of toolbars and select **Auditing.**

3 Select **OK,** as shown in Figure 0.11.

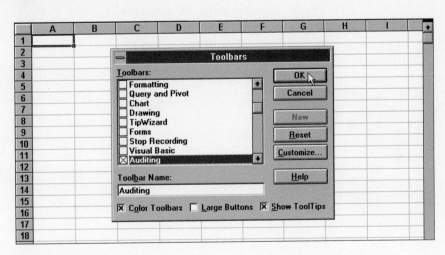

Figure 0.11

The Auditing toolbar appears in a small window of its own, "floating" on the application window. The toolbar can be moved, reproportioned, or docked against an edge.

To dock a floating toolbar:

1 Position the pointer on the Auditing toolbar's title bar.

2 Hold down the mouse button and drag the outline image of the toolbar to the bottom center of the application window, over the status bar, as shown in Figure 0.12.

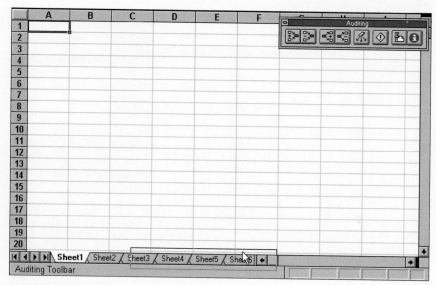

Figure 0.12

3 Release the mouse button.
The Auditing toolbar is now docked to the bottom of the application window.

Every docked toolbar has an outlined background area in which its buttons and controls are placed. If you click and drag this background, you can move the toolbar away from its docked position and make it a floating toolbar. A floating toolbar can be hidden by clicking *once* in its Control menu box.

To undock and hide a docked toolbar:

1 Position the pointer within the background of the docked Auditing toolbar.

2 Click and drag the toolbar to the center of the window.
The Auditing toolbar is once again a floating toolbar.

3 Click once in the Auditing toolbar's Control menu box to hide the toolbar.

4 Open the **View** menu, and then choose **Toolbars,** and display the Formatting toolbar.
The screen should once again appear as it did when you first started Excel.

Tip Clicking the *right* mouse button in a toolbar's background displays a shortcut menu to provide quick access to many of the commands discussed in this section.

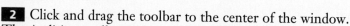

GETTING ON-SCREEN HELP

The Help system in Microsoft Excel conforms to the standard Help conventions of Windows, which may be familiar to you if you have used other Windows applications. Think of the Help system as a vast reference manual stored on disk, with convenient indexes and cross-references to help you find the information you need. You can type a word naming a topic you're interested in, and Excel will search its alphabetical list of topic areas for that word. The first few characters of the word are often sufficient for Excel to do its search. In the steps that follow, you will use the Help menu to get information on dialog boxes.

To access the Help system:

1 Open the **Help** menu, and then choose **Search for Help on.**

2 Type **dia** in the text box to get help on dialog boxes.

A list of topic areas, including the topic of dialog boxes, appears as shown in Figure 0.13. Dialog boxes is also the selected topic area in the list, because it is the first topic on the list.

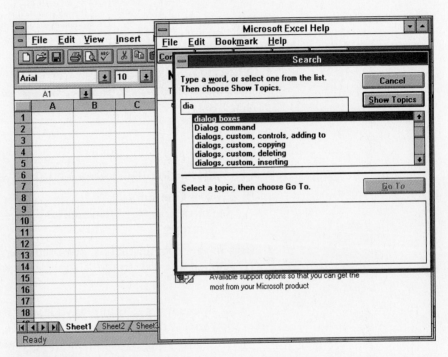

Figure 0.13

3 Select **Show Topics.**

This instructs Excel to show the specific topics concerning dialog boxes for which it can provide help. As shown in Figure 0.14, several topic areas are displayed. The first topic, Choosing dialog box options, is currently selected.

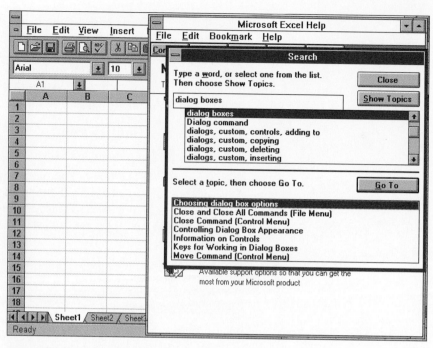

Figure 0.14

4 Select **Go To.**
Help information about choosing dialog box options now appears.

5 Select **Contents.**
A table of contents for Help appears. To read about one of the listed topics, select that topic.

6 In the Help dialog box, open the **File** menu, and then choose **Exit.** (Do not choose Exit from the application window.)

Tip If you want to return to your worksheet but wish to leave the Help window displayed for your reference, then choose Always On Top from the Help menu within the Help window.

Using the Help Tool

The Help tool allows you to get help on a topic by pointing to a particular part of the screen containing that topic or by selecting the topic from a menu. The Help tool is available on the toolbar or by pressing (SHFT) + (F1).

To use the Help tool:

1 Click the **Help** tool.
The pointer should now appear as an arrow with the word *Help.*

2 Open the **Format** menu, and then choose **Auto Format.**
A Help screen about AutoFormat appears. Note that because the Help tool was active, the AutoFormat command was not actually selected.

3 Close the Help window.

> **Tip** Using the mouse, you can also point the Help tool at a part of the screen to get help information. For example, you can activate the Help tool, point to the middle of the formula bar, and click. Help information on the formula bar appears.

Using the TipWizard

The small button depicting a light bulb near the right edge of the Standard toolbar is called the *TipWizard*. This feature monitors your work in Excel and identifies possible shortcuts and alternatives to the actions you perform. When the light bulb turns yellow (or when it displays a question mark on a monochrome screen) it has a tip for you. To see the tip, you would click the TipWizard tool. The text of the tip will appear in the TipWizard box. You can also view previous tips and get additional help on the currently displayed tip. To remove the tip from the screen, you would click the TipWizard tool again.

To use the TipWizard:

1 Click the **TipWizard** tool.
The most recent tip appears in the TipWizard box above the formula bar.

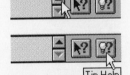

2 Click the Previous Tip button (the upward-pointing arrow near the right of the TipWizard box).
The text of the previous tip appears.

3 Click the **Tip Help** tool (to the right of the TipWizard box).
A Help and How To window opens with additional information on the currently displayed tip.

4 From the Help window's **File** menu, choose **Exit.** Select the **Close** button in the How to window if the window is displayed.

5 Click the **TipWizard** tool.
The TipWizard box disappears.

EXITING EXCEL

You will now exit the Excel program. It is not necessary to save this empty worksheet (although if you happened to have made changes to it, Excel will give you the opportunity to save it before exiting). You can use either of two methods to exit Excel.

To exit Excel:

1 Open the **File** menu, and then choose **Exit.**

2 Because you do not need to save this workbook, select No in the Save Changes dialog box if it appears.

Tip You can also exit Excel by double-clicking the Control menu box in the upper-left corner of the Excel window. Remember that there is also a smaller Control menu box that belongs to the current workbook window. Double-clicking the smaller Control menu box closes only that workbook window, not the Excel program.

Now that you've used the mouse to choose menu commands, the numbered steps will be stated in a more abbreviated form. For example,

1 Open the **File** menu, and then choose **Exit**

will be represented as

2 Choose **File** and then **Exit**.

THE NEXT STEP

Now that you are acquainted with the Excel application and workbook windows, you are ready to enter information into a worksheet and to use commands to affect the information. The next project, Building a Small Worksheet, will illustrate many of the basic aspects of Excel worksheets.

SUMMARY AND EXERCISES

Summary

- Worksheets (spreadsheets) consist of tables of information presented in rows and columns. Beyond its basic ability to perform arithmetic, Excel offers powerful formatting, data analysis, and charting features.
- You can use Excel to build workbooks composed of worksheets, chart sheets, and modules.
- The top portion of the Excel application window contains the menu bar, the Standard toolbar, the Formatting toolbar, and the formula bar.
- An Excel worksheet is composed of columns (labeled A, B, C, . . ., Z, AA, AB, . . ., IV) and rows (labeled 1 through 16384).
- The intersection of a row and a column is called a cell, which is the basic building block of a worksheet. You refer to a cell by its row and column (for example, the cell at the intersection of column C and row 15 is called cell C15).
- The selected cell is where the action takes place in a worksheet. The selected cell appears with a thick outline.
- The pointer can take a variety of shapes, depending on precisely where it is positioned on-screen and on what action it will perform.
- A range is a rectangular block of cells. You can select a range of cells by holding down the mouse button and dragging the pointer through the cells you want to select. You can also select whole columns, rows, and nonadjacent ranges.
- Toolbars contain controls that allow quick access to commands. You can rearrange and customize toolbars.

- A standard Windows Help system is available to explain Excel commands and features. You can search for topics of interest using the Search command from the Help menu.

Key Terms and Operations

Key Terms
active cell
application window
cell
cell reference
chart sheet
column
docked
fill handle
floating toolbar
formula bar
Help tool
I-beam
menu bar
module
nonadjacent selection
range
reference area

row
selection
sheet
sheet tab
split bar
spreadsheet
status bar
tab scrolling buttons
TipWizard
toolbar
ToolTip
workbook window
worksheet

Operations
Exiting Excel
Getting on-screen help

Study Questions

Multiple Choice

1 In Excel, the intersection of a column and a row is called a:
    a. block.
    b. selection.
    c. cell.
    d. range.
    e. formula.

2. How deep (how many rows) is an Excel worksheet?
    a. 100
    b. 500
    c. 1000
    d. 1024
    e. 16,384

3. To position in the upper-left corner of the worksheet (cell A1), press:
    a. CTRL + PGUP
    b. PGUP
    c. HOME
    d. CTRL + HOME
    e. ALT + PGUP

4. A new, blank workbook contains how many worksheets?
    a. 1
    b. 2
    c. 16
    d. 100
    e. 16,384

5. A rectangular block of cells is called a:
    a. data block.
    b. paragraph.
    c. data segment.
    d. code segment.
    e. range.

6. How do you use the mouse to quickly select an entire column in Excel?
   a. click any cell in the column
   b. click the column heading letter
   c. click the top cell and drag to the bottom cell
   d. click the **Column Select** tool on the toolbar
   e. click the top cell of the column and press (F8)

7. What menu command gives you control over the display of toolbars?
   a. choose **View** and then **Toolbars**
   b. ToolTips
   c. choose **Edit** and then **Bars**
   d. choose **Edit** and then **Toolbars**
   e. choose **Tools** and then **View**

Short Answer

1. The intersection of column C and row 5 is referred to as what?

2. The rectangular block of cells whose upper-left corner is B3 and whose lower-right corner is E8 is referred to as what?

3. The location where the "action" takes place in the worksheet is called what?

4. How can nonadjacent selections be made using the mouse in Excel?

For Discussion

1. Who other than accountants might benefit from Excel?

2. How might you use Excel in your own work or area of expertise?

3. What were some of the problems of spreadsheets before spreadsheet computer programs were available? What distinguishes electronic spreadsheets from their manual predecessors?

4. What distinguishes Excel from the first generation of electronic spreadsheets?

Objectives

After completing this project, you should be able to:

▶ Enter text and numeric constants

▶ Change column widths

▶ Build simple formulas

▶ Recalculate a worksheet

▶ Use arithmetic operators

▶ Automatically format a worksheet

▶ Save, close, and open a worksheet

▶ Edit cell entries

▶ Insert and name new worksheets

▶ Open a new workbook

CASE STUDY: CALCULATING NET PAY

In this project you will build a small worksheet that uses each of the three basic kinds of cell entries common to all Excel worksheets: text, numbers, and formulas. First, you will enter text to use for titles, numbers that will serve as the basic data manipulated in the worksheet, and a formula that refers to the numbers and computes a result. You will then learn how to format the worksheet to improve its appearance. Finally, you will save the workbook to disk so the workbook can be used later.

Designing the Solution

This first worksheet will calculate a person's net pay by subtracting taxes withheld from gross pay. A rough version of the worksheet follows:

Gross Pay   853
Taxes Withheld   127
                 ———
Net Pay   ?

The question mark is a reminder that you will design the Excel worksheet to compute the net pay.

ENTERING CONSTANTS

A cell can contain three basic kinds of data: *text constants, number constants,* and *formulas.* Constants do not change after you type them into a cell. *Number constants* are numbers—mathematical values that can be used in calculations; *text constants* consist of words, comments, titles, and other nonmathematical information.

Formulas compute a result, usually by performing arithmetic on information obtained from other cells. The *value* (result) of a formula can change if any of the cells the formula refers to change. Formulas do the work of a worksheet, and well-designed formulas are the key to building a worksheet that is flexible and powerful.

You will start by entering the text constants of this worksheet. Text constants are usually words that label the different parts of a worksheet to make it easier to understand.

To enter text constants:

1 Start Excel.

2 Select cell A1.

3 Type **Gross Pay**

The screen should appear similar to Figure 1.1. Notice that the text appears in the formula bar as well as in the cell.

| Cancel box | Enter box | Function Wizard |

	A	B	C	D	E	F	G	H	I	
1	Gross Pay									
2										
3										
4										
5										

Figure 1.1

> **Tip** To cancel an entry while you are typing it, you can select the Cancel box or press (ESC).

4 Select the Enter box or press (ENTER) or any arrow key to finish entering the text into cell A1.

> **Tip** From now on, when you see a step that tells you to enter something in a cell, it means to type the information and then click the Enter box or press (ENTER).

5 Select cell A2 if necessary, and enter `Taxes Withheld`

6 Enter `Net Pay` in cell A3.

Changing the Width of a Column

The text *Taxes Withheld* in cell A2 appears to spill over into column B. However, the entire text is stored in cell A2. In this section you will learn to manually adjust the width of a column so it accommodates long entries.

You can adjust the width of a column by first positioning the pointer on the right edge of a column heading and then dragging the mouse, or by using the Column command from the Format menu. If, instead of dragging the mouse, you double-click the mouse button, the width will be automatically set to *best fit* (to accommodate the longest entry in that column).

To change the width of column A:

1 Move the pointer to the right edge of the heading for column A (to the boundary line between the headings for columns A and B). The pointer should change to a double arrow.

2 Hold down the mouse button.
Notice that the current column width is displayed in the reference area.

3 Drag the column width so the column is somewhat wider than the longest text entry (*Taxes Withheld*) as shown in Figure 1.2, and then release the mouse button.

	A	B	C	D	E	F	G	H	I
1	Gross Pay								
2	Taxes Withheld								
3	Net Pay								
4									

Figure 1.2

To set the column width to best fit:

1 Position the pointer on the right edge of the heading for column A (so the pointer becomes a double arrow).

2 Double-click to set the column to best fit.

> **Tip** Sometimes best fit will actually be too narrow, and you will need to manually increase a column's width. A column is too narrow when numeric entries appear as lines of number signs (#).

Entering Numeric Constants

In general, when you type numbers in Excel, you should leave out extra punctuation such as dollar signs and commas. Although Excel will preserve this punctuation in your entry, it is best to assign a consistent appearance to a group of cells by using Excel's extensive formatting commands.

Include a decimal point only if the number has a fractional part. If you type a percent sign after a number, the number will be divided by 100 (and assigned a percent style).

This worksheet contains two numeric constants: gross pay and taxes withheld.

To enter the numeric constants:

1 Select cell B1.

2 Enter the sample gross pay amount, **853** in cell B1.

3 Enter the sample taxes withheld amount, **127** in cell B2.

Notice that Excel aligns a number against the right edge of its cell, and text against the left edge. You will learn later how to adjust the alignment of cell contents.

ENTERING FORMULAS

There are several ways to create a formula in Excel. The simplest and least prone to error is to use *point mode.* In point mode, you use the mouse or arrow keys to point to the various cells that are to be included in the formula, and Excel figures out what the actual cell references are. When you use point mode, you don't have to worry about figuring out cell addresses yourself.

Riddle

Q. How can you tell when people aren't using point mode in Excel?

A. They are trying to figure out cell references by holding a ruler or piece of paper against the computer screen to line up rows and columns.

In the following steps, you will use a formula to calculate net pay. The formula will refer to the gross pay amount and subtract the taxes withheld from that amount. Note that all formulas begin with an equal sign, and you will not press (ENTER) until the entire formula is complete.

To enter the formula to calculate net pay:

1 Select cell B3, the cell to the right of *Net Pay.*

This cell should contain the formula to calculate net pay.

2 Type =

The screen should be similar to Figure 1.3.

	B3	± X	ƒx	=						
	A	B	C	D	E	F	G	H	I
1	Gross Pay	853							
2	Taxes Withheld	127							
3	Net Pay	=							
4									
5									

Figure 1.3

3 Point to the gross pay amount you entered in cell B1 by either clicking on the cell to select it or using the arrow keys to move up to the cell. The screen should resemble Figure 1.4. Notice that Excel is building the formula for you in the formula bar.

	B1		f_x =B1								
	A	**B**	**C**	**D**	**E**	**F**	**G**	**H**	**I**		
1	Gross Pay	853									
2	Taxes Withheld	127									
3	Net Pay	=B1									
4											
5											

Figure 1.4

4 Type - (a minus sign) as shown in Figure 1.5.
The formula is supposed to subtract taxes withheld from the gross pay amount.

	B3		f_x =B1-								
	A	**B**	**C**	**D**	**E**	**F**	**G**	**H**	**I**		
1	Gross Pay	853									
2	Taxes Withheld	127									
3	Net Pay	=B1-									
4											
5											

Figure 1.5

5 Point to the taxes withheld amount by either selecting cell B2 or using the arrow keys. See Figure 1.6.

	B2		f_x =B1-B2								
	A	**B**	**C**	**D**	**E**	**F**	**G**	**H**	**I**		
1	Gross Pay	853									
2	Taxes Withheld	127									
3	Net Pay	=B1-B2									
4											
5											

Figure 1.6

6 To finish the formula, select the Enter box or press (ENTER) (see Figure 1.7).

	B2		f_x =B1-B2								
	A	**B**	**C**	**D**	**E**	**F**	**G**	**H**	**I**		
1	Gross Pay	853									
2	Taxes Withheld	127									
3	Net Pay	=B1-B2									
4											
5											

Figure 1.7

7 Select cell B3, if necessary, to examine the completed formula.

Notice that Excel has built the formula =B1-B2, as shown in the formula bar of Figure 1.8. Cell B3 contains a formula whose result, currently 726, appears in the worksheet.

B3	↓	=B1-B2							
	A	B	C	D	E	F	G	H	I
1	Gross Pay	853							
2	Taxes Withheld	127							
3	Net Pay	726							
4									
5									

Figure 1.8

Reminders Here are some reminders about building formulas using the point method:

- All formulas start with an equal sign.
- You will use the mouse or arrow keys to select the cells that the formula refers to.
- You will press (ENTER) (or select the Enter box on the formula bar) only once, when you have completed the entire formula.

Recalculating a Worksheet

The foremost advantage of an electronic spreadsheet is that its formulas can *recalculate* and show new results if there are changes in the cells to which the formulas refer. For example, suppose that the taxes withheld changed to 179.

To change and recalculate the worksheet:

1 Select cell B2, where you entered 127 as the taxes withheld.

2 Change the taxes withheld to 179 by typing **179** and pressing (ENTER) or clicking the Enter box.

As shown in Figure 1.9, the new entry replaces the previous one, and the result of the net pay formula adjusts automatically to 674.

B2	↓	179							
	A	B	C	D	E	F	G	H	I
1	Gross Pay	853							
2	Taxes Withheld	179							
3	Net Pay	674							
4									
5									

Figure 1.9

Experiment with other changes to gross pay and taxes withheld.

Arithmetic Operators

The formula you just created uses the subtraction operator. Excel has several major operators, which are listed in Table 1.1 in *priority* order. The priorities of the various operators in a formula determine the order in which Excel performs the operations. Higher priority operations are performed first. For example, because multiplication and division are operations of higher priority than addition and subtraction, =8-3*2 is calculated with implied parentheses: =8-(3*2), which results in 2, not 10. You can use parentheses to override the standard priorities: =(8-3)*2 is 10.

Table 1.1

Priority	Symbol	Operator	Function	Example Formula	Example Result
1	%	Percent	Divides a number by 100	=5%	0.05
2	^	Exponentiation	Raises a number to a power	=3^2	9
3	*	Multiplication	Multiplies two numbers	=4*2	8
	/	Division	Divides one number by another	=12/3	4
4	+	Addition	Adds two numbers	=3+2	5
	-	Subtraction	Subtracts one number from another	=7-4	3
5	&	Text joining	Connects two text strings	=''Uh''&''Oh''	UhOh
6	=	Equal to	TRUE if a=b, FALSE otherwise	=5=3	FALSE
	<	Less than	TRUE if a<b, FALSE otherwise	=6<7	TRUE
	>	Greater than	TRUE if a>b, FALSE otherwise	=2>3	FALSE
	<=	Less than or equal to	TRUE if a<=b, FALSE otherwise	=17<=17	TRUE
	>=	Greater than or equal to	TRUE if a>=b, FALSE otherwise	=16>=17	FALSE
	<>	Not equal to	TRUE if a<>b, FALSE otherwise	=6<>7	TRUE

Tip When you need to type /, *, −, or +, use the keys on the numeric keypad at the right of the keyboard. This is often quicker than searching the main keyboard for the appropriate symbol.

FORMATTING CELLS

The *format* of a cell indicates how the information in the cell should appear on-screen or in a printout. The many attributes of a cell format include number punctuation (such as dollar signs and commas), alignment, borders, and font.

In the following steps, you will use the *AutoFormat* command to have Excel automatically assign formats to the cells in your worksheet. You will learn more about cell formats in later projects.

To format the worksheet automatically:

1 Select the range A1:B3 by selecting cell A1, holding down the left mouse button, dragging to cell B3, and then releasing the mouse button.

2 Choose **Format** and then **AutoFormat**.
The AutoFormat dialog box appears.

3 Examine samples of the AutoFormat table formats available. To see a sample, click on a table format name in the list box.

4 Select **Accounting 1** from the list, and then select **OK** as shown in Figure 1.10.

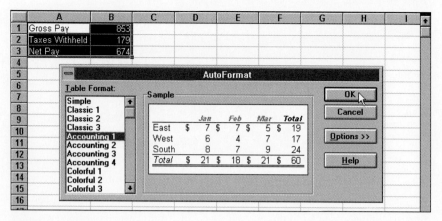

Figure 1.10

The screen should now resemble Figure 1.11.

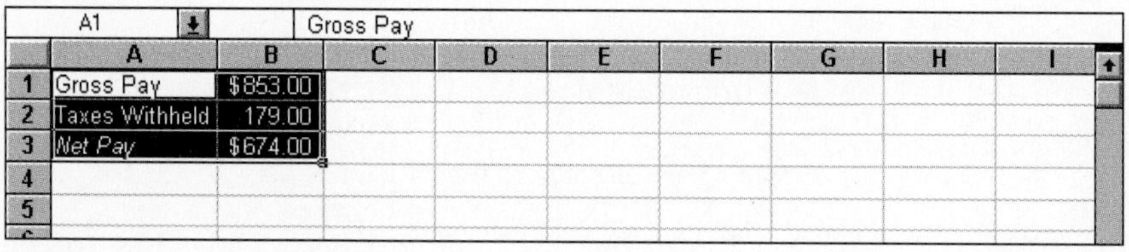

Figure 1.11

5 Click anywhere outside A1:B3 to cancel the selection.

When you use AutoFormat, Excel takes a few seconds to assign customized formats to the worksheet. Notice some of the appearance attributes affected by the AutoFormat command:

- The text *Net Pay* is italic.
- The gross pay and net pay amounts (that is, the first and last rows of numeric values in the worksheet) appear with leading dollar signs.
- All numeric values in the worksheet appear with two digits to the right of the decimal point.
- The two cells comprising the last row of the worksheet have thin top border lines and double bottom border lines.

SAVING, CLOSING, AND UPDATING WORKBOOKS

The worksheet you have built exists only in the computer's *memory* (RAM). If the computer were to be turned off or the power interrupted at this point, you would lose your work.

> ***Tip*** Save your work often, perhaps every five minutes. A rule of thumb is that it is time to save when (1) it would be troublesome to re-create the work you've done since you last saved, (2) you are about to make a major change or addition to the worksheet, or (3) you are about to use a command whose effects you are not certain of.

Saving a Workbook

You will now save a copy of the workbook to disk.

To save the workbook:

1 Choose **File** and then **Save,** or click the **Save** tool on the Standard toolbar.
Because this is a new file, Excel presents the Save As dialog box, where you can choose the disk drive on which you would like to store the file and type the name you would like to give the file. Excel proposes the name BOOK1.XLS.

2 Use the **Drives** and **Directories** list boxes to choose whatever disk drive and directory you want to save the file to.

3 Double-click in the **File Name** text box.

4 Type **pay1** in the **File Name** text box and then select **OK,** as shown in Figure 1.12.
A Summary Info dialog box appears; you can optionally provide additional descriptive information about the file.

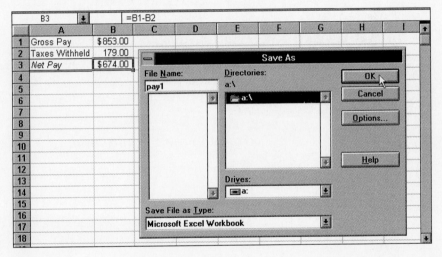

Figure 1.12

5 Type your name in the **Author** section of the Summary Info dialog box and select **OK.**

The Save command does not close the workbook window, so your worksheet remains visible. Notice that the name you just assigned to your file, PAY1.XLS, now appears in the title bar. Excel automatically assigned the file extension .XLS. Because the workbook now has a file name, subsequent uses of the Save command will be quicker; you will not be prompted to type a name.

Tip If you want to save a workbook with a different name than the one that is already assigned to it, use the Save As command from the File menu. With this command, the original file is preserved and a second file, with the new name, is created.

EXIT   If necessary, you can exit Excel now, and continue this project later.

Closing a Workbook

Closing a workbook removes it from the screen.

To close the workbook:

1 Choose **File** and then **Close,** or double-click the *workbook's* Control menu box (which is under the Excel application window's Control menu box).

If you made any changes to the workbook since you last saved it, the Save Changes dialog box will appear, asking whether you want to save the updated version of the worksheet.

2 Click **Yes,** if necessary.

Opening a Workbook

Opening the PAY1 workbook file loads a copy of the workbook from disk into memory, where you can modify the workbook. The original copy of the file remains unchanged on the disk until you save the updated workbook over the original version.

To open a workbook file:

1 Choose **File** and then **Open,** or select the **Open** tool on the Standard toolbar.

The Open dialog box appears.

2 Change the disk drive and the directory, if necessary.

3 Select the file PAY1.XLS from the alphabetical file list.

4 Select **OK.**

Tip If you save your workbooks frequently, you can return to a recently saved version if you "mess up" the workbook currently on-screen. You can use the Close command in the File menu to clear the messed-up workbook from the screen (without saving), and then use the Open command to retrieve the earlier version from disk.

Editing Cell Entries

One way to change the content of a cell is to type a new entry to replace an old one, as you did when you changed the value of the taxes withheld earlier in this project. However, there will be times when you need to change just a piece of a long entry—perhaps you will need to make a small correction to a long title or formula. In such cases, editing the cell entry can save you some typing.

You can edit a cell entry by activating the cell and clicking in the formula bar: this will display an insertion point in the formula bar. You can also double-click directly in the cell: this will allow "in-cell editing" and display the insertion point in the worksheet itself. You can position the insertion point within the text by clicking or by using the arrow keys. Pressing (BKSP) will erase characters to the left of the insertion point; pressing (DEL) will erase characters to the right.

Suppose that the title *Taxes Withheld* needed to be changed to *Tax Withheld*.

To edit a cell entry:

1 Double-click in cell A2, which contains the text *Taxes Withheld*. The insertion point appears in the cell and the Edit indicator appears in the left side of the Status bar.

2 Position the insertion point just after the *s* in *Taxes*.

3 Press (BKSP) twice.
The screen should resemble Figure 1.13.

A2			fx	Tax Withheld								
	A	**B**	**C**	**D**	**E**	**F**	**G**	**H**	**I**		
1	Gross Pay	$853.00									
2	Tax Withheld	179.00									
3	Net Pay	$674.00									
4											
5											

Figure 1.13

4 Select the Enter box or press (ENTER) to enter the revised text.

CREATING NEW WORKSHEETS AND WORKBOOKS

When you first start the program, Excel presents you with a workbook containing 16 blank worksheets. A workbook, regardless of how many worksheets it contains, is stored in a single file on disk. If you "use up" the 16 worksheets initially provided, you can insert new, blank worksheets within the workbook. In general, the worksheets within a given workbook should all be concerned with the same topic or related in some way. If you need to create worksheets for some new task unrelated to an existing workbook, then you should open a new workbook.

Inserting a New Worksheet

If at any time during your Excel session you want to insert a new, blank worksheet in the current workbook, you can choose the Worksheet command from the Insert menu. The new worksheet will be inserted immediately preceding the current sheet and will be automatically activated.

To insert a new worksheet:

1 Choose **Insert** and then **Worksheet**.
A new sheet, named Sheet17, is created and activated.

2 Click the **Sheet1** tab to switch back to the pay worksheet.

Naming Sheets

If you use multiple sheets in a workbook, it will be much easier to identify them if you assign names to appear on the sheet tabs. You can double-click on a sheet tab to rename a sheet.

> **Tip**   Though a sheet name can be up to 31 characters long, you should try to think of a good abbreviated name, because long names in sheet tabs make it harder to see multiple tabs at once on-screen. A sheet name can contain spaces but cannot be enclosed in square brackets or contain the characters \, /, :, ?, or *. Remember that sheet names are *not* workbook (file) names.

To rename a sheet:

1 Double-click on the tab for **Sheet1**.
The Rename Sheet dialog box appears.

2 Type **Payroll** and then select **OK,** as shown in Figure 1.14.

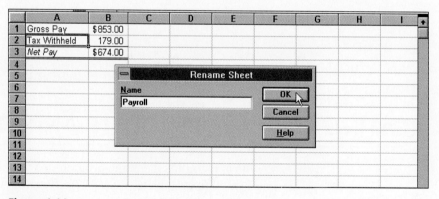

Figure 1.14

The sheet tab now shows the name Payroll.

Rearranging Sheets

By clicking and dragging a sheet tab or group of sheet tabs, you can change the order in which the sheets appear. In the steps below, you will drag Sheet17 so it appears after the Payroll sheet.

To change the order of sheet tabs:

1 Click on the tab for **Sheet17** and hold down the mouse button.
A sheet icon appears, along with a small arrowhead indicating the position at which the selected sheet will be inserted, as shown in Figure 1.15.

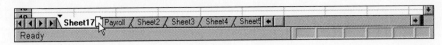

Figure 1.15

2 Drag the sheet icon so the arrowhead appears between the **Payroll** tab and the **Sheet2** tab, as shown in Figure 1.16.

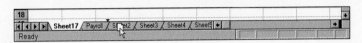

Figure 1.16

3 Release the mouse button.
The Sheet17 tab now appears after the Payroll sheet tab.
4 Close and save the PAY1 workbook.

Opening a New Workbook

To open a new workbook containing blank worksheets, you can choose the New command from the File menu or select the New Workbook tool on the Standard toolbar.

> **Tip** Remember, you can have many different workbooks open at once. If you have finished working with one workbook and want to begin a new one, you can reduce the clutter on the screen by closing the first workbook. If you need to switch between (or simultaneously view) the workbooks, you should keep them both open.

To open a new workbook:

1 Click the **New Workbook** tool on the Standard toolbar.
A new workbook window appears.

EXITING EXCEL

You will now exit the Excel program.

To exit Excel:

1 Choose **File** and then **Exit**.

THE NEXT STEP

Now that you have created basic cell entries common to most worksheets, you are ready to create them in a larger worksheet. In the next project, you will build more sophisticated formulas and learn how to copy and move cell contents. You will see how AutoFormat performs in a more complicated context, and you will begin to take more control over the appearance of the worksheet.

This concludes Project 1. You can either exit Excel, or go on to work the Study Questions, Review Exercises, and Assignments.

SUMMARY AND EXERCISES

Summary

- A cell can contain a text constant, a number constant, or a formula.
- Number constants should be entered without extra punctuation.
- A formula's result is called its value.
- You can change the width of a column in a worksheet.
- Formulas do the work in a worksheet. Formulas are built most easily by using point mode.
- When a formula in one cell depends upon the data in another cell, the formula will automatically recalculate if the contents of the other cell change.
- Arithmetic operators are prioritized, and this determines the order in which operations are performed in a formula.
- Workbooks should be saved frequently.
- The appearance of simple worksheets can be quickly improved by using the AutoFormat command.
- A cell entry can be edited rather than retyped.
- The Open command in the File menu is used to open a workbook that was saved to disk; the New command is used to open a new, blank workbook.
- New worksheets can be inserted into a workbook with the Insert command from the Edit menu.
- Worksheets can be rearranged by dragging sheet tabs.

Key Terms and Operations

Key Terms
AutoFormat
best fit
format
formula
number constant
point mode
priority
recalculate
text constant
value

Operations
Change column width
Close a workbook
Insert a worksheet
Open a saved workbook
Rearrange sheets
Rename a sheet
Save a workbook
Start a new workbook

Study Questions

Multiple Choice

1. What determines the order in which arithmetic operations are performed in an Excel formula?
   a. The order is strictly left to right.
   b. The order is strictly right to left.
   c. The order is determined by the priority of the operators used.
   d. The order doesn't matter.
   e. The settings you specify in the Operator Precedence menu determine the order.

2. What are the two types of constants?
   a. text and number
   b. formula and value
   c. label and text
   d. relative and absolute
   e. formula and number

3. If you change a cell entry upon which a formula depends (which a formula refers to), what will happen?
   a. The formula will display an error message.
   b. The formula will automatically recalculate to reflect the changed data.
   c. You will need to rebuild the formula before it will display a new result.
   d. You will need to copy the formula upon itself.
   e. Nothing will happen.

4. How many times do you press (ENTER) (or select the Enter box) when building an Excel formula?
   a. once
   b. twice
   c. as many times as there are cell references in the formula
   d. as many times as there are arithmetic operators in the formula
   e. never

5. In Excel, what is the result of the formula $= 3 + 25 + 4$?
   a. 29
   b. 72
   c. 26
   d. 17
   e. none of the above

6. In Excel, what is the result of the formula $= 3 + (4 - 2) * 3$?
   a. 15
   b. 1
   c. 3
   d. 9
   e. none of the above

7. The way information appears in a cell (such as its alignment, font, or numeric punctuation) is referred to as the cell's:
   a. style.
   b. attributes.
   c. display mode.
   d. format.
   e. AutoFormat.

8. When should you save your work in Excel?
   a. when you are about to make a major modification to the worksheet
   b. every 5 or 10 minutes
   c. when it would be time-consuming to re-create the work you've done since you last saved
   d. when you are about to experiment with an unfamiliar Excel command
   e. all of the above

9. What happens when you close a workbook in Excel?
   a. The workbook is automatically saved.
   b. Excel will automatically exit.
   c. If you made changes to the workbook since you last saved, a dialog box will appear and give you the opportunity to save again.
   d. A new, empty workbook will automatically appear.
   e. You will automatically lose all changes made since you last saved the workbook.

10. How do you begin to edit a cell entry?
    a. make the cell active and then choose **Edit** from the menu bar
    b. make the cell active and then select the formula bar or double-click the cell
    c. double-click in the formula bar
    d. all of the above
    e. none of the above

Short Answer

1. What is the result of a formula called?

2. What kind of information is usually represented with text constants?

3. If you enter a text constant that is longer than a cell's width, what does Excel do?

4. When you enter a number constant, should you include punctuation (dollar signs, commas, and so on)? Why?

5. In general what is the best method to use when building formulas that refer to other cells? Why?

6. What determines the order in which arithmetic operations are performed in Excel formulas?

7. What determines the way information in a cell will appear?

8. What command is used to automatically format a range?

9. What command is used to open a new, blank workbook?

10. What steps are required to edit an existing cell entry?

For Discussion

1. What aspects of a cell's appearance does the AutoFormat command affect?

2. What is the single most important feature of electronic spreadsheets? Why?

3. Describe the point method for building formulas.

Review Exercises

Simple Income Statement

Build and format a worksheet based on the information shown in Figure 1.17. Income is calculated by subtracting the cost of goods sold from the sales. Pick out any one of the Accounting table formats when you use the AutoFormat command. Save the workbook as INCOME1.

	A	B	C	D	E	F	G	H	
1	Sales	$57,189.00							
2	Cost of Goods Sold	33,202.00							
3	Income	?							
4									
5									

Figure 1.17

Population Report

Build and format a worksheet similar to Figure 1.18. Use an addition formula to compute the total population of the United States, Canada, and Mexico combined. If the column containing the numbers is too narrow, Excel displays a number sign (#) or scientific notation. Once you use AutoFormat or manually widen the columns, the numbers themselves will appear. Pick out any one of the Classic or Colorful table formats. Save the workbook as POPREP1.

	A	B	C	D	E	F	G	H	I	
1	Country	Population								
2	United States	248710000								
3	Mexico	90007000								
4	Canada	26835500								
5	Total	?								
6										

Figure 1.18

Assignments

Detailed Income Statement

Build a worksheet based on Figure 1.19. Gross income is the sales minus the cost of goods sold. Net income is the gross income minus the expenses. Use AutoFormat and the Accounting 1 table format. Save the file as INCOME2.

	A	B	C	D	E	F	G	H	
1	Sales	$93,126.00							
2	Cost of Goods Sold	32,117.00							
3	Gross Income	?							
4	Expenses	$16,909.00							
5	Net Income	?							
6									

Figure 1.19

Population Density

Build a worksheet based on Figure 1.20. The population density is the number of people per square mile; calculate it by dividing the population of a city by the city's area. Use AutoFormat and experiment with the various non-Accounting table formats. Notice that AutoFormat does not limit the number of digits that display to the right of the decimal point in the non-Accounting formats. Save the file as DENSITY1.

	A	B	C	D	E	F	G	H	
1	City	Population	Area (sq. mi.)	Density					
2	Hong Kong	5693000	23	?					
3	Los Angeles	10130000	1110	?					
4									
5									
6									

Figure 1.20

Coffee House Income

Figure 1.21 shows cost and price information for the top-selling coffee at Clem's Coffee Clutch. Enter the data as shown in Figure 1.21. The formula that calculates income will subtract the cost from the selling price and multiply the result by the number sold. You will need to use parentheses in the formula. Adjust column widths as necessary, but do not format the worksheet; it will be used for an exercise in a later project. Save the worksheet as COFFEE1.

	A	B	C	D	E	F	G	H	I	
1	Coffee	Cost	Selling Price	No. Sold	Income					
2	House Blend	0.39	0.95	60	?					
3										

Figure 1.21

PROJECT 2: BUILDING A LARGER WORKSHEET

Objectives

After completing this project, you should be able to:

- Move a cell
- Check the spelling of worksheet data
- Use preselected ranges for data entry
- Copy the contents of a cell
- Use relative cell references in formulas
- Use the SUM function and the AutoSum tool

CASE STUDY: SALES OF AUDIO RECORDINGS

From 1975 to 1990, the popularity of the kinds of media used for recorded music shifted dramatically. These changes are illustrated in Figure 2.1. In this project, you will build this Excel worksheet and add formulas to calculate the totals (indicated by question marks in the figure).

	A	B	C	D	E	F	G	H
1	Shipments of Audio Recordings							
2	(in millions of dollars)							
3		1975	1980	1985	1990			
4	Phonograph Records							
5	LP Albums	1485	2290.3	1280.5	86.5			
6	Singles	211.5	269.3	281	94.4			
7	Total Records	?	?	?	?			
8	Tapes							
9	8-tracks	583	526.4	25.3	0			
10	Cassettes	98.8	776.4	2411.5	3472.4			
11	Total Tapes	?	?	?	?			
12	Compact Discs							
13	Regular CDs	0	0	389.5	3451.6			
14	CD Singles	0	0	0	6			
15	Total CDs	?	?	?	?			
16	Grand Total	?	?	?	?			
17								

Figure 2.1

Designing the Solution

The formulas you will create for this worksheet will calculate totals for each year in each media category (records, tapes, and CDs) and grand totals (the totals of records, tapes, and CDs combined). You will then format the worksheet so the information is more readable.

In the steps that follow, as important new concepts and features are introduced, you can refer to Figure 2.1 to orient yourself in the worksheet. Although you might be tempted to jump ahead and type everything in immediately, please follow the steps carefully.

BUILDING THE SKELETON OF A WORKSHEET

When you create a worksheet, it is often easiest to enter the static (unchanging) information first. To establish an overall skeleton or shape for the worksheet, you will enter the row and column titles before you enter the number constants and formulas. In general you should wait until the worksheet is complete and functioning correctly before doing detailed formatting.

To enter the main titles:

1 Start Excel.

2 Select cell A1 on Sheet1 and enter the text **Shipments of Audio Recordings**

3 Enter **(in millions of dollars)** in cell A2.

Moving Cells

In the following steps, you will enter the first row title, *Phonograph Records*, in the wrong cell. You will then use Excel's **drag-and-drop** feature to move the title to the correct cell. In Excel, to **move** means that you pick up an object from one location (in this case, the original cell) and place it in another location.

To move a cell:

1 Enter **Phonograph Records** in cell A3.
Notice that the sample worksheet in Figure 2.1 shows the first row title, *Phonograph Records*, in row 4, one row *below* the row containing the years. Rather than retyping the information you just entered, you can move it to the correct location, cell A4.

2 Select cell A3, which should contain the text constant *Phonograph Records*.

3 Position the pointer to touch any edge of the active-cell rectangle so the pointer becomes an arrow (Figure 2.2).

2	(in millions of dollars)					
3	Phonograph Records					
4						
5						

Figure 2.2

4 Hold down the mouse button and drag the dimmed image of the cell outline to cell A4, as shown in Figure 2.3. Release the mouse button. The screen should now look like Figure 2.4, with *Phonograph Records* in the new location.

2	(in millions of dollars)						
3	Phonograph Records						
4							
5							

Figure 2.3

2	(in millions of dollars)						
3							
4	Phonograph Records						
5							

Figure 2.4

Entering Row Titles

Notice that the row subtitles in Figure 2.1 are slightly indented to create an outline format. One simple way to accomplish this in Excel is to precede each text entry with two space characters.

To enter the row titles:

1 Select cell A5.

2 Press (SPACE) twice, and then enter **LP Albums**

3 Select cell A6, press (SPACE) twice, and then enter **Singles**

4 Select cell A7, press (SPACE) twice, and then enter **Total Records**

5 Refer back to Figure 2.1 to enter all the remaining row titles. Remember to indent where indicated in the figure.

> **Reminder** If you discover that you have made an incorrect entry in a cell, you can select the cell and double-click in it, or click in the formula bar. As shown in Project 1, you will then be able to type new information or use the editing keys to correct your mistake.

Checking the Spelling in a Worksheet

Once you have entered all the text constants into a worksheet, you can use Excel to check your spelling. The spelling checker will begin its check on the currently selected cell, and then it will proceed toward the lower-right corner of the worksheet. When it finishes checking the lower-right part of the worksheet, you can optionally have it check the upper-left portion. If you plan to check the spelling of the entire worksheet, it is most convenient to start at the top left corner by making A1 the active cell.

The spelling checker will pause on any word in the worksheet that it does not find in the spelling dictionary. The Spelling dialog box will suggest replacements for the possibly misspelled word. If the original word you typed is spelled correctly, you can select Ignore All in the dialog box; the spelling checker then skips over all subsequent occurrences of that spelling. (Choosing Ignore causes only the current occurrence to be skipped.) If the spelling needs to be corrected, you can choose from the list of suggestions or type a new spelling and then select Change. As illustrated in Figure 2.5, the spelling checker paused on an incorrect spelling of the word *Phonograph*. The two suggested words are *Phonograph* and *Photograph*. Because *Phonograph* is selected in the Change To box, you would select Change. The spelling will be corrected, and the spelling checker will continue to any other words that may have been misspelled, giving you a chance to correct them.

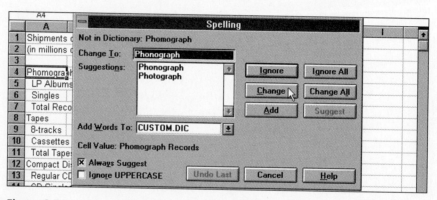

Figure 2.5

To check spelling in the worksheet:

1 Move the active cell to the top left cell (cell A1).
A quick way to do this is by pressing (CTRL) + (HOME)

2 Choose **Tools** and then **Spelling** or select the **Spelling** tool.

3 Correct any misspelled words that occur in your worksheet.

Entering Column Titles

The years *1975*, *1980*, *1985*, and *1990* need to be entered as column titles. In the steps that follow, you will use several methods for entering data.

To enter the column titles:

1 To make it easier to read the worksheet as you enter data, make column A slightly wider than *Phonograph Records*, the longest of the individual row titles.

2 Select cell B3, type **1975** and press (ENTER)
Depending on how Excel was installed on the system you are using, the active-cell rectangle may move down automatically after you press (ENTER). You can change this option if you wish.

> **Tip** To control whether the active cell (the selection) is moved after you press (ENTER), you can choose Options from the Tools menu, select the Edit tab, and select (or clear) the Move Selection After Enter check box. If the check box is cleared, the effect of pressing (ENTER) is the same as that of clicking the Enter button in the formula bar. If the check box is checked, the active cell will move down after you press (ENTER).

3 Select cell C3, type **1980** and press ⊕

4 Enter the other two years **1985** and **1990** in the appropriate cells.

> **Tip** Pressing an arrow key after you type data will automatically enter the data and position the selection one cell in the direction of the arrow key.

Using Selection to Speed Data Entry

The various sales figures need to be entered in the main section of the worksheet. Although the sales figures could always be entered without the use of a preselected range, in the steps that follow you will learn how to make repetitive entry more convenient by preselecting a data-entry range. At the lower-right corner of a selection, pressing (TAB) or (ENTER) moves to the upper left; at the upper left of a selection, pressing (SHIFT)+(TAB) moves to the lower right. You can use these keys to change which cell is active within a selected range. If (TAB) does not behave in this way, you can choose Options from the Tools menu, select the Transition tab, and clear the Transition Navigation Keys check box. Using (TAB) or (ENTER) will make your entry of multiple columns of numbers somewhat more convenient, because as you complete the last entry in a column, the active cell will "wrap around," or continue, to the next column automatically.

To use selection to speed data entry:

1 Select B5:E6 (as shown in Figure 2.6), the range where you will place sales amounts for LP albums and singles.

	A	B	C	D	E	F	G	H	
1	Shipments of Audio Recordings								
2	(in millions of dollars)								
3		1975	1980	1985	1990				
4	Phonograph Records								
5	LP Albums								
6	Singles								
7	Total Records								

Figure 2.6

2 Practice pressing (ENTER) to move down and (TAB) to move to the right within the selection.

3 Use (TAB) or (ENTER) to make cell B5 the active cell in the selected range, and type **1485** as shown in Figure 2.7.

	A	B	C	D	E	F	G	H	
1	Shipments of Audio Recordings								
2	(in millions of dollars)								
3		1975	1980	1985	1990				
4	Phonograph Records								
5	LP Albums	1485							
6	Singles								
7	Total Records								

Figure 2.7

4 Press (ENTER)

5 Enter the remaining figures for phonograph-record sales in the appropriate cells.

6 Enter the other sales figures for tapes and compact discs. As you enter the data, remember that the cells in Figure 2.1 that have question marks are kept blank for now.

SAVING THE WORKBOOK

In the following steps, you will save the workbook to disk, giving it the name AUDIO1.

To save the workbook:

1 Choose **File** and then **Save,** or click the **Save** tool. The Save As dialog box appears.

2 Select the appropriate disk drive and directory.

3 Enter **audio1** for the file name and select **OK.**

4 Enter your name in the Author section of the Summary Info dialog box and select **OK.**

 EXIT If necessary, you can quit Excel now and continue this project later.

CONSTRUCTING FORMULAS AND FUNCTIONS

In the steps that follow, you will use point mode to build a formula that calculates total record sales for 1975.

To enter the formula for total record sales:

1 Select cell B7. You will build a formula that adds the sales of LP albums and singles.

2 Type = to activate the formula bar.

3 Use the mouse or arrow keys to select cell B5, which contains sales of LP albums for 1975.

4 Type +

5 Use the mouse or arrow keys to select cell B6, which contains sales of singles for 1975.

6 Click the formula bar Enter box, or press (ENTER) to complete the formula.
Compare the screen with Figure 2.8.

	B7	=B5+B6						
	A	B	C	D	E	F	G	H
1	Shipments of Audio Recordings							
2	(in millions of dollars)							
3		1975	1980	1985	1990			
4	Phonograph Records							
5	LP Albums	1485	2290.3	1280.5	86.5			
6	Singles	211.5	269.3	281	94.4			
7	Total Records	1696.5						
8	Tapes							

Figure 2.8

A formula's result is called its value. The value of this formula is 1696.5, which appears in cell B7. If you look in the formula bar, you will see the formula itself: =B5+B6.

Copying Formulas

In Excel, any type of cell entry—text constant, number constant, or formula—can be duplicated in other cells, but duplication of formulas is most useful. Worksheets tend to have repeating patterns. For example, total record sales for 1980, 1985, and 1990 are all calculated in a manner similar to the calculation of total record sales for 1975. Copying allows you to create a formula once and then have its operation duplicated in other cells that require the same computation.

You will now copy the formula to the cells in the range C7:E7, so that you can also calculate total record sales for 1980, 1985, and 1990.

To copy a formula using the fill handle:

1 Select cell B7, which contains the total records formula for 1975.

2 Position the pointer on the lower-right corner of the active-cell rectangle.
As shown in Figure 2.9, the pointer changes to a small plus sign, which is called the *fill handle*.

	B7	=B5+B6						
	A	B	C	D	E	F	G	H
1	Shipments of Audio Recordings							
2	(in millions of dollars)							
3		1975	1980	1985	1990			
4	Phonograph Records							
5	LP Albums	1485	2290.3	1280.5	86.5			
6	Singles	211.5	269.3	281	94.4			
7	Total Records	1696.5						
8	Tapes							

Figure 2.9

3 Press and hold down the mouse button and drag the fill handle across the row through column E for 1990, as shown in Figure 2.10.

	=B5+B6						
	A	**B**	**C**	**D**	**E**	**F**	**G**	**H**
1	Shipments of Audio Recordings							
2	(in millions of dollars)							
3		1975	1980	1985	1990			
4	Phonograph Records							
5	LP Albums	1485	2290.3	1280.5	86.5			
6	Singles	211.5	269.3	281	94.4			
7	Total Records	1696.5						
8	Tapes							

Figure 2.10

4 Release the mouse button.
Totals should now appear for the years 1980 through 1990, as shown in Figure 2.11.

B7	=B5+B6						
	A	**B**	**C**	**D**	**E**	**F**	**G**	**H**
1	Shipments of Audio Recordings							
2	(in millions of dollars)							
3		1975	1980	1985	1990			
4	Phonograph Records							
5	LP Albums	1485	2290.3	1280.5	86.5			
6	Singles	211.5	269.3	281	94.4			
7	Total Records	1696.5	2559.6	1561.5	180.9			
8	Tapes							

Figure 2.11

The steps that follow show an alternative method of copying a cell. You will first use the Undo command, which will undo the copy performed in the previous steps. The Undo command reverses the effect of the most recent command performed and returns the worksheet to the state it was in before the command was issued.

To copy a formula using the Copy and Paste commands:

1 Choose **Edit** and then **Undo Auto Fill.**
Because Auto Fill was the most recently issued command, Excel undoes that command.

2 Select cell B7, which contains the formula for calculating total records for 1975.

3 Choose **Edit** and then **Copy,** or select the **Copy** tool.
Notice the message at the bottom of the application window: *Select destination and press ENTER or choose Paste.*

4 Select the destination range, C7:E7.

5 Press (ENTER) to complete the copy operation.

Tip The drag-and-drop move operation you used at the beginning of this project takes data from one location and places it in another. The Copy command *duplicates* the data—the original data remains.

Recognizing Relative Cell References

What was copied when you performed the previous steps? It wasn't the value 1696.5, because different numbers appear in each of the cells showing totals. To see what is actually in a cell, you can activate that cell and then look in the formula bar.

To examine the relative cell references:

1 Select cell B7, which contains the original formula for total record sales for 1975.

2 Examine the formula bar. The formula is $=B5+B6$.

3 Select cell C7, which contains the formula for 1980.
The formula in this cell is a copy of the original formula, but the formula bar shows that this formula is $=C5+C6$.

4 Examine the formulas for 1985 and 1990. These formulas read $=D5+D6$ and $=E5+E6$, respectively.

$=B5+B6$ was not literally copied. In a formula, Excel treats cell references as being *relative* to the cell containing the formula. Although the original formula reads $=B5+B6$, Excel interprets the formula to mean "Take what is two cells above (the formula) and add to it what is one cell above." Unless you instruct the program otherwise, Excel will interpret cell references in formulas as being *relative* to the location of the formula; this is called a **relative cell reference**. When cell B7's formula is copied to cell C7, Excel shifts all the references one cell to the right, so the formula in cell C7 reads $=C5+C6$.

Relative cell referencing is why the duplicated formulas each read differently from the original. This adjustment of a copied formula to reflect a new location is most often what you will want Excel to do. For example, the formula that calculates total record sales for 1990 *should* read $=E5+E6$ and not $=B5+B6$.

Using Excel Functions

The total sales for tapes and compact discs also need to be calculated. You could use an addition formula identical to that used to calculate total record sales, but instead you will now try another approach: you will build a formula that contains an Excel function.

A *function* is an operation whose use simplifies formula building. Functions are similar to the keys on an electronic calculator that perform specialized calculations. For example, a financial calculator will have a button to calculate the periodic payment amount for a loan. Excel has more than 300 functions, including mathematical, financial, engineering, statistical, date, and text functions. Each function has an identifying name, such as SUM, AVERAGE, and PMT.

When you enter a function as part of a formula, you must follow the function name with a pair of parentheses. For most functions, you also must provide additional items of information inside the parentheses. These additional items, called **arguments** to the function, give the function the data it needs to complete its task and compute a **result**. If you are supplying multiple arguments, you should separate them with commas. Table 2.1 lists several basic Excel functions and provides examples based on Figure 2.12.

	A	B	C	D	E
1	Principal	$16,000			
2	Interest	10% per year			
3	Term	5 years			
4					
5	**Vehicle**	**Mileage**	**Price**		
6	Velocipede	10,000	$12,000		
7	Steam Cart	20,000	$8,000		
8	Sedan Chair	30,000	$16,000		
9					
10					

Figure 2.12

Table 2.1

Function	Syntax	Description	Example Formula	Example Result
SUM	SUM(range)	Totals a range	=SUM(C6:C*)	$36,000
AVERAGE	AVERAGE(range)	Averages a range	=AVERAGE(B6:B8)	20,000
MIN	MIN(range)	Gets smallest value in range	=MIN(C6:C8)	$8,000
MAX	MAX(range)	Gets largest value in range	=MAX(B6:B8)	30,000
COUNT	COUNT(range)	Counts values in range	=COUNT(A5:C8)	6
IF	IF (test, result if true, result if false)	Performs test; result of function depends on whether test is true or false	=IF(B2<0.12,5,10)	5
PMT	PMT (periodic interest rate, number of periods, principal amount)	Calculates periodic payment for a loan	=PMT(B2/ 12,B3*12,B1)	($339.95)

The SUM function, in its basic form, is designed to total the values in a range of cells. The argument you provide to the function indicates the range it is to sum. For example, =SUM(H1:H12) totals all the values in the range H1:H12. The much longer addition formula =H1+H2+H3+H4+H5+H6+H7+H8+H9+H10+H11+H12 arrives at the same result as =SUM(H1:H12), but the SUM function is a more efficient way of creating the formula.

In the steps that follow, you will use point mode to build a SUM function formula that calculates total tape sales for 1975. As with all formulas, you will start by typing an equal sign, followed by SUM and an open parenthesis. Then, using pointing techniques, you will select the range to be summed, and finally you will end the formula with a close parenthesis.

To enter the SUM function to calculate total tape sales for 1975:

1 Select cell B11.

2 Type =sum(

SUM can be in upper- or lowercase letters. The screen should resemble Figure 2.13.

B11		fx	=sum(						
	A	B	C	D	E	F	G	H	
1	Shipments of Audio Recordings								
2	(in millions of dollars)								
3		1975	1980	1985	1990				
4	Phonograph Records								
5	LP Albums	1485	2290.3	1280.5	86.5				
6	Singles	211.5	269.3	281	94.4				
7	Total Records	1696.5	2559.6	1561.5	180.9				
8	Tapes								
9	8-tracks	583	526.4	25.3	0				
10	Cassettes	98.8	776.4	2411.5	3472.4				
11	Total Tapes	=sum(							
12	Compact Discs								
13	Regular CDs	0	0	389.5	3451.6				

Figure 2.13

3 Select cell B10, cassette sales for 1975, and drag up to cell B9, 8-track sales for 1975. Once the range B9:B10 is selected, release the mouse button. The screen should appear similar to Figure 2.14. Notice that a range selection made in point mode appears with a moving border.

B10		fx	=sum(B9:B10						
	A	B	C	D	E	F	G	H	
1	Shipments of Audio Recordings								
2	(in millions of dollars)								
3		1975	1980	1985	1990				
4	Phonograph Records								
5	LP Albums	1485	2290.3	1280.5	86.5				
6	Singles	211.5	269.3	281	94.4				
7	Total Records	1696.5	2559.6	1561.5	180.9				
8	Tapes								
9	8-tracks	583	526.4	25.3	0				
10	Cassettes	98.8	776.4	2411.5	3472.4				
11	Total Tapes	=sum(B9:B10							
12	Compact Discs								
13	Regular CDs	0	0	389.5	3451.6				

Figure 2.14

4 Type) and press (ENTER) to complete the formula.
5 Select cell B11.
The completed formula reads =SUM(B9:B10), as shown in Figure 2.15.

| B11 | ↓ | =SUM(B9:B10) |

	A	B	C	D	E	F	G	H
1	Shipments of Audio Recordings							
2	(in millions of dollars)							
3		1975	1980	1985	1990			
4	Phonograph Records							
5	LP Albums	1485	2290.3	1280.5	86.5			
6	Singles	211.5	269.3	281	94.4			
7	Total Records	1696.5	2559.6	1561.5	180.9			
8	Tapes							
9	8-tracks	583	526.4	25.3	0			
10	Cassettes	98.8	776.4	2411.5	3472.4			
11	Total Tapes	681.8						
12	Compact Discs							
13	Regular CDs	0	0	389.5	3451.6			

Figure 2.15

For totaling such a small range, the SUM function might appear to have little advantage over a regular addition formula. But functions are more flexible. For example, if you insert a new row between 8-track and cassette sales—such as a row for sales of cassette singles—the range reference in the SUM function automatically expands to include the new information. A simple addition formula would not change to include this new row.

The formula =SUM(B9:B10) uses relative cell references; the formula means "sum up the two-cell range immediately above the formula." Because it uses relative addresses, the formula will work correctly if copied. You will now learn about a shortcut method of building SUM formulas before you copy the SUM formula to other cells.

Using the AutoSum Tool

You can always write a SUM formula manually, but *AutoSum* is a convenient feature that writes a SUM formula for you. The AutoSum button is located on the Standard toolbar. It is labeled with a Greek capital sigma (Σ), which is traditionally used in mathematics to indicate summation.

When you choose the AutoSum command, it looks for ranges surrounding the active cell, and makes a guess about what range you want to total. You have the option of accepting AutoSum's proposed range or selecting another range.

To use the AutoSum tool:

1 Select cell C11, which is to contain total tape sales for 1980.

2 Click the AutoSum tool.

AutoSum writes a formula for you. As shown in Figure 2.16, the formula =SUM(C9:C10) appears in the formula bar. After examining the contents of cells neighboring C11, AutoSum guesses that the range you want to sum is C9:C10, which is correct. At this point, if you wanted to select a different range to be summed, you could.

C9	↓ X	f_x	=SUM(C9:C10)					
	A	B	C	D	E	F	G	H
1	Shipments of Audio Recordings							
2	(in millions of dollars)							
3		1975	1980	1985	1990			
4	Phonograph Records							
5	LP Albums	1485	2290.3	1280.5	86.5			
6	Singles	211.5	269.3	281	94.4			
7	Total Records	1696.5	2559.6	1561.5	180.9			
8	Tapes							
9	8-tracks	583	526.4	25.3	0			
10	Cassettes	98.8	776.4	2411.5	3472.4			
11	Total Tapes	681.8	=SUM(C9:C10)					
12	Compact Discs							
13	Regular CDs	0	0	389.5	3451.6			

Figure 2.16

3 Accept this formula by clicking the formula bar Enter box or by pressing (ENTER)

4 Copy the formula for 1980 total tape sales to the other cells designated for total tapes (for the years 1985 and 1990).

5 Select B15:E15, the range of cells that are to contain total CD sales.

6 Select the AutoSum tool.
A SUM formula is entered automatically in each cell of the selected range. The screen should now resemble Figure 2.17.

B15	↓		=SUM(B13:B14)					
	A	B	C	D	E	F	G	H
1	Shipments of Audio Recordings							
2	(in millions of dollars)							
3		1975	1980	1985	1990			
4	Phonograph Records							
5	LP Albums	1485	2290.3	1280.5	86.5			
6	Singles	211.5	269.3	281	94.4			
7	Total Records	1696.5	2559.6	1561.5	180.9			
8	Tapes							
9	8-tracks	583	526.4	25.3	0			
10	Cassettes	98.8	776.4	2411.5	3472.4			
11	Total Tapes	681.8	1302.8	2436.8	3472.4			
12	Compact Discs							
13	Regular CDs	0	0	389.5	3451.6			
14	CD Singles	0	0	0	6			
15	Total CDs	0	0	389.5	3457.6			
16	Grand Total							

Figure 2.17

Calculating Grand Totals

You can compute the grand total for a year by adding total records, total tapes, and total CDs. This cannot be calculated using a SUM function of a single range, because you need to add the values of three nonadjacent cells. If you were to construct the formula manually, you would make an addition formula that referred to three separate cells. For example, the grand total for 1975 would be calculated by the formula $=B15+B11+B7$. In the steps that follow, you will not build such an addition formula but will instead learn how AutoSum can automatically generate grand totals. If you select a range that contains subtotals and then select AutoSum, the AutoSum command will analyze the range and write grand total formulas in the first row of blank cells below the range.

To build the grand total formulas using AutoSum:

1 Select the range B5:E15, as shown in Figure 2.18.

	A	B	C	D	E	F	G	H
	B5	1485						
1	Shipments of Audio Recordings							
2	(in millions of dollars)							
3		1975	1980	1985	1990			
4	Phonograph Records							
5	LP Albums	1485	2290.3	1280.5	86.5			
6	Singles	211.5	269.3	281	94.4			
7	Total Records	1696.5	2559.6	1561.5	180.9			
8	Tapes							
9	8-tracks	583	526.4	25.3	0			
10	Cassettes	98.8	776.4	2411.5	3472.4			
11	Total Tapes	681.8	1302.8	2436.8	3472.4			
12	Compact Discs							
13	Regular CDs	0	0	389.5	3451.6			
14	CD Singles	0	0	0	6			
15	Total CDs	0	0	389.5	3457.6			
16	Grand Total							
17								

Figure 2.18

2 Select the AutoSum tool.
Grand total formulas appear in the grand total row, B16:E16.

3 Select cell B16.
The screen should now resemble Figure 2.19. The grand total formula for 1975, created by AutoSum, reads = SUM(B15,B11,B7).

	A	B	C	D	E	F	G	H
	B16	=SUM(B15,B11,B7)						
1	Shipments of Audio Recordings							
2	(in millions of dollars)							
3		1975	1980	1985	1990			
4	Phonograph Records							
5	LP Albums	1485	2290.3	1280.5	86.5			
6	Singles	211.5	269.3	281	94.4			
7	Total Records	1696.5	2559.6	1561.5	180.9			
8	Tapes							
9	8-tracks	583	526.4	25.3	0			
10	Cassettes	98.8	776.4	2411.5	3472.4			
11	Total Tapes	681.8	1302.8	2436.8	3472.4			
12	Compact Discs							
13	Regular CDs	0	0	389.5	3451.6			
14	CD Singles	0	0	0	6			
15	Total CDs	0	0	389.5	3457.6			
16	Grand Total	2378.3	3862.4	4387.8	7110.9			
17								

Figure 2.19

4 Double-click the **Sheet1** tab and rename the sheet **Audio Sales**

5 Save the file.

THE NEXT STEP

In this project, you built the functional parts of a worksheet. In the next project, your primary concern will be the appearance of the worksheet—its format. You will retrieve the worksheet, modify it, format it, print it, and learn more about several different formatting techniques.

This concludes Project 2. You can either exit Excel, or go on to work the Study Questions, Review Exercises, and Assignments.

SUMMARY AND EXERCISES

Summary

- The first step in building a large worksheet is to enter the row and column titles, followed by any other constant information. You can then construct formulas. You should complete the worksheet before doing detailed formatting.
- A cell's contents can be moved easily with the mouse.
- Excel can check the spelling of worksheet data.
- You can use preselection of a range to speed the entry of large amounts of data.
- You can copy a cell using the fill handle, the Copy tool, or the Copy command in the Edit menu. When a formula containing relative cell references is copied, those cell references will change relative to the new cell.
- A function is a built-in mathematical procedure that can be used in a formula. The SUM function, which totals a range of cells, can be typed in or entered using the AutoSum tool.

Key Terms and Operations

Key Terms	Operations
argument (to a function)	Copy cell contents
AutoSum	Move cell contents
drag-and-drop	Paste cell contents
function	Spell check
move	Undo a command
relative cell reference	
result	

Study Questions

Multiple Choice

1. What should usually be done first when building a large worksheet?
   a. formatting
   b. entry of text and number constants
   c. entry of formulas
   d. saving
   e. column-width adjustment

2. Which of the following best describes what happens when a cell is moved?
   a. The cell's contents are duplicated in another location and you have to erase the contents from the original.
   b. The cell's contents are removed from their original location and placed in a new location.
   c. The Move command is used to reposition the active cell in a new location.
   d. The Move command extends the current selection so it is larger than a single cell.
   e. none of the above

3. What key can be used to move within a preselected data-entry range?
   a. ↓   d. →
   b. ENTER   e. all of the above
   c. F1

4. What kinds of cell entries can be copied?
   a. formulas   d. all of the above
   b. text constants   e. none of the above
   c. number constants

5. Items of information provided to a function are called:
   a. values.   d. parameters.
   b. formulas.   e. arguments.
   c. variables.

6. What is a shorter way of computing
   $= C1 + C2 + C3 + C4 + C5 + C6 + C7 + C8$?
   a. $=ADD(C1..C8)$ d. $=SUMMATION(C1:C8)$
   b. $=TOTAL(C1:C8)$ e. $=C1:C8$
   c. $=SUM(C1:C8)$

7. What tool can be used to quickly create SUM formulas?
   a. Summation
   b. $=SUM$
   c. AutoSum
   d. Sum-O-Matic
   e. Sum command from the Formula menu

8. To have Excel skip all occurrences of a word that it doesn't have in its dictionary, what should you select in the Spelling dialog box?
   a. Ignore   d. Change All
   b. Ignore All   e. Cancel
   c. Change

9. When you use the mouse to copy a cell, the pointer will change to an:
   a. fill handle.   d. insertion symbol.
   b. double arrow.   e. hollow arrow.
   c. hollow plus sign.

10. Suppose the formula $=SUM(A1:A5)$ was entered in cell A6. What best describes the meaning of the formula?
    a. Total the cells A1 and A5.
    b. Total the five-cell range immediately above.
    c. Count the number of entries in the range A1 through A5.
    d. Total the cells A1, A2, A3, and A4.
    e. none of the above

Short Answer

1. What is a more efficient way to compute $= E7 + E8 + E9 + E10 + E11 + E12 + E13$ and what are the reasons to use it?

2. What effect does the Undo command have on a worksheet?

3. If the spelling checker pauses on a word in the worksheet, does this mean the word is misspelled? If so, what can be done?

4. What technique can be used to speed the entry of a block of data in a worksheet?

5. When a formula is copied to another cell, is it the value (result) of the formula that appears in the new cell?

6. What does the AutoSum tool do?

7. Approximately how many built-in functions does Excel have?

8. If the formula $= SUM(B2:B5)$ were entered into cell B6, how would the formula change if copied to cell C6?

9. What is a simple way to indent text entries?

10. What menu commands can be used to copy a cell?

For Discussion

1. Describe the general steps you should follow when building a worksheet.

2. Describe how to move a cell.

3. Describe how to copy a cell.

4. Describe relative cell referencing and how this affects the way formulas are copied.

5. Describe functions and their components. Use the example of the SUM function.

Review Exercises

Municipal Waste Trends

The Environmental Protection Agency (EPA) reports the information shown in Figure 2.20 about the composition of municipal waste and how it has changed over time (the figures reflect pounds per day per person). Build a worksheet to present this data and calculate the various totals. Use the SUM function to compute the required totals. Save an unformatted version of the workbook to disk, under the name EPA1, for use in a Review Exercise at the end of Project 3. After you save the workbook, experiment with AutoFormat options but do not save the formatted version.

	A	B	C	D	E	F	G	H	I
1	Municipal Waste								
2		1960	1970	1980	1990				
3	Nonfood Wastes								
4	Paper	0.91	1.19	1.32	1.6				
5	Glass	0.2	0.34	0.36	0.28				
6	Plastics	0.01	0.08	0.19	0.32				
7	Total Nonfood	?	?	?	?				
8	Other								
9	Food	0.37	0.34	0.32	0.29				
10	Yard	0.61	0.62	0.66	0.7				
11	Total Other	?	?	?	?				
12	Grand Total	?	?	?	?				
13									

Figure 2.20

Winter Olympic Medals

Figure 2.21 shows the number of medals won by selected countries during the 1992 Winter Olympic Games. Create a worksheet that presents this information and calculates the required totals. Note that both row and column totals are computed. Save an unformatted version of the workbook to disk; use the name OLYMPIC1. Experiment with AutoFormat if you wish.

	A	B	C	D	E	F	G	H	I
1	1992 Winter Olympiad								
2									
3	Country	Gold	Silver	Bronze	Total				
4	Germany	10	10	6	?				
5	Unified Team	9	6	8	?				
6	Austria	6	7	8	?				
7	Norway	9	6	5	?				
8	Total	?	?	?	?				
9									

Figure 2.21

Assignments

Coffee House Income

Open the file COFFEE1 that you created in an assignment at the end of Project 1. Modify the worksheet, as shown in Figure 2.22, to show sales figures for other kinds of coffee. Note that the original formula for income uses relative addresses and can be copied down to compute income for the other coffee flavors. Create SUM formulas that compute totals for the number sold and income. Do not format the worksheet. Use the Save As command from the File menu to save the updated workbook under a new name, COFFEE2.

	A	B	C	D	E	F	G	H	I
1	Coffee	Cost	Selling Price	No. Sold	Income				
2	House Blend	0.39	0.95	60	?				
3	Espresso	0.61	1.25	12	?				
4	Cappuccino	0.74	1.5	22	?				
5	Cafe Mocha	0.55	1.45	35	?				
6	Total			?	?				
7									
8									

Figure 2.22

Personal Budget

Build a personal budget that describes your income and expenses for a typical month. Begin with income items such as salary, tips, and interest earned, grouped and indented under the heading *Income*. Build a formula that calculates a total of the income items. Similarly, group expense items such as food, rent, electricity, and insurance, and calculate their total. Finally, build a formula to calculate the difference between total income and total expenses. Do not format the worksheet, but save it to disk under the name BUDGET1 for use in another project.

Space Payloads

Figure 2.23 documents the number of payloads (objects carried into space) launched by various countries for the years 1988 through 1991. Construct a worksheet to present this data and compute the totals. You can use the SUM function to calculate column totals; you can calculate the average payloads per year for each country by dividing its row total by 4 or by using the AVERAGE function. Do not format the worksheet; save it to disk under the name SPACE1. You will use it in an assignment in Project 3.

	A	B	C	D	E	F	G	H	I
1	Space Payloads								
2									
3		1988	1989	1990	1991	Average			
4	USSR	107	95	96	101	?			
5	United States	15	22	31	30	?			
6	Japan	2	4	7	2	?			
7	Total	?	?	?	?	?			
8									

Figure 2.23

Objectives

After completing this project, you should be able to:

► Identify and analyze formulas in a worksheet

► Insert blank cells into a worksheet

► Recognize and correct circular references

► Clear cells

► Center titles across columns

► Change row height

► Print the worksheet

► Change the standard format

► Understand and modify styles

► Use information windows

CASE STUDY: SALES OF AUDIO RECORDINGS

In this project you will continue to work with the audio recordings worksheet from Project 2. Sales of cassette singles, shown below, will need to be included in the worksheet. The new data will appear in between the rows labeled *Cassettes* and *Compact Discs*.

	1975	1980	1985	1990
Cassette Singles	0	0	0	87.4

Once this information is added, some formulas in the worksheet will need to be adjusted to reflect the new information. In the final phase of the project, you will format the worksheet and learn about cell styles.

Designing the Solution

First you will need to make room for the new information on sales of cassette singles. You could move the lower half of the worksheet (A11:E16) down one row to create the needed space, but for this exercise you will use the Insert command. Using the Insert command is easier because it does not require that you select as large an area.

MODIFYING A WORKSHEET

When you modify a worksheet, you must consider how the change will affect other parts of the worksheet. You need to analyze carefully the way formulas depend on other cells. Usually formulas adjust automatically as you'd like them to, but in some cases they do not. Consider the consequences of inserting a new row: the area where you want to place extra cells might be quite small, but if you choose to insert an entire row, a new blank row will extend across the entire worksheet, perhaps inserting blank space through the middle of some other portion of the worksheet that you do not want to affect. Deleting an entire row or column is even more sensitive, because information is removed all the way across or down the worksheet.

> **Reminder**   You should save a workbook before performing a command that might significantly affect it. You should also consider the possible side effects of using a command. Save before you perform a command, then if the workbook is adversely affected by the command, you can close the damaged workbook without saving, return to your previously saved copy, and try again.

Tracing Precedents and Dependents

The Excel Auditing toolbar (and the Auditing option in the Tools menu) has several features that make it easier for you to understand the formulas in a worksheet. If you select a cell containing a formula and then select the Trace Precedents tool, Excel will draw *tracer arrows* on the screen from all the cells upon which that formula directly depends. These cells are called *direct precedents*. Selecting the Trace Precedents tool again will draw tracer arrows from *indirect precedents*—cells upon which the direct precedent cells depend. The Trace Precedents tool can be used repeatedly to trace back to the original precedents. If the precedent cells comprise a range, a box is drawn around the range.

You can also use the Trace Dependents tool to draw tracer arrows to direct and indirect *dependents*—cells that contain formulas that refer to (depend on) a particular cell. Whether you are tracing dependents or precedents, the tracer arrows have large dots on one end to show precedent cells and arrowheads on the other end to show dependent cells. The arrowheads indicate the direction of information flow.

In the following steps, you will use these tools to review how the formulas work in the audio sales worksheet.

To open and prepare the AUDIO1 workbook:

1 Choose **File** and then **Open,** and open the AUDIO1.XLS workbook file you saved in Project 2.

2 Click the **Audio Sales** sheet tab, if necessary.

To display the Auditing toolbar:

1 Choose **View** and then **Toolbars,** and display the Auditing toolbar.

2 Dock the Auditing toolbar on the right side of the vertical scroll bar. The screen should resemble Figure 3.1.

	A	B	C	D	E	F	G	H
1	Shipments of Audio Recordings							
2	(in millions of dollars)							
3		1975	1980	1985	1990			
4	Phonograph Records							
5	LP Albums	1485	2290.3	1280.5	86.5			
6	Singles	211.5	269.3	281	94.4			
7	Total Records	1696.5	2559.6	1561.5	180.9			
8	Tapes							
9	8-tracks	583	526.4	25.3	0			
10	Cassettes	98.8	776.4	2411.5	3472.4			
11	Total Tapes	681.8	1302.8	2436.8	3472.4			

Figure 3.1

To trace direct precedents:

1 Select cell B16, which contains the formula for the grand total for 1975.

2 Click the **Trace Precedents** tool.

The screen should resemble Figure 3.2. Large dots appear in cells B7, B11, and B15; these dots mark precedent cells. The arrowhead points to cell B16, indicating that the information from the marked precedent cells feeds into the formula in cell B16.

B16		=SUM(B15,B11,B7)						
	A	B	C	D	E	F	G	H
1	Shipments of Audio Recordings							
2	(in millions of dollars)							
3		1975	1980	1985	1990			
4	Phonograph Records							
5	LP Albums	1485	2290.3	1280.5	86.5			
6	Singles	211.5	269.3	281	94.4			
7	Total Records	1696.5	2559.6	1561.5	180.9			
8	Tapes							
9	8-tracks	583	526.4	25.3	0			
10	Cassettes	98.8	776.4	2411.5	3472.4			
11	Total Tapes	681.8	1302.8	2436.8	3472.4			
12	Compact Discs							
13	Regular CDs	0	0	389.5	3451.6			
14	CD Singles	0	0	0	6			
15	Total CDs	0	0	389.5	3457.6			
16	Grand Total	2378.3	3862.4	4387.8	7110.9			
17								

Figure 3.2

The formula in cell B16 depends *directly* on the three cells marked with dots. Remember that the three cells are themselves totals; in the next steps, you will select the indirect precedents of the grand total formula.

To trace indirect precedents:

1 Click the **Trace Precedents** tool again.
The screen should now resemble Figure 3.3, which shows indirect precedents along with direct precedents. For example, cell B11 depends on the range B9:B10, so this range is outlined, a dot appears in the first cell of the range, and the connected arrow points into cell B11.

	A	B	C	D	E	F	G	H
	B16	=SUM(B15,B11,B7)						
1	Shipments of Audio Recordings							
2	(in millions of dollars)							
3		1975	1980	1985	1990			
4	Phonograph Records							
5	LP Albums	1485	2290.3	1280.5	86.5			
6	Singles	211.5	269.3	281	94.4			
7	Total Records	1696.5	2559.6	1561.5	180.9			
8	Tapes							
9	8-tracks	583	526.4	25.3	0			
10	Cassettes	98.8	776.4	2411.5	3472.4			
11	Total Tapes	681.8	1302.8	2436.8	3472.4			
12	Compact Discs							
13	Regular CDs	0	0	389.5	3451.6			
14	CD Singles	0	0	0	6			
15	Total CDs	0	0	389.5	3457.6			
16	Grand Total	2378.3	3862.4	4387.8	7110.9			
17								

Figure 3.3

 2 Click the **Trace Precedents** tool again.
Excel beeps, signaling that there are no further precedents to be traced.

3 Click the **Remove Precedent Arrows** tool.
The last traced precedence arrows are cleared; the screen should once again resemble Figure 3.2.

It is sometimes useful, when analyzing a worksheet with multiple levels of precedent cells, to be able to jump quickly from a cell to its precedent. The following steps demonstrate this feature.

 ## To use tracer arrows to activate dependent and precedent cells:

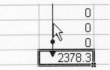

1 Position the pointer so it forms an arrow shape, just touching anywhere along the tracer arrow.

2 Double-click.
The active cell switches to cell B7, at the opposite end of the tracer arrow.

3 Make sure the pointer arrow just touches the tracer arrow and double-click.
The active cell switches back to cell B16.

 4 Click the **Remove All Arrows** tool.
No precedence arrows are visible now. The Remove Precedent Arrows tool could also have been used.

To trace dependents:

1 Select cell B5, LP album sales for 1975.

2 Click the **Trace Dependents** tool.

A tracer arrow appears, showing that cell B7, which computes total record sales for 1975, depends on the selected cell. The screen should resemble Figure 3.4.

	A	B	C	D	E	F	G	H
	B5	1485						
1	Shipments of Audio Recordings							
2	(in millions of dollars)							
3		1975	1980	1985	1990			
4	Phonograph Records							
5	LP Albums	1485	2290.3	1280.5	86.5			
6	Singles	211.5	269.3	281	94.4			
7	Total Records	1696.5	2559.6	1561.5	180.9			
8	Tapes							

Figure 3.4

3 Click the **Trace Dependents** tool again.

Another tracer arrow appears, showing that cell B16, which computes the grand total for 1975, depends indirectly on the selected cell. The screen should resemble Figure 3.5.

	A	B	C	D	E	F	G	H
	B5	1485						
1	Shipments of Audio Recordings							
2	(in millions of dollars)							
3		1975	1980	1985	1990			
4	Phonograph Records							
5	LP Albums	1485	2290.3	1280.5	86.5			
6	Singles	211.5	269.3	281	94.4			
7	Total Records	1696.5	2559.6	1561.5	180.9			
8	Tapes							
9	8-tracks	583	526.4	25.3	0			
10	Cassettes	98.8	776.4	2411.5	3472.4			
11	Total Tapes	681.8	1302.8	2436.8	3472.4			
12	Compact Discs							
13	Regular CDs	0	0	389.5	3451.6			
14	CD Singles	0	0	0	6			
15	Total CDs	0	0	389.5	3457.6			
16	Grand Total	2378.3	3862.4	4387.8	7110.9			
17								

Figure 3.5

4 Click the **Trace Dependents** tool again.

There are no further dependent cells.

5 Click the **Remove All Arrows** tool.

No tracer arrows should be visible.

Bearing in mind the modification planned for this worksheet, you will want to make sure that the data for sales of cassette singles, once entered into the worksheet, is also included in the total tape sales formula. You shouldn't have to worry about the grand total formula in this case, because it depends on the total tape sales formula.

Inserting Cells in a Worksheet

A range of blank cells needs to be inserted directly above the total tapes row. Excel lets you insert either a range of cells or an entire column or row. It is often safest to insert a range, because the effect doesn't stretch as far across the worksheet as it does when an entire column or row is inserted.

To insert blank cells:

1 Select cell A11, the cell containing the text *Total Tapes*, and then select the range A11:E11.

2 Choose **Insert** and then **Cells.**

The Insert dialog box appears, as shown in Figure 3.6. Because the selected range is wider than it is deep, Excel presumes that you want to shift the selected range (and everything underneath it) down, which is correct.

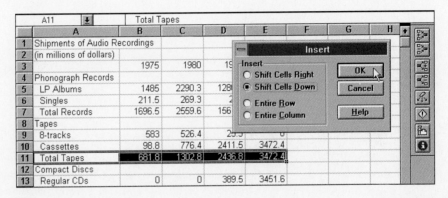

Figure 3.6

3 Select **OK.**

A new range of blank cells is now available.

To enter the new information:

1 Select cell A11.

2 Press (SPACE) twice and enter **Cassette Singles**

3 Enter **0** in cells B11, C11, and D11.

4 Enter **87.4** in cell E11.

Your worksheet should now resemble Figure 3.7.

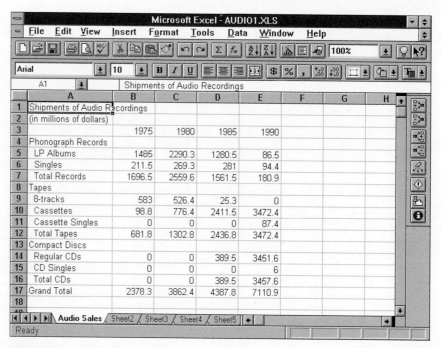

Figure 3.7

Assessing the Effects of a Command

Now that the data for sales of cassette singles is entered, you can determine whether adjustments are required to accommodate the new information. The sales of cassette singles should be included in the computation of total tapes, so you should examine the formulas in the total tapes row.

To examine the total tapes formulas:

1 Select cell E12.
The formula reads =SUM(E9:E10), so the range being summed does *not* include the new information in cell E11.

2 Trace the direct precedents of cell E12.
As shown in Figure 3.8, this confirms visually that the range being totaled, B9:B10, is not correct. For the total tape sales formula to be correct, it should depend not only on the sales of 8-tracks and cassettes, but on cassette singles as well.

	A	B	C	D	E	F	G	
8	Tapes							
9	8-tracks	583	526.4	25.3	0			
10	Cassettes	98.8	776.4	2411.5	3472.4			
11	Cassette Singles	0	0	0	87.4			
12	Total Tapes	681.8	1302.8	2436.8	3472.4			
13	Compact Discs							

Figure 3.8

3 Remove all tracer arrows.

Because cassette singles had no sales for 1975 through 1985, you might conclude that the only formula that needs to be fixed is the one for 1990. But leaving the other total tape sales formulas unchanged would be a serious design mistake; it would create an inconsistency in the worksheet that could later prove troublesome. What if the worksheet were reused and different years' data (all with sales of cassette singles) was entered over the older data? If the incorrect tape sales formulas were still present, their results would not include the new amounts.

You may have wondered why the range referred to in the SUM function did not automatically adjust. Excel will automatically adjust a range reference within a formula if the newly inserted row is *within* the existing top and bottom rows of the range, but not if the inserted row lies outside the existing range. Had the row for cassette singles been inserted between the 8-track and cassette rows, Excel would have adjusted the range reference in the formula.

In the steps that follow, you will build a new SUM formula for total tape sales for 1975 and copy the formula to the other total tape cells. Please follow the steps carefully, because the steps will purposefully instruct you to make a common mistake that you will then learn how to correct. *Do not use AutoSum for these steps.*

To build a self-referential SUM formula:

1 Select cell B12, where the formula for total tape sales for 1975 resides.

2 Type =**sum(**

3 Select cell B9, 8-track tape sales for 1975.

4 Drag the selection down through cell B12 to highlight the range B9:B12.

5 Type **)** and press (ENTER)
A dialog box appears with the message "Cannot resolve circular references."

6 Select **OK** to bypass the dialog box.

7 Select cell B12.

8 Trace the direct precedents of cell B12.

9 Select another cell away from the tracer area to see the tracer arrow more clearly.
As shown in Figure 3.9, cell B12 is dependent upon itself. Note that the Status bar shows "Circular: B17."

	A	B	C	D	E	F	G	H
1	Shipments of Audio Recordings							
2	(in millions of dollars)							
3		1975	1980	1985	1990			
4	Phonograph Records							
5	LP Albums	1485	2290.3	1280.5	86.5			
6	Singles	211.5	269.3	281	94.4			
7	Total Records	1696.5	2559.6	1561.5	180.9			
8	Tapes							
9	8-tracks	583	526.4	25.3	0			
10	Cassettes	98.8	776.4	2411.5	3472.4			
11	Cassette Singles	0	0	0	87.4			
12	Total Tapes	0	1302.8	2436.8	3472.4			
13	Compact Discs							
14	Regular CDs	0	0	389.5	3451.6			
15	CD Singles	0	0	0	6			
16	Total CDs	0	0	389.5	3457.6			
17	Grand Total	2378.3	3862.4	4387.8	7110.9			
18								

Ready Circular: B17

Figure 3.9

10 Remove all tracer arrows.

Understanding Circular References

A *circular reference* occurs when a formula refers, either directly or indirectly, to itself. This kind of formula usually doesn't make any sense, so it is considered an error. The erroneous formula you just entered is an example of one of the more common places where circular references can occur. When using the mouse or arrow keys to select a range within a formula, you should drag or select away from the formula: this will reduce the chance of inadvertently including the formula's own cell within the selected range.

In the following steps, you will rebuild the formula. Although it is not necessary to clear the old formulas first, you will do so to learn about the Clear command.

To clear a range of cells:

1 Select the range B12:E12, which contains the total tape formulas.

2 Choose **Edit** and then **Clear.**
The Clear submenu appears.

3 Select **All.**
The formulas in the range B12:E12 should now be erased.

> **Tip** Another way to clear the contents of a selection is click the right mouse button to access the shortcut menu, and then choose Clear Contents. An even quicker way is to press (DEL) after making the selection.

Clearing cells is not the same as deleting them. When cells are cleared, their contents are erased but the cells themselves remain. Deleting cells, which you haven't done yet, removes the cells from the worksheet and shifts neighboring cells into take up the space.

You will now create the correct formula, copy it to the total tapes cells, and save the workbook.

To build the correct total tapes formula:

1 Select the range B12:E12, the cells that will contain total tape sales for each year.

2 Click the **AutoSum** tool.
SUM formulas appear in each of the selected cells.

3 Select cell B12.
The correct formula, =SUM(B9:B11), is visible in the formula bar.

4 Click the **Trace Precedents** tool, and then select another cell away from the trace area.
A tracer arrow and range outline appear, confirming that the range being totaled is correct, as shown in Figure 3.10.

8	Tapes				
9	8-tracks	583	526.4	25.3	0
10	Cassettes	98.8	776.4	2411.5	3472.4
11	Cassette Singles	0	0	0	87.4
12	Total Tapes	681.8	1302.8	2436.8	3559.8
13	Compact Discs				

Figure 3.10

5 Click the **Remove All Arrows** tool.

6 Undock and close the Auditing toolbar.
The screen should look like Figure 3.11.

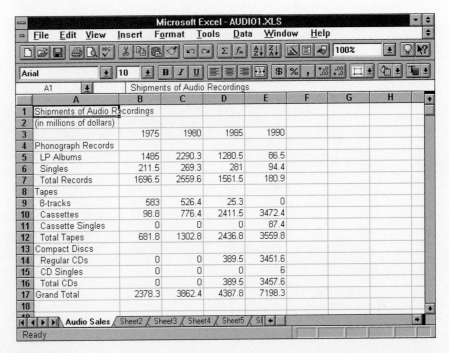

	A	B	C	D	E	F	G	H
1	Shipments of Audio Recordings							
2	(in millions of dollars)							
3		1975	1980	1985	1990			
4	Phonograph Records							
5	LP Albums	1485	2290.3	1280.5	86.5			
6	Singles	211.5	269.3	281	94.4			
7	Total Records	1696.5	2559.6	1561.5	180.9			
8	Tapes							
9	8-tracks	583	526.4	25.3	0			
10	Cassettes	98.8	776.4	2411.5	3472.4			
11	Cassette Singles	0	0	0	87.4			
12	Total Tapes	681.8	1302.8	2436.8	3559.8			
13	Compact Discs							
14	Regular CDs	0	0	389.5	3451.6			
15	CD Singles	0	0	0	6			
16	Total CDs	0	0	389.5	3457.6			
17	Grand Total	2378.3	3862.4	4387.8	7198.3			
18								

Figure 3.11

7 Save the workbook using the Save command from the File menu
or the Save button.
It is very important to save at this point, because in later steps you will
need to use this version of the workbook.

ENHANCING THE WORKSHEET

As in Project 1, you will use AutoFormat to format a worksheet. The
AutoFormat command works best on worksheets that have a relatively
simple and consistent structure. This worksheet will require several manual
adjustments after you use AutoFormat.

To use AutoFormat with the worksheet:

1 Select the range A1:E17.
A quick way to do this, provided you did not type any extraneous information
after the grand total for 1990, is to select cell A1 by pressing (CTRL) + (HOME)
and then press (CTRL) + (SHFT) + (END) (use (END) on the numeric keyboard
with (NUM LOCK) off).

2 Choose **Format** and then **AutoFormat**.
The AutoFormat dialog box appears.

3 Select the **Accounting 1** table format and select **OK**, as shown in
Figure 3.12.

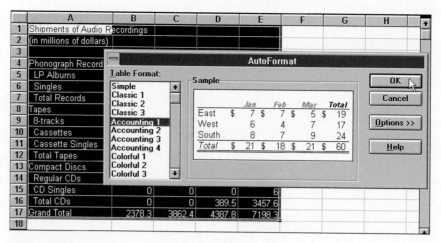

Figure 3.12

The worksheet is automatically formatted. Notice that in the Accounting 1 table format, values of zero are displayed as centered hyphens.

4 Select cell A1 to cancel the larger selected range.
You will notice that AutoFormat made column A too wide. It based its decision on the length of the worksheet's main title, *Shipments of Audio Recordings*. You will center this title across all the columns of the worksheet in the next series of steps, so column A does not need to be this wide.

5 Adjust the width of column A to about 22, so it is slightly wider than Phonograph Records, as shown in Figure 3.13.

Width: 22.00	Shipments of Audio Recordings						
	A	B	C	D	E	F	G
1	Shipments of Audio Recordings						
2	(in millions of dollars)						
3		1975	1980	1985	1990		
4	**Phonograph Records**						
5	LP Albums	$1,485.00	$2,290.30	$1,280.50	$ 86.50		
6	Singles	211.50	269.30	281.00	94.40		
7	*Total Records*	$1,696.50	$2,559.60	$1,561.50	$ 180.90		
8	**Tapes**						
9	8-tracks	$ 583.00	$ 526.40	$ 25.30	$ -		
10	Cassettes	98.80	776.40	2,411.50	3,472.40		
11	Cassette Singles	-	-	-	87.40		
12	*Total Tapes*	$ 681.80	$1,302.80	$2,436.80	$3,559.80		
13	**Compact Discs**						
14	Regular CDs	$ -	$ -	$ 389.50	$3,451.60		
15	CD Singles	-	-	-	6.00		
16	*Total CDs*	$ -	$ -	$ 389.50	$3,457.60		

Figure 3.13

Centering Text across Columns

The main title, *Shipments of Audio Recordings*, and the subtitle, *(in millions of dollars)*, would look better centered over the worksheet. You can use the Center Across Columns tool in the Formatting toolbar to center the contents of one cell over a selected group of columns. This tool requires that you select a range whose leftmost cells contain the text you want to center; the selected range should extend across the columns that you want the text centered within.

To center text across columns:

1 Select cell A1, which contains the text *Shipments of Audio Recordings*.

2 As shown in Figure 3.14, extend the selection to include A1:E2, which includes the subtitle row (row 2) and the column for 1990 (column E).

	A	B	C	D	E	F	G
1	Shipments of Audio Recordings						
2	(in millions of dollars)						
3		1975	1980	1985	1990		
4	Phonograph Records						
5	LP Albums	$1,485.00	$2,290.30	$1,280.50	$ 86.50		
6	Singles	211.50	269.30	281.00	94.40		
7	Total Records	$1,696.50	$2,559.60	$1,561.50	$ 180.90		
8	Tapes						
9	8-tracks	$ 583.00	$ 526.40	$ 25.30	$ -		
10	Cassettes	98.80	776.40	2,411.50	3,472.40		
11	Cassette Singles	-	-	-	87.40		
12	Total Tapes	$ 681.80	$1,302.80	$2,436.80	$3,559.80		
13	Compact Discs						
14	Regular CDs	$ -	$ -	$ 389.50	$3,451.60		
15	CD Singles	-	-	-	6.00		
16	Total CDs	$ -	$ -	$ 389.50	$3,457.60		

Figure 3.14

3 Release the mouse button and click the **Center Across Columns** tool on the Formatting toolbar.

4 Click any cell to cancel the selection.

The title and subtitle should now be centered above the worksheet, as shown in Figure 3.15. *Note that the text for these titles is still stored in cells A1 and A2.*

	A	B	C	D	E	F	G
1	Shipments of Audio Recordings						
2	(in millions of dollars)						
3		1975	1980	1985	1990		
4	Phonograph Records						
5	LP Albums	$1,485.00	$2,290.30	$1,280.50	$ 86.50		
6	Singles	211.50	269.30	281.00	94.40		
7	Total Records	$1,696.50	$2,559.60	$1,561.50	$ 180.90		
8	Tapes						
9	8-tracks	$ 583.00	$ 526.40	$ 25.30	$ -		
10	Cassettes	98.80	776.40	2,411.50	3,472.40		
11	Cassette Singles	-	-	-	87.40		
12	Total Tapes	$ 681.80	$1,302.80	$2,436.80	$3,559.80		
13	Compact Discs						
14	Regular CDs	$ -	$ -	$ 389.50	$3,451.60		
15	CD Singles	-	-	-	6.00		
16	Total CDs	$ -	$ -	$ 389.50	$3,457.60		

Figure 3.15

EX-72

Microsoft Excel 5 for Windows

Changing Row Height

The worksheet might look better if there were more vertical space between the titles and the years. To create this extra space, you could insert a new row. However, you will have more precise control over the spacing if instead you change the height of the years' row. This process is very similar to that of changing the width of a column.

Whereas the width of a column is measured in characters, the height of a row is measured in **points**, a traditional type-measurement unit employed by printers and typographers. A point, abbreviated as *pt.*, is equal to one-72nd of an inch.

To change row height:

1 Position the pointer so it is over the *lower* edge of the heading for row 3 (on the line separating rows 3 and 4). The pointer should change to a vertical double arrow.

2 Hold down the mouse button and drag downward slightly to extend the lower edge of row 3. The reference area in the formula bar shows the height. Drag the mouse to set the height anywhere between 23 and 28 points, and then release the mouse button, as shown in Figure 3.16.

Height: 25.50							
	A	B	C	D	E	F	G
1	Shipments of Audio Recordings						
2	(in millions of dollars)						
3		1975	1980	1985	1990		
4	Phonograph Records						
5	LP Albums	$1,485.00	$2,290.30	$1,280.50	$ 86.50		
6	Singles	211.50	269.30	281.00	94.40		
7	Total Records	$1,696.50	$2,559.60	$1,561.50	$ 180.90		

Figure 3.16

Saving the Workbook under a Different Name

The worksheet has once again changed significantly. In the steps that follow, you will save the workbook before you print it. Because you will need to work with the earlier, unformatted version of the audio worksheet in later steps, you will save this formatted workbook with a different name.

To save the workbook with a different name:

1 Choose **File** and then **Save As.**
The Save As dialog box appears.

2 Type **audio2** for the file name and select **OK.**

EXIT If necessary, you can quit Excel now, and continue this project later.

PRINTING THE WORKSHEET

Before you print a worksheet, you should check your printer to make sure it is turned on, has paper, and is online (communicating with the computer). If it is a dot-matrix printer, you should ensure that the paper is properly lined up.

To print the worksheet:

1 Make sure your printer is ready.

2 Choose **File** and then **Print.**
The Print dialog box appears.

3 Select **OK.**
You may notice dotted lines on the screen—these indicate page breaks in the worksheet.

Removing Cell Gridlines

Your printout should look something like Figure 3.17. Worksheets that have been formatted with border lines usually look better (and are less confusing to use) if the cell gridlines are turned off.

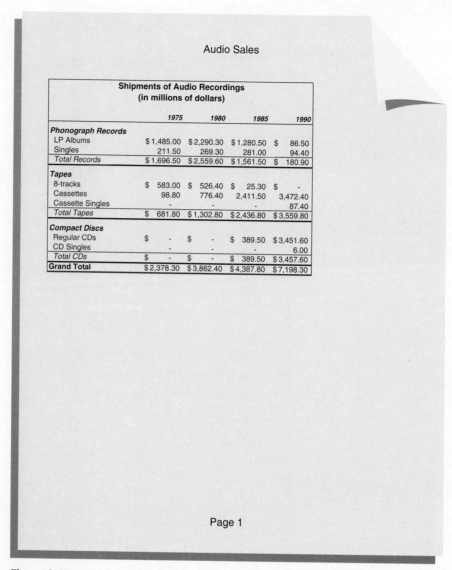

Audio Sales

Shipments of Audio Recordings (in millions of dollars)				
	1975	1980	1985	1990
Phonograph Records				
LP Albums	$1,485.00	$2,290.30	$1,280.50	$ 86.50
Singles	211.50	269.30	281.00	94.40
Total Records	$1,696.50	$2,559.60	$1,561.50	$ 180.90
Tapes				
8-tracks	$ 583.00	$ 526.40	$ 25.30	$ -
Cassettes	98.80	776.40	2,411.50	3,472.40
Cassette Singles	-	-	-	87.40
Total Tapes	$ 681.80	$1,302.80	$2,436.80	$3,559.80
Compact Discs				
Regular CDs	$ -	$ -	$ 389.50	$3,451.60
CD Singles	-	-	-	6.00
Total CDs	$ -	$ -	$ 389.50	$3,457.60
Grand Total	$2,378.30	$3,862.40	$4,387.80	$7,198.30

Page 1

Figure 3.17

To remove cell gridlines:

1 Choose **Tools** and then **Options.**
The Options dialog box appears.

2 Click the **View** tab.

3 Clear the **Gridlines** check box and select **OK,** as shown in Figure 3.18.

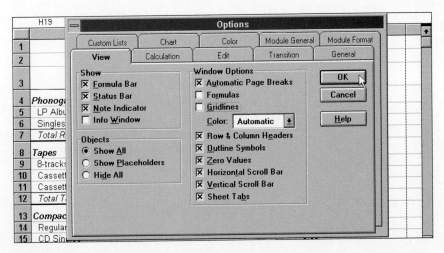

Figure 3.18

The worksheet now appears without gridlines. It will also print without gridlines.

 4 Click the **Print** tool as a shortcut to print the file again. Your printout should look similar to Figure 3.19.

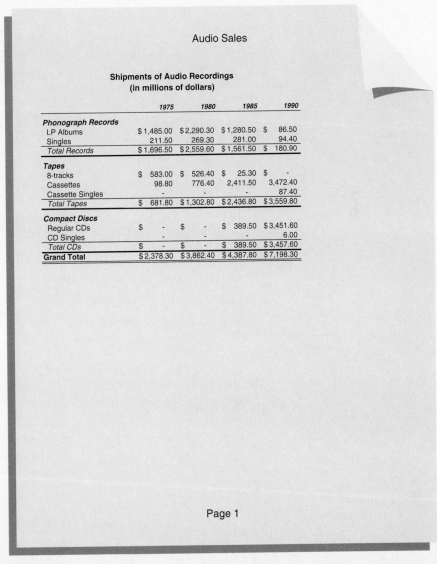

Figure 3.19

5 Close (and save) the AUDIO2 workbook. You will use the original AUDIO1 workbook for the remainder of this project.

> **Tip** If you want to preserve cell gridlines on-screen but do not want to have them appear on printouts, first choose Options from the Tools menu, select the View tab, and select the Gridlines check box so it is checked. Then choose Page Setup from the File menu, select the Sheet tab, and clear the Gridlines check box.

WORKING WITH STYLES

In Excel, a *style* is a group of format settings that are collected and referred to by a name. The Normal style is what is used by default for all cell entries, unless you specify a different style.

In the steps that follow, you will work with the original, unformatted AUDIO1 workbook. You will be changing some of the characteristics of the Normal style, but you will not be switching any cells from one style (Normal) to another (such as Comma style). Normal style is the only style used in this project.

Changing the Standard Font

With most printers, you will achieve the best printouts with the smoothest lines and clearest type if you use TrueType fonts. A *font* in Excel is a typeface—the form or design of letters and characters. The TrueType font technology is built directly into Windows. Several basic TrueType fonts are also provided with Windows. TrueType has the additional advantage of making the screen appear very similar to the printout. Excel's default font, called Arial, is a TrueType font.

The Style dialog box includes a brief description of the style. Six check boxes correspond to the formatting attributes that a style can include: Number, Alignment, Font, Border, Patterns, and Protection. The Normal style specifies all of these. In this section, you will learn how to change the Normal style setting for a worksheet so Courier New, another TrueType font, is used.

To change the standard font:

1 Open the AUDIO1 workbook.

2 Choose **Format** and then **Style**.
The Style dialog box appears.
The name Normal should appear in the Style Name list box. The font currently being used for the Normal style is Arial 10 (Arial, size of 10 points). You will change this to Courier New.

3 Select **Modify**.
A Format Cells dialog box appears, with tabs for each formatting attribute, as shown in Figure 3.20. You will now change the font.

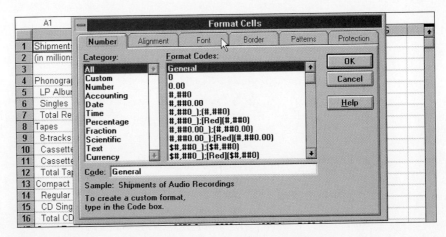

Figure 3.20

4 Click the **Font** tab.
The Font tab appears. Names of TrueType fonts are preceded by a "TT" logo.

5 Select the TrueType **Courier New** font in the list box (you may need to scroll through the alphabetical list) as shown in Figure 3.21, and then select **OK.**

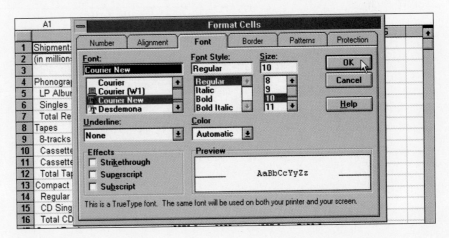

Figure 3.21

6 Select **OK** in the Style dialog box to complete the new definition of the Normal style.
All existing cell entries in this worksheet are in the Normal style and now appear in the TrueType Courier New font. The Normal style will also be in effect if you type new cell entries, so future entries will also appear in the Courier New font.

Formatting the Worksheet

In the steps that follow, you will format and adjust the worksheet, just as you did at the beginning of this project. These steps are condensed; refer back to the beginning of the project if necessary.

To format the worksheet:

1 Perform an AutoFormat on the range A1:E17, using the Accounting 1 table format.

2 Narrow column A to a width of about 20.

3 Center the main title and subtitle across columns A through E.

4 Turn off cell gridlines.

5 Increase the height of row 3 to about 25 points.

Your worksheet should look similar to Figure 3.22.

	A	B	C	D	E	F
1	Shipments of Audio Recordings					
2	(in millions of dollars)					
3		1975	1980	1985	1990	
4	Phonograph Records					
5	LP Albums	$1,485.00	$2,290.30	$1,280.50	$ 86.50	
6	Singles	211.50	269.30	281.00	94.40	
7	Total Records	$1,696.50	$2,559.60	$1,561.50	$ 180.90	
8	Tapes					
9	8-tracks	$ 583.00	$ 526.40	$ 25.30	$ –	
10	Cassettes	98.80	776.40	2,411.50	3,472.40	
11	Cassette Singles	–	–	–	87.40	
12	Total Tapes	$ 681.80	$1,302.80	$2,436.80	$3,559.80	
13	Compact Discs					
14	Regular CDs	$ –	$ –	$ 389.50	$3,451.60	

Figure 3.22

6 Save the workbook under the name AUDIO3.

7 Print the worksheet.

Compare your new printout with the earlier ones you made. Notice that the Courier New font resembles typewriter-style characters. You may wish to experiment with the other TrueType fonts on the system you are using.

USING INFORMATION WINDOWS

You have seen that several kinds of data can be stored in a cell and that a wide variety of formatting attributes can be applied to a cell. An *information window* lets you examine a cell's contents more closely. In the steps that follow, you will open an information window and then use it to find out more about the cells in your worksheet. Remember that some of these cells were extensively changed by the AutoFormat command. By studying these changes, you will better understand how to control worksheet formatting without using AutoFormat.

To activate an information window:

1 Select cell A1.

2 Choose **Tools** and then **Options.**
The Options dialog box appears.

3 Click the **View** tab.

4 Make sure the Info Window option is checked, and then select **OK.**

A new window will appear. If the AUDIO3 workbook was maximized prior to this, the new information window will completely cover the worksheet window, as shown in Figure 3.23; otherwise, a small information window will appear on top of the worksheet window. Notice that a different menu appears on the menu bar: this is because an information window is not a worksheet, and a different set of commands applies.

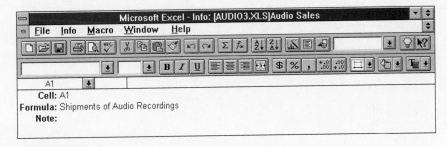

Figure 3.23

Switching between Windows

If several windows are visible on the screen at once, you can make a particular window active by clicking anywhere in that window. The active window will appear with a darker title bar. You can also use the list in the Window menu to choose a window by name; the names of currently open windows are included in the Window menu.

To switch between windows using the Window menu:

1 Activate the AUDIO3.XLS workbook window by opening the **Window** menu and choosing **AUDIO3.XLS.**
The information window seems to disappear, but it is just underneath the AUDIO3 worksheet window.

2 To reactivate the information window, open the **Window** menu and choose **Info: [AUDIO3.XLS]Audio Sales.**

Arranging Multiple Windows

For you to use the information window effectively, both it and the worksheet window must be visible at the same time. One way to achieve this is to *tile* the windows; doing so places them side by side, rather than one on top of the other. In the following steps, you will tile the two windows and then decrease the width of the information window to make more room for the worksheet window. Figure 3.24 shows the two windows tiled with their sizes being adjusted.

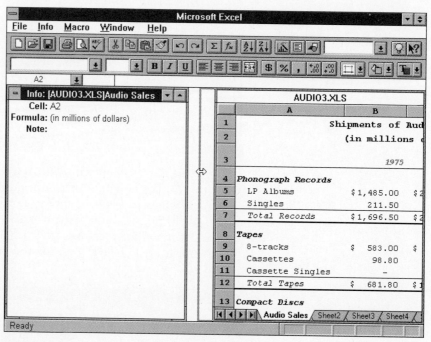

Figure 3.24

To arrange windows:

1 Choose **Window** and then **Arrange.**
The Arrange Windows dialog box appears.

2 Select **Tiled,** and then select **OK.**
The two windows are now tiled.

3 Select the information window by clicking it.

4 Decrease the width of the information window slightly by dragging its sizing border.

5 Select the worksheet window and increase its width, as shown in Figure 3.24.

Setting Up an Information Window

The standard display of an information window is not very informative. You can control what information about a cell is shown. In the following steps, you will instruct the information window to provide more details about a cell.

To set up an information window:

1 Activate the information window.

2 Choose **Info** and then **Value.**
Notice that Cell, Formula, and Note are already checked in the menu.

3 Choose **Info** and then **Format.**
Cell, Formula, Value, Format, and Note should all be checked.

4 Select the worksheet window.

5 Select cell G1.
Observe the information window. It should appear similar to Figure 3.25.

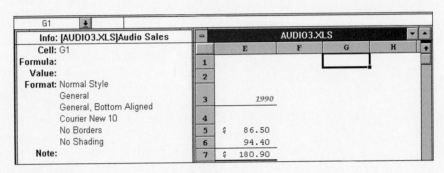

Figure 3.25

Using Information Windows to Examine Styles and Formats

The information window indicates that the active cell is G1; nothing appears next to Formula and Value because cell G1 is blank. The first line of the Format section reads *Normal Style.* This tells you that the Normal style applies to this cell. The subsequent lines provide details on what specifications of the Normal style apply. Because this cell was not included in the AutoFormat range, it has only the basic formatting attributes of the Normal style (without any additions or modifications).

General means the General Number format applies; this format does not include any special punctuation for numerical values.

General, Bottom Aligned describes the horizontal and vertical *alignment* of information in a cell. The horizontal alignment is *General;* this will cause numbers (and the results of formulas) to appear aligned right in their cells, and text to appear aligned left. The vertical alignment is *Bottom Aligned,* meaning that a cell's contents will appear to "sit" on the bottom edge of the cell.

Courier New 10 refers to the font—10-point Courier New. You will recall that earlier in this project you changed the font for Normal style to Courier New.

No Borders means no border lines will appear for this cell.

No Shading means no shading will be used in the cell.

To see information on cell A1:

1 Select cell A1.

2 Observe the information window; it will be similar to Figure 3.26.

A1	⬇	Shipments of Audio Recordings

Info: [AUDIO3.XLS]Audio Sales		AUDIO3.XLS		
Cell: A1		**A**	**B**	**C**
Formula: Shipments of Audio Recordings	1		Shipments of Audio	
Value: "Shipments of Audio Recordings"	2		(in millions of d	
Format: Normal Style	3		1975	
General	4	*Phonograph Records*		
+ Center Across, Bottom Aligned	5	LP Albums	$1,485.00	$2,290
+ Courier New 11, Bold	6	Singles	211.50	269
+ No Borders	7	*Total Records*	$1,696.50	$2,559
+ No Shading	8	*Tapes*		
Note:	9	8-tracks	$ 583.00	$ 526

Figure 3.26

The Formula line shows what was literally typed into the cell (similar to what you would see in the formula bar); the Value line indicates, in the case of formulas, what the result of the formula is. The quotation marks around *Shipments of Audio Recordings* serve to remind you that this is a *text* entry.

The Format section indicates that the Normal style applies to this cell; certain aspects of this style still apply, but others have been overridden. The Format section of an information window will first name the style that applies to the cell, list the aspects of the style that have *not* changed (if any), and then list the formats that preempt those originally specified in the style. These overriding formats are preceded by a plus sign.

You may have noticed that some of the overriding formats (such as *No Shading*) do not differ from those in the original Normal style. These are still considered to be overriding because they were set specifically by the AutoFormat command.

The definition of the Normal style has not changed; rather, some cells in the worksheet have been given customized formats that take precedence over the formats indicated in the Normal style. If you were to change the definition of the Normal style—for example, if you changed the font specified in the style—the change would affect any cell to which the Normal style had been applied, provided that an overriding format had not been applied to the cell.

In this worksheet, if you redefined the Normal style to use the font Times New Roman 12, cell A5 would reflect the change, but not cell A4. Examine both of these cells (A4 and A5) in the information window to make sure you understand why a redefinition of the Normal style would affect cell A5 but not cell A4.

To see information on cell B7:

1 Select the cell that contains total records for 1975 (B7).
Note that the cell's literal contents are =B5+B6, as indicated on the Formula line of the information window. The *value* of the cell is the result of this formula, 1696.5. Do not be alarmed by the strange-looking number format. Examine other cells with the information window.

2 Close the information window by selecting it and then double-clicking in its Control menu box.

3 Maximize the workbook window.

CUSTOMIZING TOOLBARS

Suppose that you frequently made use of information windows and wanted to avoid having to repeatedly use the Options dialog box. You could keep the Auditing toolbar open most of the time—it contains a button, called the Show Info Window tool, that creates information windows. But if you didn't want the extra screen space used up by the entire Auditing toolbar, you could add just the Show Info Window tool to one of the toolbars already on-screen.

Excel allows you to customize toolbars—to decide which tools you want to display on any toolbar. You do this graphically by dragging the desired tool from the Customize dialog box to the toolbar you want to contain the tool. You can remove a tool from a toolbar by dragging it from the toolbar to the Customize dialog box.

The Customize dialog box groups the dozens of available tools by category. For example, the show Info Window tool is in the Auditing category. You may need to examine several different categories before you find the particular tool you want to add to a toolbar.

In the steps that follow, you will customize the Standard toolbar by removing the Drawing button and adding a Show Info Window tool.

To customize a toolbar:

1 Choose **View** and then **Toolbars**.
The Toolbars dialog box appears.

2 Select **Customize**.
The Customize dialog box appears.

3 Click the **Drawing** tool on the Standard toolbar, drag its outline into the Customize dialog box (as shown in Figure 3.27), and release the mouse button.
The Drawing tool is removed from the Standard toolbar.

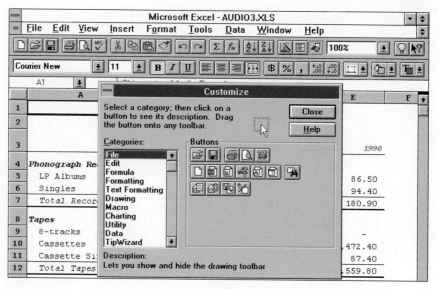

Figure 3.27

4 Scroll down the list of tool categories and click the **Auditing** category. This category contains the same set of buttons and tools that are on the Auditing toolbar.

5 Click the **Show Info Window** tool, as shown in Figure 3.28. A description of the tool appears in the Customize dialog box.

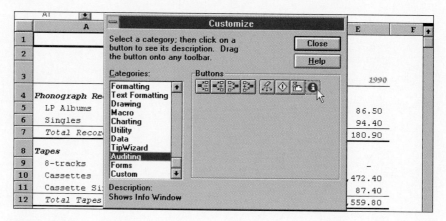

Figure 3.28

6 Drag the tool to the Standard toolbar, so it is placed where the Drawing tool used to be.

7 Select **Close**.
The Standard toolbar is now customized, as shown in Figure 3.29.

Figure 3.29

In the steps that follow, you will return the Standard toolbar to its default set of tools. You can reset a toolbar by opening the Toolbars dialog box, making sure the toolbar name is selected and checked in the list, and then selecting the Reset button.

To reset a toolbar to its default tools:

1 Choose **View** and then **Toolbar.**

2 Make sure the Standard toolbar is selected (highlighted) *and* checked.

3 Select the **Reset** button, and then select **OK.**
Notice that the Standard toolbar reverts to its default collection of tools.

4 Exit Excel, saving the workbook if necessary.
For many Excel operations, the most convenient access method is through a toolbar tool. You should feel free to customize toolbars to suit your particular needs as you work with Excel.

> **Tips** You can create a fully customized toolbar with a name of your choice by choosing Toolbars from the View menu, double-clicking in the Toolbar Name box, typing a name, and then selecting OK. A floating toolbar will appear along with the Customize dialog box. You can then drag whatever tools you want to the new toolbar.
>
> The file EXCEL5.XLB, normally stored in the Windows subdirectory, contains the most recently saved toolbar settings, including any customized toolbars you may have created. If you want to guarantee that Excel reverts to all of its original toolbar settings, you can delete this file before starting Excel. You can also rename the file (preserving the .XLB extension) and open it later, using the Open command from the File menu in Excel, to activate .XLB file's particular toolbar settings. Placing the file in the XLSTART subdirectory will cause the file to automatically open whenever Excel is started.

THE NEXT STEP

You are now ready to build a larger and more powerful worksheet. With the insight you have gained about formatting, you will be able to begin taking direct control over the formatting of your worksheets, because, as you have seen, AutoFormat won't always do what you want it to.

In the next project, you will build and format a worksheet on energy conservation that estimates the electricity used by a household and allows you to identify high-energy-cost appliances.

This concludes Project 3. You can either exit Excel, or go on to work the Study Questions, Review Exercises, and Assignments.

SUMMARY AND EXERCISES

Summary

- When you make major additions or changes to a worksheet, you must consider the effect those changes might have on existing parts of the worksheet—especially formulas.
- A formula's precedents are those cells on which the formula depends; a cell's dependents are other cells containing formulas that refer to that cell.
- You can insert blank cells into a worksheet, shifting existing cells to make room. However, if you do this, formulas do not always automatically adjust the way you might want them to.
- A circular-reference error occurs when a cell either directly or indirectly refers to itself.
- Clearing a range of cells erases the contents of the cells but does not remove the cells from the worksheet. Deleting removes both the contents and the cells.
- You can center cell entries across multiple columns; this is especially useful for worksheet titles.
- Row height can be changed in a manner similar to that for changing column width.
- You can remove the cell gridlines from a worksheet if you do not want them to appear on the screen or on printouts.
- A style is a named set of format attributes that can be applied to a cell to affect the cell's appearance. The default style is called *Normal*.
- TrueType fonts are preferable in most cases, because their appearance on-screen and on printouts is nearly identical, and because they produce sharper type on printouts.
- Information windows are used to find out detailed information about a cell, including its contents, value, and format.
- Customized formats applied to a cell override corresponding formats specified in the cell's style.

Key Terms and Operations

Key Terms	Operations
alignment	Arrange
circular reference	Clear a cell or range
dependent	Insert a cell or range
direct precedent	Print a worksheet
font	Trace Dependents
indirect precedent	Trace Precedents
information window	
points	
style	
tile	
tracer arrow	

Study Questions

Multiple Choice

1. The cells that a formula either directly or indirectly refers to are called its:
   - a. descendants.
   - b. ancestors.
   - c. lineage.
   - d. dependents.
   - e. precedents.

2. Cells (containing formulas) that refer either directly or indirectly to a particular cell are called that cell's:
   - a. referents.
   - b. dependents.
   - c. terminal nodes.
   - d. signs.
   - e. descendants.

3. Which statement about the Edit Insert command is correct?
   - a. Any information present in the insert area is automatically cleared before the inserted text is added.
   - b. The command will prompt you to type the text or numeric constants to be inserted.
   - c. The command works on cells containing formulas.
   - d. Existing cells in the insertion range will be shifted to accommodate the inserted, blank cells.
   - e. None of the above.

4. The formula $=SUM(B3:E3)$ is stored in cell E3. What (if anything) is the problem with the formula?
   - a. It contains a circular reference, and should probably be $=SUM(B3:D3)$.
   - b. It should be $=SUM(B3+C3+D3+E3)$.
   - c. It contains a circular reference, and should probably be $=SUM(E3:B3)$.
   - d. It should be $=B3+C3+D3+E3$.
   - e. Nothing is wrong with the formula.

5. What font technology, built into Windows, can usually improve the printed quality of worksheets?
   - a. TrueType
   - b. PostScript
   - c. TypeTrue
   - d. Linotype
   - e. monotype

6. What menu command is used to arrange multiple windows?
   - a. Window Sort
   - b. Sort Window
   - c. Edit Arrange
   - d. Window Arrange
   - e. Format Windows

7. What menu command can be used to change from one window to another?
   - a. Options Goto
   - b. Edit Window
   - c. Window
   - d. File Window
   - e. Only mouse and keyboard shortcuts are available for this action.

8. What feature can be used to get detailed information on a particular cell?
   a. an information window
   b. the reference area
   c. the formula bar
   d. the Edit menu
   e. the Format menu

9. What term is used to describe a particular typeface design in Excel?
   a. style   d. format
   b. face   e. regular
   c. font

10. What command should be used to save a file under a new name?
    a. New in the File menu
    b. Save in the File menu
    c. Rename in the File menu
    d. Save As in the File menu
    e. Save As in the Edit menu

Short Answer

1. The formula $=A1-A2+A3$ is stored in cell A2. What (if anything) is wrong with the formula?

2. What mouse action or command is used to find the direct precedents of the currently selected cell?

3. Will centering text across columns change the cells where the text is stored? Will it break up the text and distribute the pieces to be stored in various cells?

4. List the formatting settings that can be included within a style.

5. Is inserting a blank row the best way to increase the space between rows of information in a worksheet? If not, what is a better way?

6. Are cell gridlines and border lines the same thing?

7. What font technology is usually the best choice for clear printouts?

8. What menu command is used to switch among multiple windows?

9. What kinds of information can be displayed in an information window?

10. What command is used to arrange multiple windows?

For Discussion

1. Why should you be careful when making major changes to a worksheet? What things should you do before you make a change? What should you check after the change?

2. What is a circular reference? Give an example.

3. Describe what happens when a customized format is applied to a cell. How does this affect the corresponding formats specified in the cell's style?

Review Exercises

Municipal Waste Trends

In the first review exercise in Project 2, you built a workbook about municipal waste and saved it under the name EPA1. If you haven't already created that worksheet, refer to Project 2 to build it. Then proceed to add the new information shown in Figure 3.30 for metals in the nonfood category.

	A	B	C	D	E	F	G	H
2		1960	1970	1980	1990			
3	Nonfood Wastes							
4	Paper	0.91	1.19	1.32	1.6			
5	Glass	0.2	0.34	0.36	0.28			
6	Plastics	0.01	0.08	0.19	0.32			
7	Metals	0.32	0.38	0.35	0.34			
8	Total Nonfood	1.44	1.99	2.22	2.54			
9	Other							
10	Food	0.37	0.34	0.32	0.29			
11	Yard	0.61	0.62	0.66	0.7			
12	Total Other	0.98	0.96	0.98	0.99			
13	Grand Total	2.42	2.95	3.2	3.53			
14								

Figure 3.30

Use the Insert command to create a blank row for this new information; the information should be between the rows for plastics and total nonfood. Check, adjust, and copy formulas as necessary. Format the worksheet using AutoFormat with a nonaccounting table format. Additional opportunity for numeric formatting will be possible after you complete the next project. Save the workbook under the name EPA2.

Winter Olympic Games Medals

In the second review exercise of Project 2, you built and saved OLYMPIC1, a workbook that tabulates medals won by selected countries during the 1992 Winter Olympic Games. If you haven't already created that workbook, refer to Project 2 to build it.

Use the information shown in Figure 3.31 to add Italy to the worksheet. Use the Insert command to create a blank row for this new information; Italy should be the last country in the list. Check, adjust, and copy formulas as necessary. Format the worksheet using AutoFormat with a nonfinancial table format. Additional opportunities for numeric formatting will be possible after you complete the next project. Save the workbook under the name OLYMPIC2.

	A	B	C	D	E	F	G	H	I
1	1992 Winter Olympiad								
2									
3	Country	Gold	Silver	Bronze	Total				
4	Germany	10	10	6	26				
5	Unified Team	9	6	8	23				
6	Austria	6	7	8	21				
7	Norway	9	6	5	20				
8	Italy	4	6	4	?				
9	Total	34	29	27	90				
10									

Figure 3.31

Assignments

Space Payloads

In the third assignment in Project 2, you built and saved SPACE1, a workbook that tabulates rocket payloads put into space by selected countries. If you haven't already created that workbook, refer to Project 2 to build it.

Add the information for the European Space Agency (ESA) as shown in Figure 3.32. Try using Move rather than Insert to make space for the new information. Adjust and copy formulas as necessary, change the standard font to a TrueType font of your choice, format the worksheet using AutoFormat and a nonaccounting table format, and save the workbook under the name SPACE2.

	A	B	C	D	E	F	G	H	I
1	Space Payloads								
2									
3		1988	1988	1988	1988	Average			
4	USSR	107	95	96	101	99.75			
5	United States	15	22	31	30	24.5			
6	ESA	2	2	1	4	?			
7	Japan	2	4	7	2	3.75			
8	Total	126	123	135	137	130.25			
9									

Figure 3.32

Coffee House Income

Starting with the third assignment in Project 1 and continuing in the first assignment in Project 2, you built and saved COFFEE2, a spreadsheet that calculates the income derived from sales of various coffees at Clem's Coffee Clutch. If you haven't already created that workbook, refer to Projects 1 and 2 to build it.

Add information for Cafe Royale, as shown in Figure 3.33. Adjust and copy formulas as necessary, change the standard font to a TrueType font of your choice, format the worksheet using AutoFormat, and save the workbook under the name COFFEE3.

	A	B	C	D	E	F	G	H
1	Coffee	Cost	Selling Price	No. Sold	Income			
2	House Blend	0.39	0.95	60	33.6			
3	Espresso	0.61	1.25	12	7.68			
4	Cappuccino	0.74	1.5	22	16.72			
5	Cafe Mocha	0.55	1.45	35	31.5			
6	Cafe Royale	0.68	1.85	55	?			
7	Total			184	89.5			
8								

Figure 3.33

Open an information window, set it to display values and formats, adjust the COFFEE3 and information windows in a tiled arrangement, and examine the format and style settings in the worksheet.

Additions to AUDIO3

Modify the AUDIO3 worksheet to include data for 1991, as well as figures for shipments of music videos, as shown in Figure 3.34. After inserting the new information, adjust and copy formulas as necessary, reformat the worksheet, and save the workbook under the name AUDIO4.

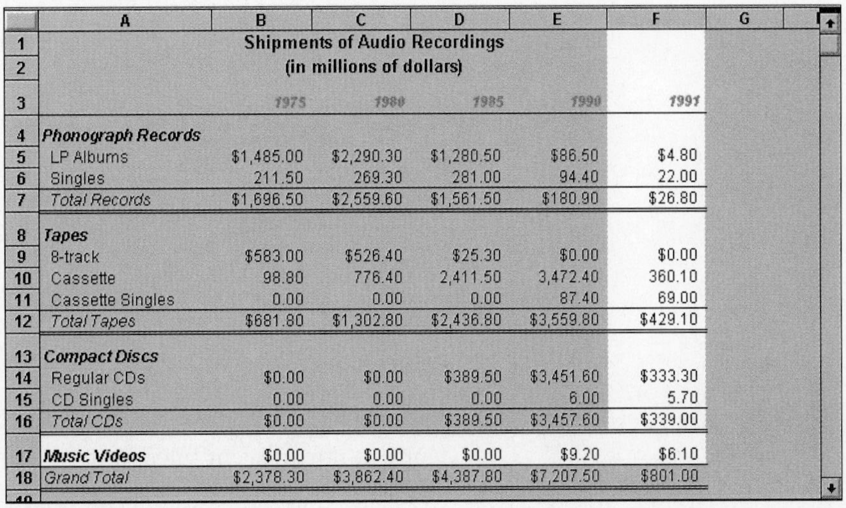

	A	B	C	D	E	F	G
1	Shipments of Audio Recordings						
2	(in millions of dollars)						
3		1975	1980	1985	1990	1991	
4	*Phonograph Records*						
5	LP Albums	$1,485.00	$2,290.30	$1,280.50	$86.50	$4.80	
6	Singles	211.50	269.30	281.00	94.40	22.00	
7	*Total Records*	$1,696.50	$2,559.60	$1,561.50	$180.90	$26.80	
8	*Tapes*						
9	8-track	$583.00	$526.40	$25.30	$0.00	$0.00	
10	Cassette	98.80	776.40	2,411.50	3,472.40	360.10	
11	Cassette Singles	0.00	0.00	0.00	87.40	69.00	
12	*Total Tapes*	$681.80	$1,302.80	$2,436.80	$3,559.80	$429.10	
13	*Compact Discs*						
14	Regular CDs	$0.00	$0.00	$389.50	$3,451.60	$333.30	
15	CD Singles	0.00	0.00	0.00	6.00	5.70	
16	*Total CDs*	$0.00	$0.00	$389.50	$3,457.60	$339.00	
17	*Music Videos*	$0.00	$0.00	$0.00	$9.20	$6.10	
18	*Grand Total*	$2,378.30	$3,862.40	$4,387.80	$7,207.50	$801.00	

Figure 3.34

PROJECT 4:   USING FORMULAS IN A WORKSHEET

After completing this project, you should be able to:

► Create customized numeric formats

► Magnify or reduce your view of a worksheet

► Change the alignment of cell entries

► Define and use names for constants and ranges

► Copy to nonadjacent selections

► Recognize and use absolute cell references

► Change the font style and size of a cell entry

► Apply borders to the worksheet

► Produce landscape printouts

CASE STUDY: ANALYZING HOME ENERGY USAGE

One way to decide how to save on home-electric bills—and reduce electricity consumption and related power-plant pollution—is to determine how each electrical appliance in your home or apartment contributes to your total monthly bill. Along with your personal electricity-usage patterns, many other factors, such as season, climate, and the availability of alternative energy sources, will influence the total bill. Excel is the ideal tool for making sense of these variables and simplifying the task of estimating electricity consumption.

Designing the Solution

In this project, you will build a worksheet that lists various electrical appliances and estimates their monthly consumption of electricity. The worksheet will describe a basic, all-electric home during a mild winter month in a moderate climate. Constructing this worksheet will involve calculating the monthly energy used by each appliance, a calculation based on each appliance's energy-consumption rate and the amount of time the appliance is used during a month.

There are several ways you could design a worksheet to implement the calculation described above. You could construct one giant formula to perform all calculations on all variables, but the worksheet will be easier to understand and modify if you break the process into smaller steps comprising a series of simpler formulas. This is the approach you will take in this project.

Figure 4.1 shows the completed worksheet. Separate columns designate each of the major variables involved in the calculation. The flexibility of this electronic worksheet will make easy experimentation and adaptation possible with variables such as different appliances, different electricity-usage habits, and so on.

Residential Electricity Usage
Based on a cost of
$0.08 per kilowatt-hour

Appliance	Wattage	Mon	Tue	Wed	Thu	Fri	Sat	Sun	Operating Hours per Month	Kilowatt-hours per month	Estimated Cost per Month
Heating/Cooling											
Heat pump (3 ton)	4,800	4.00	4.00	4.00	4.00	4.00	6.00	6.00	128	614	$49.15
Portable heater	1,500	1.00	1.00	1.00	1.00	1.00	2.00	2.00	36	54	4.32
Water heater	4,100	2.00	2.00	2.00	2.00	2.00	4.00	4.00	72	295	23.62
Kitchen											
Frost-free refrigerator	460	15.00	15.00	15.00	15.00	15.00	15.00	15.00	420	193	15.46
Convection oven	3,000	0.00	0.00	0.00	0.00	0.00	3.00	3.00	24	72	5.76
Microwave oven	1,500	0.25	0.25	0.25	0.25	0.25	0.50	1.00	11	17	1.32
Dishwasher	1,200	1.00	0.00	1.00	0.00	1.00	1.00	1.00	20	24	1.92
Laundry											
Washing machine	510	0.00	0.00	0.00	0.00	0.00	3.00	3.00	24	12	0.98
Clothes dryer	4,850	0.00	0.00	0.00	0.00	0.00	3.00	3.00	24	116	9.31
Lighting											
Incandescent	150	5.00	5.00	5.00	5.00	5.00	5.00	5.00	140	21	1.68
Fluorescent (twin)	96	5.00	5.00	5.00	5.00	5.00	5.00	5.00	140	13	1.08
Fluorescent (compact)	18	5.00	5.00	5.00	5.00	5.00	5.00	5.00	140	3	0.20
Electronics											
Color television	145	2.00	2.00	2.00	2.00	4.00	6.00	7.00	100	15	1.16
Personal computer	160	1.00	1.00	1.00	1.00	1.00	2.00	3.00	40	6	0.51
Total											**$116.46**

(Page 1)

Figure 4.1

ENTERING THE WORKSHEET CONSTANTS

You will first enter some of the worksheet titles and number constants. You will do some formatting early, to make subsequent data entry and formula construction easier to follow. You can refer to Figure 4.2 to see a partial, unformatted version of the worksheet. As in the previous project, the more intricate formatting steps will be completed in the final phase of worksheet construction.

	A	B	C	D	E	F	G	H	I	J	K	L	M
1	Residential Electricity Usage												
2	Based on a cost of												
3		0.08											
4				Hours Cycled-On									
5	Appliance	Wattage	Mon	Tue	Wed	Thu	Fri	Sat	Sun	Operating	Kilowatt-hc	Estimated	Cost per Month
6	Heating/Cooling												
7	Heat pump (3 ton)												
8	Portable heater												
9	Water heater												
10	Kitchen												
11	Frost-free refrigerator												
12	Conventional oven												
13	Microwave oven												
14	Dishwasher												
15	Laundry												
16	Washing machine												
17	Clothes dryer												
18	Lighting												
19	Incandescent												
20	Fluorescent (twin)												
21	Fluorescent (compact)												
22	Electronics												
23	Color television												
24	Personal computer												
25	Total												
26													

Figure 4.2

To enter the main title and first subtitle:

1 Open a new workbook, select the **Sheet1** tab, and ensure that the font of the Normal style is Arial 10.

2 Enter `Residential Electricity Usage` in cell A1.

3 Enter `Based on a cost of` in cell A2.

Creating Customized Formats

In Figure 4.1, the second subtitle, *$0.08 per kilowatt-hour*, might appear to be a text entry. If it *were* a text entry, formulas in the worksheet could not meaningfully refer to it when calculating. In fact, it is a numeric entry, 0.08, assigned a ***customized format***. Any time you want to have a value appear in some form other than the standard formats available, you can create your own format. For example, you might want a special date format, a format designed to represent amounts in a foreign currency, or a format that includes an abbreviation for a special unit of measurement. For this worksheet, you will create a format that will display whatever number is typed in the cell, preceded by a dollar sign and followed by the phrase *per kilowatt-hour*.

To enter and custom-format the second subtitle:

1 Enter `0.08` in cell A3.

2 Make sure cell A3 is still selected; choose **Format** and then **Cells**. The Format Cells dialog box appears.

3 Select the **Number** tab, if necessary. The Number format tab is displayed.

4 Double-click in the **Code** edit box. The Code edit box is where you can enter formatting codes to specify how you want numbers to appear.

5 Type the formatting code `$0.00 "per kilowatt-hour"` in the **Code** box.

Note the use of quotation marks. The screen should resemble Figure 4.3. The format code instructs Excel to display a value in cell A3 with a leading dollar sign, show a leading zero before the decimal point for numbers less than one, always show two digits to the right of the decimal, and follow the number with the phrase *per kilowatt-hour*.

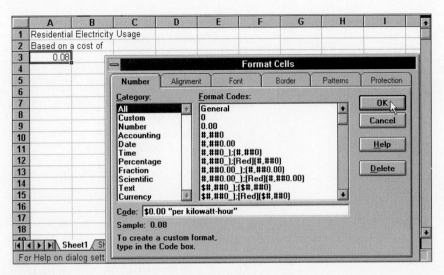

Figure 4.3

6 Select **OK** to complete the format specification.

Now you have assigned a customized format to cell A3. Number signs (#) appear in the cell, indicating that the column is too narrow to display the number 0.08 in the new format.

7 Widen column A to about 25 characters, so that all three cell entries (A1, A2, and A3) are accommodated.

It is very important to recognize that for calculation purposes, cell A3 contains the *number* 0.08. Formatting affects the way a cell entry *appears* but does not change the value of the entry or its data type (text constant, number constant, or formula).

Tip If you want to force every entry in a range to be converted to text, you can choose the Text format from the Number tab of the Format Cells dialog box. The Text format is the only format that actually changes the underlying data type of a cell entry.

Changing the View of a Worksheet Window

At normal magnification, a worksheet is rarely visible in its entirety; the screen and the worksheet window restrict your view. Excel is capable of *zooming out* (reducing) or *zooming in* (magnifying) to let you see more or less of the worksheet.

Occasionally, you will zoom in for a closer look, but more often you will zoom out to see more of the worksheet at once. A disadvantage of zooming out is that because you see more of the worksheet in a reduced size, it is more difficult to position correctly on specific cells.

You can also change to *full-screen view,* which temporarily removes the toolbars and status bar to allow more room for the worksheet itself. Switching to full-screen view does not in itself change the magnification of the worksheet, though full-screen view can be used in conjunction with the zoom command.

In the steps that follow, you will experiment with the Zoom and Full Screen commands.

To magnify a worksheet:

1 Open the **Zoom Control** list box on the Standard toolbar. A list box opens, showing various magnifications.

2 Select **200%** in the **Zoom Control** list box. Each worksheet cell appears much larger, but you can't see as many cells.

To reduce a worksheet:

1 Open the **Zoom Control** list box on the Standard toolbar.

2 Select **50%** in the **Zoom Control** list box. You can see many more cells in the worksheet, but individual cells become more difficult to read. This is especially true when Windows is running with standard VGA video (rather than with SuperVGA).

To set a custom magnification:

1 Click on the **50%,** which is currently displayed in the **Zoom Control** box.

2 Type **85** for the magnification and press (ENTER)

To return to 100% magnification:

1 Click the **Zoom Control.**

2 Select **100%** in the **Zoom Control** list box.

Tip If you want to magnify or reduce the worksheet so it accommodates a particular range of cells, select the range first and then choose Selection from the Zoom Control list box.

The Zoom commands are also available by selecting Zoom from the View menu.

From now on, you should change your view of the worksheet whenever you want.

To change to full-screen view:

1 Choose **View** and then **Full Screen.** The toolbars and status bar disappear, and more rows of the worksheet are visible. A single-tool floating toolbar also appears, called the Full Screen toolbar; if you select this tool, you can switch back to normal view. You will now close the toolbar so it does not clutter the screen.

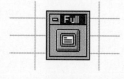

2 Click the Control menu box of the floating toolbar to close the toolbar. The toolbar disappears. You can always return to normal view by using the View menu. Excel will now remember your preference of not having the Full Screen toolbar appear in full-screen view.

3 Choose **View** and then **Full Screen.**

This "unchecks" the Full Screen option, returning the screen to normal view.

Using Series Fill

In the sections that follow, you will enter and partially format the column titles. To make it easier to see what you're typing, you will first zoom to a 75% magnification of the worksheet. As you work, you can refer to Figure 4.4.

You could manually enter the days of the week as the column headings in C5:I5, but Excel provides a shortcut called *AutoFill* that you can use when entering the days of the week or names of months. When you use the fill handle to copy information that represents part of a standard sequence or series, Excel automatically fills in the other members of the series. For example, if you use the fill handle to copy a cell that contains the text *Feb* and select a range three cells to the right, Excel will enter *Mar*, *Apr*, and *May*. If you don't want the series-fill effect to take place, hold down (CTRL) while dragging the fill handle.

A1	↓	Residential Electricity Usage								
	A	B	C	D	E	F	G	H	I	J	K
1	Residential Electricity Usage										
2	Based on a cost of										
3	$0.08 per kilowatt-hour										
4			Hours Cycled-On								
5	Appliance	Wattage	Mon	Tue	Wed	Thu	Fri	Sat	Sun	Operating	Kilowat
6											
7											

Figure 4.4

To enter the column titles:

1 Use the **Zoom Control** list box to reduce magnification of the worksheet to 75 percent.

2 Enter `Appliance` in cell A5.

3 Enter `Wattage` in cell B5.

4 Enter `Mon` in cell C5.

5 With cell C5 selected, position the pointer at the lower-right corner of the cell so the pointer forms the fill handle; drag the fill handle to cell I5 and release the mouse button.
The range now contains abbreviations for the days of the week, as shown in Figure 4.4.

6 In cell C4, *above* the column title *Mon*, enter `Hours Cycled-On`

7 In cell J5, enter `Operating Hours per Month`
This column is used to estimate how many hours per month an appliance is used. Do not be concerned if a column title or other cell entry appears either to spill over into a neighboring cell or to be cut off by a neighboring cell.

8 In cell K5, enter `Kilowatt-hours per Month`
Later you will construct a formula to calculate the number of kilowatt-hours used each month.

9 In cell L5, enter `Estimated Cost per Month`

This column will contain a formula that computes the electricity cost.

10 Press (CTRL) + (HOME)

The worksheet should resemble Figure 4.4.

Adjusting the Width of Multiple Columns

The columns for weekdays should be narrowed. Instead of setting each column width separately, you can adjust the width of a group of columns by selecting the group and then adjusting the width of any column in the group.

To adjust the width of a group of columns:

1 Select columns C through I by dragging across column headings C through I, and then release the mouse button.

2 Position the pointer on the *right* edge of any selected column heading. Using the width information provided in the reference area, drag the mouse to select a new width of about 5 characters, as shown in Figure 4.5.

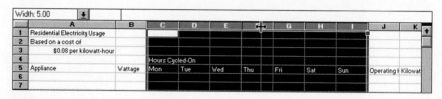

Figure 4.5

3 Release the mouse button.

Changing the Alignment of Cell Entries

A text entry is automatically aligned against the left edge of its cell, and a number entry against the right edge, but you can change this alignment. Text titles appearing above numeric entries will look better if they are aligned at the center or to the right.

Notice that Figure 4.1 shows the long column titles, such as *Operating Hours per Month*, wrapping in their cells. *Wrapping* means to break a long entry into separate lines.

In the steps that follow, you will align to the right the column titles *Wattage* through *Estimated Cost per Month* and specify that long entries be wrapped.

To align to the right and wrap selected column titles:

1 Select cell B5.

2 Select B5:L5, the range of text entries to be aligned.

3 Choose **Format** and then **Cells.**

The Format Cells dialog box appears.

4 Select the **Alignment** tab.

The Alignment tab appears.

5 Select the **Right** option button in the **Horizontal** group.

6 Select the **Wrap Text** check box if it is not already checked. The screen should resemble Figure 4.6.

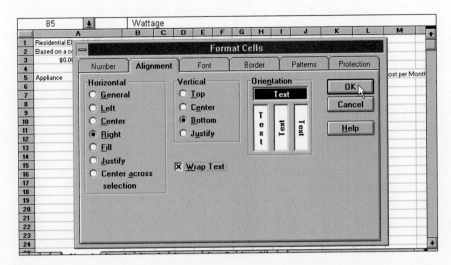

Figure 4.6

7 Select **OK** to complete the alignment.
The column headings should now be aligned to the right and, where necessary, wrap within their cells. Notice that wrapping automatically adjusted the height of row 5.

8 To make the worksheet look less cramped, increase the width of columns J, K, and L to about 10 characters.

Entering the Remaining Text Constants

In the following steps, you will enter the text constants for the row titles. Note that two levels of indentation are used for the row titles to visually outline the list of appliances. Section titles such as *Heating/Cooling* are indented two spaces, and individual appliance names, such as *Water heater*, are indented four spaces. You can use Figure 4.7 as a reference.

	A	B	C	D	E	F	G	H	I	J	K	L
1	Residential Electricity Usage											
2	Based on a cost of											
3	$0.08 per kilowatt-hour											
4			Hours Cycled-On									
5	Appliance	Wattage	Mon	Tue	Wed	Thu	Fri	Sat	Sun	Operating Hours per Month	Kilowatt-hours per Month	Estimated Cost per Month
6	Heating/Cooling											
7	Heat pump (3 ton)											
8	Portable heater											
9	Water heater											
10	Kitchen											
11	Frost-free refrigerator											
12	Conventional oven											
13	Microwave oven											
14	Dishwasher											
15	Laundry											
16	Washing machine											
17	Clothes dryer											
18	Lighting											
19	Incandescent											
20	Fluorescent (twin)											
21	Fluorescent (compact)											
22	Electronics											
23	Color television											
24	Personal computer											
25	Total											
26												

Figure 4.7

To enter the row titles:

1 Select A1:L5, the entire functional area of the worksheet.

2 Click the **Zoom Control** list box and choose **Selection** to fit the magnification to the selected range.

3 Select cell A6.

4 In cell A6, press (SPACE) twice, type **Heating/Cooling** and press (ENTER)

5 In cell A7, press (SPACE) four times, type **Heat pump (3 ton)** and press (ENTER)

6 Refer to Figure 4.7 to enter the remaining row titles.
Note that *Total* is not indented; *Kitchen*, *Laundry*, *Lighting*, and *Electronics* are indented by preceding the text with two spaces, and the remaining titles are indented four spaces.

7 Press (CTRL) + (HOME) and then choose **Tools** and then **Spelling** to check the spelling of the worksheet.

8 Save the worksheet under the name ENERGY1. The worksheet should resemble Figure 4.7.

> **Tip** If you are building a worksheet that requires several levels of indentation, you can use separate columns for each indentation level, rather than using spaces. Although this approach slightly increases the complexity of the worksheet, adjustment (via column-width changes) of the amount of indentation for each level is much easier.

Entering the Number Constants

You will now enter the constants for wattage and hours cycled-on. Note that the numbers in the hours cycled-on section are ordinary decimal numbers: an hour-and-a-half is written as 1.50, not 1:30. In the following steps, you will also learn a data-entry shortcut that allows you to fill a large selection easily with a single entry.

The first step in calculating the energy used by an appliance over the course of a month is to determine the appliance's power consumption, or the rate at which it uses up energy. The amount of electrical power an appliance consumes is measured in *watts*. A typical light bulb uses 100 watts; a typical microwave oven uses 1500 watts.

If you need to know how many watts an appliance uses, check the appliance's operating manual or look on the appliance itself. If watts are not listed on the appliance, then volts (V) and amps (A) will likely be listed. You can multiply volts by amps to calculate watts. Note that sometimes the appliance's power supply will list the maximum rated power consumption, not what the appliance actually uses under normal operating conditions.

To enter the appliance-wattage constants:

1 Enter **4800** in cell B7.

This is the wattage of the 3-ton heat pump.

2 Referring to Figure 4.1 or 4.8, carefully enter the remaining number constants for the wattage column *only*.

Reminder Because all punctuation is added through formatting, do not type commas in any of the numbers.

	A	Wattage	Mon	Tue	Wed	Thu	Fri	Sat	Sun	Operating Hours per Month	Kilowatt-hours per Month	Estimated Cost per Month
1	Residential Electricity Usage											
2	Based on a cost of											
3	$0.08 per kilowatt-hour											
4			Hours Cycled-On									
5	Appliance	Wattage	Mon	Tue	Wed	Thu	Fri	Sat	Sun	Operating Hours per Month	Kilowatt-hours per Month	Estimated Cost per Month
6	Heating/Cooling											
7	Heat pump (3 ton)	4800	4	4	4	4	4	6	6			
8	Portable heater	1500	1	1	1	1	1	2	2			
9	Water heater	4100	2	2	2	2	2	4	4			
10	Kitchen											
11	Frost-free refrigerator	460	15	15	15	15	15	15	15			
12	Conventional oven	3000	0	0	0	0	0	3	3			
13	Microwave oven	1500	0.25	0.25	0.25	0.25	0.25	0.5	1			
14	Dishwasher	1200	1	0	1	0	1	1	1			
15	Laundry											
16	Washing machine	510	0	0	0	0	0	3	3			
17	Clothes dryer	4850	0	0	0	0	0	3	3			
18	Lighting											
19	Incandescent	150	5	5	5	5	5	5	5			
20	Fluorescent (twin)	96	5	5	5	5	5	5	5			
21	Fluorescent (compact)	18	5	5	5	5	5	5	5			
22	Electronics											
23	Color television	145	2	2	2	2	4	6	7			
24	Personal computer	160	1	1	1	1	1	2	3			
25	Total											
26												

Figure 4.8

Your next step is to estimate how many hours per month the appliance is used. With many appliances you can estimate how many hours the appliance runs each day of the week, total these times, and then approximate a month's worth of use by multiplying the total by four (since there are about four weeks in a month).

Notice in Figure 4.8 that all three types of lighting are estimated to run at five hours per day, every day of the week. Rather than using the Copy command or typing 5 in each of the 21 cells, you will use an alternative method for this type of repetitive entry.

To quickly enter the usage times for lighting:

1 Select C19:I21, the range encompassing hours cycled-on for each of the lighting types for all of the days.

2 Type **5** and press (CTRL) + (ENTER)
The number 5 should be entered in all the cells of the selected range.

Other appliances vary in their consumption of electricity. For example, an air conditioner or oven consumes significant amounts of electricity, but only when actually in use. When calculating the hours cycled-on in your own home, you may need to refer to published approximations of typical running times for certain appliances.

To enter the remaining usage times:

1 Enter the remaining numbers for hours cycled-on. Use the various shortcut methods you've learned so far to do this quickly and easily.

2 Save the worksheet.
Your worksheet should now resemble Figure 4.8.

Electric bills are based on the number of hours each appliance runs, and the billing units are *kilowatt-hours*. A kilowatt is 1000 watts, and one kilowatt-hour is the energy consumed by running a 1000-watt appliance for one hour. If you run a 1000-watt hair dryer for three hours a month, you have consumed 3000 watt-hours or 3 kilowatt-hours of energy. The formula for energy consumption is generally written as (watts/1000) * hours. Remember to divide watts by 1000 when converting to kilowatts.

To estimate the monthly energy cost of an appliance, multiply the kilowatt-hours the appliance consumes by the cost per kilowatt-hour. With typical residential electric rates, electricity costs between $0.03 and $0.15 per kilowatt-hour. Check an electric bill or call your utility company to find out the rate for your area. The worksheet you build in this project will presume that electricity is billed at a flat rate.

You have already entered an electric rate of 8 cents ($0.08) per kilowatt-hour in cell A3. The monthly cost of the hair dryer mentioned above is 24 cents. As you can see in Figure 4.1, large appliances used for heating or cooling are the major consumers of electricity in the home.

Documenting Formulas

The total time an appliance is operated in a month is calculated by multiplying a week's operating time by four, because there are about four weeks in a month. For example, to compute the total monthly operating hours for the heat pump, the formula =SUM(C7:I7)*4 could be entered in cell J7. The SUM function computes a week's operating hours, and the result is then multiplied by 4.

It may seem that anyone examining the formula would understand that the 4 represents the four weeks in a month, but the 4 is a rather benign example of a *magic number*. Magic numbers are undocumented constants that show up in formulas. The problem with magic numbers is twofold. First, magic numbers carry little intrinsic meaning, so when people (even the worksheet's author) examine the worksheet long after it was first created, they may not understand the purpose of the number. Second, magic numbers buried within formulas make it harder to change the worksheet. For example, suppose you created and copied the formula just described and later wanted to use a more precise definition of a typical month as 4.345 weeks. You would have to first edit or rebuild the formula and then recopy it to replace the old formula.

Defining Names

One alternative to using magic numbers is to present such constants explicitly in the worksheet, in their own easily changed cells. This is an approach that you have already taken when you entered the information about the electric rate of $0.08 per kilowatt-hour. Excel offers another approach: defined names.

A ***defined name*** is a name you create that refers to other cells or to constants, such as the number of weeks per month. Each workbook has its own dictionary of defined names to which you can add or delete definitions.

In the following steps, you will define the name *WeeksPerMonth* to stand for 4. You will then use this name in the formulas for operating hours per month.

To define names for constants:

1 Choose **Insert** and then **Name**.

2 Choose **Define**.
The Define Name dialog box appears.

3 Type `WeeksPerMonth` in the **Names in Workbook** box, replacing any text that might have initially appeared in the box.
Remember to type the name with no spaces, and with mixed upper- and lowercase letters.

4 Type `4` in the box labeled **Refers to,** replacing any text that might have initially appeared in the box.

5 Select the **Add** button.
The dialog box should now resemble Figure 4.9. The newly defined name is added to the dictionary, which is listed under Names in Workbook. An equal sign is also automatically inserted.

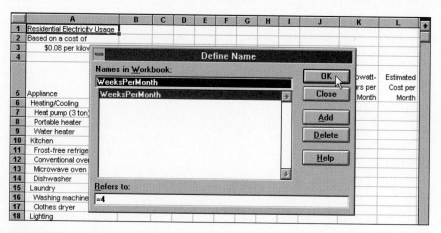

Figure 4.9

6 Select **OK** to close the dialog box.

Instead of typing the constant *4*, you can now use the name *WeeksPerMonth* in formulas within this worksheet.

> ***Tip*** When you define a name, follow these guidelines:
>
> ■ Make the name meaningful. Don't use names such as *X* or *N*. If a name refers to the marginal tax rate then make the name *MarginalTaxRate*, not *X*.
>
> ■ Make the name readable by mixing uppercase and lowercase letters; *MarginalTaxRate*, not *MARGINALTAXRATE*. You can also use underscores: *Marginal__Tax__Rate*.
>
> ■ Use only letters, underscores, and numbers in a name; never use spaces; and don't make a name look like a cell address or formula. Excel will prevent you from creating invalid names, such as *F16, B1,* and *Quarter-1*, which are all ambiguous.

Using Names in Formulas

To use a defined name within a formula, you type the name as part of the formula. When computing the formula's result, Excel automatically refers to the dictionary and substitutes the name with its definition. In the following steps, you will build and copy a formula to compute the operating hours per month for each appliance.

To build the formula for operating hours per month:

1 Select cell J7, which will contain the operating hours per month for the heat pump.

2 Type **=sum(**

3 Using point mode, select the range to be summed, C7:I7, by selecting away from the formula (Sunday's through Monday's operating hours).

4 Type **)*WeeksPerMonth** and then press (ENTER)

The formula reads =SUM(C7:I7)*WeeksPerMonth, and it means "total the seven cells to the left and multiply the total by WeeksPerMonth."

The formula's relative addressing will work when you copy the formula to the other cells in the column.

The result of this formula is 128. If you want to change the value of WeeksPerMonth, you can do so in the Define Name dialog box. The change would then be reflected in every formula that uses the name *WeeksPerMonth*.

Copying to Nonadjacent Selections

The formula you just completed needs to be copied to calculate operating hours per month for the other appliances. The fill handle could be used in a single step to copy the formula; however, this would leave copies in certain cells that should be blank (J10, for example). In the following steps, you will copy the formula to a nonadjacent selection—only those cells that should receive the copy.

To copy to a nonadjacent selection:

1 Select cell J7, which contains the formula to be copied.

2 Click the **Copy** tool from the Standard toolbar.

3 Hold down (CTRL) while dragging to select the ranges of cells that should receive the copy: J8:J9, J11:J14, J16:J17, J19:J21, and J23:J24, as shown in Figure 4.10.

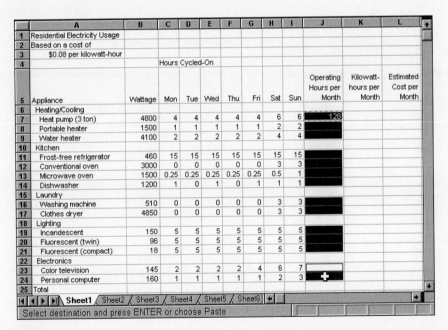

Figure 4.10

4 Press (ENTER) to paste the formula into the selected cells.

Calculating Kilowatt-hours per Month

The kilowatt-hours of energy used by an appliance in a month are the number of kilowatts it consumes multiplied by the number of hours it is cycled-on.

To build the formula for kilowatt-hours per month:

1 Select cell K7, which will contain kilowatt-hours per month for the heat pump.

2 Type =(

3 Select the wattage for this appliance, in cell B7.

4 Type /1000)*

5 Select the operating hours per month for this appliance, in cell J7.

6 Press (ENTER) to complete the formula.

The result of the formula is 614.4. This formula's relative addressing will work when the formula is copied to other cells. The completed formula, =(B7/1000)*J7, can be interpreted as "Take what is nine cells to the left, divide it by 1000, and multiply that result by what is one cell to the left."

7 Copy the completed formula to the cells in column K that should contain the formula.

The parentheses inserted in this formula are not required by the rules of operator priority, nor do they affect the result of the formula. They are used to help convey the logic of the computation to people who might later examine the formula.

Computing Estimated Cost per Month

The final column will compute the monthly cost of operating each appliance. This value is calculated by multiplying the cost per kilowatt-hour (currently 0.08, in cell A3) by the kilowatt-hours calculated for each appliance in column K.

Follow the next steps carefully. You will first change the view of the worksheet and then, to illustrate a common error, you will build a formula that is mathematically correct but does not work when copied to other cells. Later, you will correct the formula and copy it again.

To change the view of the worksheet:

1 Press (CTRL)+(HOME), then choose **View** and then **Full Screen.** Close the floating Full Screen toolbar if it appears.

The toolbars and status bar disappear. You will need the Standard toolbar for quick adjustment of magnification and access to the Copy tool, and you will need the Auditing toolbar to analyze formulas.

2 Choose **View** and then **Toolbars,** select the Standard and Auditing toolbars, and then select **OK.**

3 Drag the Auditing toolbar toward the upper-right corner of the worksheet window so the toolbar is positioned above blank cells but does not cover the column headings, as shown in Figure 4.11.

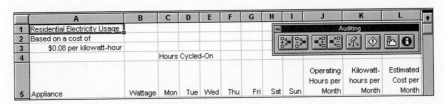

Figure 4.11

4 Choose **View** and then **Formula bar.**
The Formula bar appears.

5 Select the range A1:L25, the entire area of the worksheet that is needed. *Make sure column L is included in the selection.*

6 Click the **Zoom Control** list box and choose **Selection** to fit the magnification to the selected range.
The screen should resemble Figure 4.12.

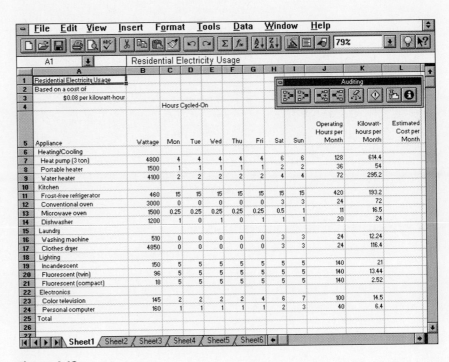

Figure 4.12

Reminder The cost per month is the cost per kilowatt-hour multiplied by the number of kilowatt-hours used in a month.

To build the formula for estimated cost per month (first attempt):

1 Select cell L7, which will contain the cost per month of the heat pump.

2 Type =

3 Select the cost per kilowatt-hour, in cell A3.

4 Type *

5 Select the number of kilowatt-hours used, in cell K7.

6 Press (ENTER)

The completed formula reads =A3*K7.

7 Using the skills you learned earlier for copying to nonadjacent selections, copy this formula to the other cells that require it in column L. The worksheet should now resemble Figure 4.13.

		L8	⬇		=A4*K8								

	A	B	C	D	E	F	G	H	I	J	K	L
1	Residential Electricity Usage											
2	Based on a cost of								Auditing			
3	$0.08 per kilowatt-hour											
4					Hours Cycled-On							
5	Appliance	Wattage	Mon	Tue	Wed	Thu	Fri	Sat	Sun	Operating Hours per Month	Kilowatt-hours per Month	Estimated Cost per Month
6	Heating/Cooling											
7	Heat pump (3 ton)	4800	4	4	4	4	4	6	6	128	614.4	49.152
8	Portable heater	1500	1	1	1	1	1	2	2	36	54	0
9	Water heater	4100	2	2	2	2	2	4	4	72	295.2	#VALUE!
10	Kitchen											
11	Frost-free refrigerator	460	15	15	15	15	15	15	15	420	193.2	#VALUE!
12	Conventional oven	3000	0	0	0	0	0	3	3	24	72	#VALUE!
13	Microwave oven	1500	0.25	0.25	0.25	0.25	0.25	0.5	1	11	16.5	#VALUE!
14	Dishwasher	1200	1	0	1	0	1	1	1	20	24	#VALUE!
15	Laundry											
16	Washing machine	510	0	0	0	0	0	3	3	24	12.24	#VALUE!
17	Clothes dryer	4850	0	0	0	0	0	3	3	24	116.4	#VALUE!
18	Lighting											
19	Incandescent	150	5	5	5	5	5	5	5	140	21	#VALUE!
20	Fluorescent (twin)	96	5	5	5	5	5	5	5	140	13.44	#VALUE!
21	Fluorescent (compact)	18	5	5	5	5	5	5	5	140	2.52	#VALUE!
22	Electronics											
23	Color television	145	2	2	2	2	4	6	7	100	14.5	#VALUE!
24	Personal computer	160	1	1	1	1	1	2	3	40	6.4	#VALUE!
25	Total											

Figure 4.13

Analyzing Problem Formulas

There is obviously something wrong with the copied formulas. The formula in cell L8 gives a result of 0, and the other cells display the error message *#VALUE!*.

Consider the original formula in cell L7. As do the other formulas you have created, =A3*K7 uses relative cell references. The formula means "Take what is 4 cells up and 11 cells to the left, and multiply that by what is 1 cell to the left." This can be visualized by tracing the precedents of the formula.

To trace the precedents of the original formula:

1 Select cell L7, the estimated cost per month for the heat pump.

2 Click the **Trace Precedents** tool.

The direct precedents are cell A3, the cost per kilowatt-hour, and cell K7, the kilowatt hours used per month for this appliance.

To trace the precedents of a copy of the formula:

1 Select cell L8, the estimated cost per month for the portable heater.

2 Click the **Trace Precedents** tool.

The screen should resemble Figure 4.14. The direct precedents are cell A4, which is blank, and cell K8, the kilowatt hours used per month for this appliance.

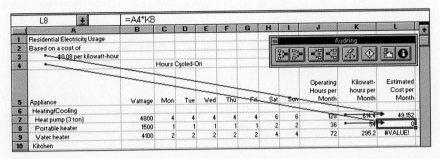

Figure 4.14

The formula in cell L8 attempts to take the contents of cell A4, which is 4 cells up and 11 cells to the left, and multiply those contents by cell K8, which is 1 cell to the left.

The K8 part is correct; the A4 reference is wrong. Cell A4 is blank, and because blank cells have a value of zero, the result of the formula is 0. The results of the other formulas give the error message *#VALUE!* because the other formulas attempt to multiply by cells that contain text, which is considered an error.

Another way of analyzing these formulas is to consider cell A3, which contains the cost per kilowatt-hour. This cell should be a direct precedent of all the formulas that compute estimated cost per month.

To trace the dependents of cell A3:

1 Click the **Remove All Arrows** tool.
All tracer arrows disappear.

2 Select cell A3, the cost per kilowatt-hour.

3 Click the **Trace Dependents** tool.
Your screen should resemble Figure 4.15. Only one cell, L7, depends on cell A3.

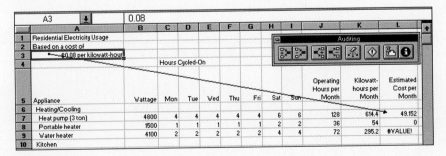

Figure 4.15

4 Click the **Remove All Arrows** tool.

Using Absolute Cell References

The formula in cell L7 (and in all the other cells in the estimated cost per month column) should instead mean "Take what is in cell A3, and multiply it by what is one cell to the left (of the cell in which this formula is located)." Using Excel terminology, the reference to cell A3 should not be a relative reference, but an ***absolute reference.***

An absolute cell reference in a formula is frozen so the reference will not change even if the formula that contains the reference is copied. A fully absolute reference is indicated with dollar signs preceding both the column letter and the row number. For example, in $A$3, the dollar sign in front of the *A* means "Don't change the *A*," and the dollar sign in front of the *3* means "Don't change the *3*."

The most convenient way to make a reference absolute is with the Absolute function key, (F4), which will work either while you are building a formula in point mode or when you are editing a formula. You can also type the dollar signs directly into a formula. In the steps that follow you will rebuild the formula, this time making the reference to cell A3 absolute.

> *Tip* Any time you are pointing to a cell while building a formula, and that cell alone provides the required information for the formula and for future copies of the formula, the reference to the cell should be absolute. In short: if you're building a formula to be copied, any references to specific cells should be made absolute.

To build the formula for estimated cost per month (second attempt):

1 Select cell L7, which will contain the cost per month of the heat pump.

2 Type =

3 Select the cost per kilowatt-hour, in cell A3, and press (F4)
Notice that the dollar signs for absolute addressing appear in the formula bar. Don't hold down (F4), because it will cycle through absolute, mixed, and relative address forms. If this cycling happens, tap (F4) several times to cycle back to where both the row and the column part of the address are frozen.

4 Type *

5 Point to the number of kilowatt-hours used, in cell K7.

6 Press (ENTER)
The completed formula reads =$A$3*K7.

7 Copy this formula to the other cells that require it in column L.
The worksheet should now resemble Figure 4.16.

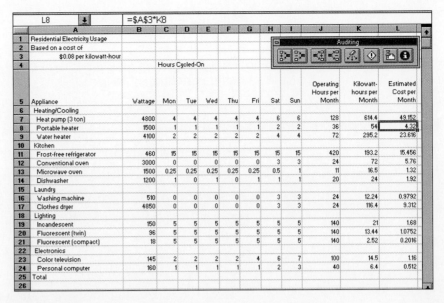

Figure 4.16

Once again, the formula you just created and copied means "Take what is in cell A3 and multiply it by what is one cell to the left (of the cell containing this formula)." You can use tracer arrows to confirm that all the estimated cost per month formulas now depend on cell A3.

To trace the dependents of cell A3:

1 If necessary, select the **Remove All Arrows** tool.
All tracer arrows disappear.

2 Select cell A3, the cost per kilowatt-hour.

3 Click the **Trace Dependents** tool.
The screen should resemble Figure 4.17. All the cells that calculate estimated cost per month now depend on cell A3.

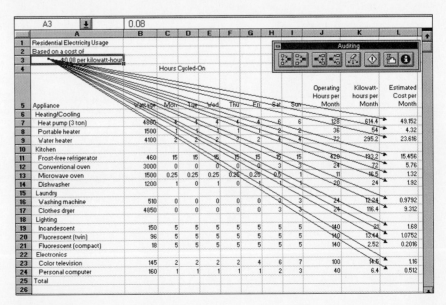

Figure 4.17

4 Click the **Remove All Arrows** tool.

Tip Printouts will include tracer arrows unless you clear the arrows before printing.

Building the Grand Total Formula

The only remaining formula to enter on the spreadsheet is the grand total of estimated monthly electricity costs.

To build the total formula:

1 Select cell L25, which will contain the total monthly cost of all appliances.

2 Type **=sum(**

3 Select the range encompassing all the cost formulas, L7:L24.
You can select the range by moving backward, if you wish. It's okay for the range to include blank cells—they won't affect the total.

4 Type **)** and press **ENTER**
The completed formula reads =SUM(L7:L24). The worksheet should now resemble Figure 4.18.

	A	B	C	D	E	F	G	H	I	J	K	L
					Hours Cycled-On					Operating Hours per Month	Kilowatt-hours per Month	Estimated Cost per Month
1	Residential Electricity Usage											
2	Based on a cost of											
3	$0.08 per kilowatt-hour											
5	Appliance	Wattage	Mon	Tue	Wed	Thu	Fri	Sat	Sun			
6	Heating/Cooling											
7	Heat pump (3 ton)	4800	4	4	4	4	4	6	6	128	614.4	49.152
8	Portable heater	1500	1	1	1	1	1	2	2	36	54	4.32
9	Water heater	4100	2	2	2	2	2	4	4	72	295.2	23.616
10	Kitchen											
11	Frost-free refrigerator	460	15	15	15	15	15	15	15	420	193.2	15.456
12	Conventional oven	3000	0	0	0	0	0	3	3	24	72	5.76
13	Microwave oven	1500	0.25	0.25	0.25	0.25	0.25	0.5	1	11	16.5	1.32
14	Dishwasher	1200	1	0	1	0	1	1	1	20	24	1.92
15	Laundry											
16	Washing machine	510	0	0	0	0	0	3	3	24	12.24	0.9792
17	Clothes dryer	4850	0	0	0	0	0	3	3	24	116.4	9.312
18	Lighting											
19	Incandescent	150	5	5	5	5	5	5	5	140	21	1.68
20	Fluorescent (twin)	96	5	5	5	5	5	5	5	140	13.44	1.0752
21	Fluorescent (compact)	18	5	5	5	5	5	5	5	140	2.52	0.2016
22	Electronics											
23	Color television	145	2	2	2	2	4	6	7	100	14.5	1.16
24	Personal computer	160	1	1	1	1	1	2	3	40	6.4	0.512
25	Total											116.464

Figure 4.18

5 Rename the Sheet1 tab **Electricity**

6 Close the Auditing toolbar.

7 Save the workbook.

EXIT If necessary, you can quit Excel now and continue this project later.

FORMATTING THE WORKSHEET

As you can see from Figure 4.1, the finished worksheet has several formatting features. In the remainder of this project, you will assign formats to the worksheet and arrive at a completed document very similar to Figure 4.1.

Changing Numeric Formats

Apart from the custom-formatted 0.08 in the subtitle, three kinds of numeric formats are appropriate for this worksheet:

- A comma-punctuated format with zero decimal places, used for wattage, operating hours per month, and kilowatt-hours per month.
- A format showing values two digits to the right of the decimal, used for the hours cycled-on and for most of the values in the estimated cost per month columns. Although the values in these areas are currently small numbers, in later use of the worksheet they could become larger, so a comma-punctuated format wouldn't hurt.
- A currency or accounting format, showing two decimal places, for the first entry and grand total in the estimated cost per month column.

You can change numeric formats in a worksheet in two ways: you can apply a style that contains the desired format or you can apply the numeric format directly. The main advantage to using styles is that you can later change the style definition and have the change take effect on all cells that have that style. There are six standard styles that will work for most situations; however, if no existing style includes the format you want, you can create your own style or modify an existing one.

In the following steps, you will use both approaches—styles and direct formatting—to change numeric formats. You will start by applying the Comma style to a nonadjacent selection composed of the columns for wattage, operating hours per month, and kilowatt-hours per month.

To apply the Comma style to a selection:

1 Staying in full-screen view, display the Formatting toolbar.

2 Zoom the worksheet to 73 percent magnification.

3 Make a nonadjacent selection that includes the values in the wattage, operating hours per month, and kilowatt-hours per month columns.

4 Click the **Comma Style** tool.
The screen should resemble Figure 4.19.

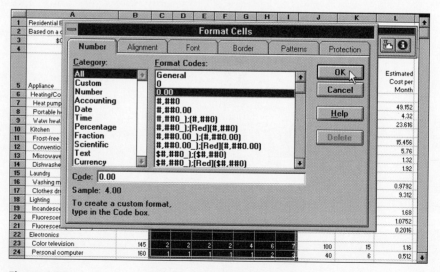

Figure 4.19

5 Click the **Decrease Decimal** tool twice.
The affected values will now always appear with no digits to the right of the decimal and with commas in values of 1000 and higher.

To apply a number format directly from the Format menu:

1 Select C7:I24, the range for hours cycled-on for Monday through Sunday.

2 Choose **Format** and then **Cells.**

3 Click the **Number** tab.

4 Select **0.00** from the **Format Codes** list box.
The screen should resemble Figure 4.20.

Figure 4.20

5 Select **OK** to apply the format.

The numbers for hours cycled-on now appear with two digits to the right of the decimal point.

The final numeric formatting involves the column for estimated cost per month. Because the numbers in this column are dollar amounts, they should appear with two digits to the right of the decimal. Even though all the figures in the column represent dollar amounts, preceding each by a dollar sign would make the column more difficult to read. In traditional financial-spreadsheet style, a dollar sign is used only in the first entry and the total of such a column.

The regular Comma style displays two digits to the right of the decimal; the regular Currency style is similar to Comma, except that a dollar sign precedes the displayed value.

To apply the Comma style to a selection:

1 Make a nonadjacent selection of L8:L24, the values for estimated cost per month, *excluding* the first and last figures.

2 Click the **Comma Style** tool to apply the style.

To apply the Currency style to a selection:

1 Select the estimated cost per month for the heat pump and the total estimated cost in L7 and L25, respectively.

2 Click the **Currency Style** tool.

The worksheet should resemble Figure 4.21.

	A	B	C	D	E	F	G	H	I	J	K	L	M
1	Residential Electricity Usage												
2	Based on a cost of												
3	$0.08 per kilowatt-hour												
4				Hours Cycled-On									
5	Appliance	Wattage	Mon	Tue	Wed	Thu	Fri	Sat	Sun	Operating Hours per Month	Kilowatt-hours per Month	Estimated Cost per Month	
6	Heating/Cooling												
7	Heat pump (3 ton)	4,800	4.00	4.00	4.00	4.00	4.00	6.00	6.00	128	614	$ 49.15	
8	Portable heater	1,500	1.00	1.00	1.00	1.00	1.00	2.00	2.00	36	54	4.32	
9	Water heater	4,100	2.00	2.00	2.00	2.00	2.00	4.00	4.00	72	295	23.62	
10	Kitchen												
11	Frost-free refrigerator	460	15.00	15.00	15.00	15.00	15.00	15.00	15.00	420	193	15.46	
12	Conventional oven	3,000	0.00	0.00	0.00	0.00	0.00	3.00	3.00	24	72	5.76	
13	Microwave oven	1,500	0.25	0.25	0.25	0.25	0.25	0.50	1.00	11	17	1.32	
14	Dishwasher	1,200	1.00	0.00	1.00	0.00	1.00	1.00	1.00	20	24	1.92	
15	Laundry												
16	Washing machine	510	0.00	0.00	0.00	0.00	0.00	3.00	3.00	24	12	0.98	
17	Clothes dryer	4,850	0.00	0.00	0.00	0.00	0.00	3.00	3.00	24	116	9.31	
18	Lighting												
19	Incandescent	150	5.00	5.00	5.00	5.00	5.00	5.00	5.00	140	21	1.68	
20	Fluorescent (twin)	96	5.00	5.00	5.00	5.00	5.00	5.00	5.00	140	13	1.08	
21	Fluorescent (compact)	18	5.00	5.00	5.00	5.00	5.00	5.00	5.00	140	3	0.20	
22	Electronics												
23	Color television	145	2.00	2.00	2.00	2.00	4.00	6.00	7.00	100	15	1.16	
24	Personal computer	160	1.00	1.00	1.00	1.00	1.00	2.00	3.00	40	6	0.51	
25	Total											$ 116.45	

Figure 4.21

3 Save the worksheet.

Tip   The Currency Style tool uses an Accounting number format. If you would prefer having a format that places dollar signs immediately in front of numbers, you should use one of the Currency number formats available on the Number tab of the Format Cells dialog box. You can also redefine the Currency style to use a different number format.

If you use the Increase Decimal or Decrease Decimal tool on a cell, the tool overrides the number format specified in the cell's style. Unfortunately, this means subsequent changes to the style definition will not affect the cell (unless you reapply the style).

Changing the Font Style and Size

As you learned in a previous project, a *font* is a typeface design. Arial, New Courier, and Times New Roman are names of different fonts.

Along with choosing a font, you can decide whether the font should appear in a particular *font style.* The basic font styles, which should not be confused with worksheet-cell formatting styles, are Regular, **Bold,** *Italic,* and <u>Underline</u>. You can also combine font styles, as in ***Bold Italic.*** The size of a font is measured in units called *points.* One point is 1/72 of an inch; the default font size in Excel is 10 points.

Figure 4.22

As shown in Figure 4.22, the Formatting toolbar contains a group of convenient controls that can be used for the following functions: changing the font; changing the point size; turning bold formatting on or off; turning italic formatting on or off; and turning underline formatting on or off. More extensive control over fonts is available in the Font tab, accessed from the Format Cells menu command.

The only font used in the completed version of this worksheet is Arial, although a variety of point sizes and font styles are employed. In the next series of steps, you will change the main title to appear in 18-point bold italic.

To change the font style and size for the main title:

1 Select cell A1, which contains the title *Residential Electricity Usage.*

2 Select **18** points from the **Font Size** list box.

3 Click the **Bold** tool.

4 Click the **Italic** tool.

The screen should resemble Figure 4.23.

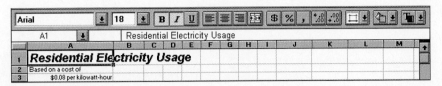

Figure 4.23

The title text should now appear in bold and italic and in a larger point size. Notice that the Bold and Italic buttons on the toolbar are highlighted; this indicates that the current selection has both the bold and the italic font styles.

The two subtitle lines each use a font size of 11 points. You can change this with the Font Size tool on the Formatting toolbar or in the Font tab of the Format Cells dialog box.

 To increase the font size of the two subtitles:

1 Select A2:A3, the range containing the two subtitles.

2 Click inside the **Font Size** list box and change the size to 11 points.

Changing Font Style and Size for Other Cell Entries

Here's a list of the remaining cell entries whose font styles and sizes need to be changed:

- The title *Hours Cycled-On* should be 10-point bold.
- All of the column titles in B5:L5 should be 10-point italic.
- The titles *Appliance* and *Total* should be 16-point bold.
- The titles *Heating/Cooling, Kitchen, Laundry, Lighting,* and *Electronics* should be 11-point bold.
- The formula result for total estimated cost per month in cell L25 should be 11-point bold.

 To change other font attributes in the worksheet:

1 Select cell C4, which contains the text *Hours Cycled-On.*

2 Click the **Bold** tool.

3 Select the range B5:L5, which contains the column titles.

4 Click the **Italic** tool.

This changes the font style to italic. On some systems, it may be necessary to slightly adjust the width of the columns after changing the column titles to italic.

5 Select cell A5, which contains the text *Appliance.*

6 Change the font size and style to 16-point bold.

Copying Only the Format of a Cell

The title *Total* in cell A25 is supposed to have the same font style and size as *Appliance* in cell A5. Excel has the ability to copy just the format (and not the contents) of one cell to another cell.

To copy the format of cell A5 to cell A25:

1 Select cell A5, which contains *Appliance*.

2 Select the **Format Painter** tool on the Standard toolbar. The pointer changes to a paintbrush.

3 Scroll down if necessary, and then select cell A25, which contains *Total*.

Tip The Paste Special command from the Edit menu can also be used to copy selected attributes of a cell and to change these copies in various ways.

To complete the font settings for the worksheet:

1 Press (CTRL) + (HOME)

2 Make a nonadjacent selection to include *Heating/Cooling* (cell A6), *Kitchen* (cell A10), *Laundry* (cell A15), *Lighting* (cell A18), *Electronics* (cell A22), and the grand total formula in cell L25.

3 Set these cells to 11-point bold.

Centering Selected Titles

The titles in A1:A3 should be centered across the whole worksheet; the title *Hours Cycled-On* should be centered across the weekday columns.

To center titles across selected columns:

1 Select the range A1:L3, as shown in Figure 4.24.

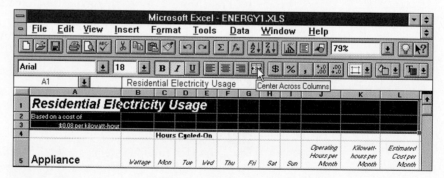

Figure 4.24

2 Click the **Center Across Columns** tool, as shown in Figure 4.24.

3 Change the height of row 4 to about 30 points.

4 Select the range C4:I4. This is the selection in which *Hours Cycled-On* should be centered.

5 Center *Hours Cycled-On* across the selection.

6 Save the workbook.

Adding Borders to a Worksheet

A *border* is a line that lends visual organization to the information in a worksheet. The completed worksheet will have several kinds of borders. You may want to turn cell gridlines off after performing a Border command, because the gridlines make it harder to see the borders.

> **Tip** When you are applying borders, it is usually a good idea to work from within the worksheet toward the outside perimeter: that is, you should create the innermost borders first, and then proceed to the next layer, and so forth.

The innermost borders in this worksheet are those for the hours cycled-on values. Next you will add the horizontal section borders, separating appliance categories. Finally, you will set the thick outer border.

To add borders to the hours cycled-on cells:

1 Remove the Formatting toolbar from the screen.

2 Select the range C5:I24, the hours cycled-on column headings and values.

3 Choose **Format** and then **Cells**.

4 Click the **Border** tab.

The Border dialog box appears. Notice that in the Style section, a rectangle surrounds the currently selected line style. Figure 4.25 shows the names of the various line styles.

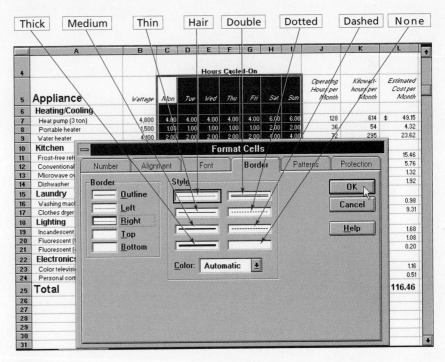

Figure 4.25

5 Select **Outline** in the **Border** group.

A thin line appears next to Outline indicating that this line style will be used to form an outline around the entire selected area.

6 Select **Left** in the **Border** group.
The left edge of each cell in the selected range will have a thin border.

7 Select the Hair line in the upper left of the **Style** group.
This selects a different line style—one that will be used for the left and right borders for each cell in the selected range.

8 Select **Right** in the **Border** group.
The Hair line style should appear for both the Left and Right borders, and the Thin line for the Outline, as shown in Figure 4.25.

9 Select **OK** to apply the chosen borders.

10 Choose **Tools** and then **Options,** click the **View** tab, and turn off cell gridlines, and then select OK.
The effect of the Border command is now more apparent, as shown in Figure 4.26. Notice that outline borders override individual cell borders.

	A	Wattage	Mon	Tue	Wed	Thu	Fri	Sat	Sun	Operating Hours per Month	Kilowatt-hours per Month	Estimated Cost per Month	M
1					*Residential Electricity Usage*								
2					Based on a cost of								
3					$0.08 per kilowatt-hour								
4						Hours Cycled-On							
5	**Appliance**												
6	**Heating/Cooling**												
7	Heat pump (3 ton)	4,800	4.00	4.00	4.00	4.00	4.00	6.00	6.00	128	614	$ 49.15	
8	Portable heater	1,500	1.00	1.00	1.00	1.00	1.00	2.00	2.00	36	54	4.32	
9	Water heater	4,100	2.00	2.00	2.00	2.00	2.00	4.00	4.00	72	295	23.62	
10	**Kitchen**												
11	Frost-free refrigerator	460	15.00	15.00	15.00	15.00	15.00	15.00	15.00	420	193	15.46	
12	Conventional oven	3,000	0.00	0.00	0.00	0.00	0.00	3.00	3.00	24	72	5.76	
13	Microwave oven	1,500	0.25	0.25	0.25	0.25	0.25	0.50	1.00	11	17	1.32	
14	Dishwasher	1,200	1.00	0.00	1.00	0.00	1.00	1.00	1.00	20	24	1.92	
15	**Laundry**												
16	Washing machine	510	0.00	0.00	0.00	0.00	0.00	3.00	3.00	24	12	0.98	
17	Clothes dryer	4,850	0.00	0.00	0.00	0.00	0.00	3.00	3.00	24	116	9.31	
18	**Lighting**												
19	Incandescent	150	5.00	5.00	5.00	5.00	5.00	5.00	5.00	140	21	1.68	
20	Fluorescent (twin)	96	5.00	5.00	5.00	5.00	5.00	5.00	5.00	140	13	1.08	
21	Fluorescent (compact)	18	5.00	5.00	5.00	5.00	5.00	5.00	5.00	140	3	0.20	
22	**Electronics**												
23	Color television	145	2.00	2.00	2.00	2.00	4.00	6.00	7.00	100	15	1.16	
24	Personal computer	160	1.00	1.00	1.00	1.00	1.00	2.00	3.00	40	6	0.51	
25	**Total**											$ 116.46	

Figure 4.26

11 Turn gridlines back on to make it easier to position the active cell.

To set the horizontal section borders:

1 Make a nonadjacent selection to include the rows for the appliance categories and the total. The selected ranges are A6:L6, A10:L10, A15:L15, A18:L18, A22:L22, and A25:L25.

2 Choose **Format** and then **Cells,** select the **Border** tab, and specify a Thin top border, as shown in Figure 4.27.
In the dialog box, the Left and Right boxes are shaded because not all cells within the selection currently have the same setting for left and right borders.

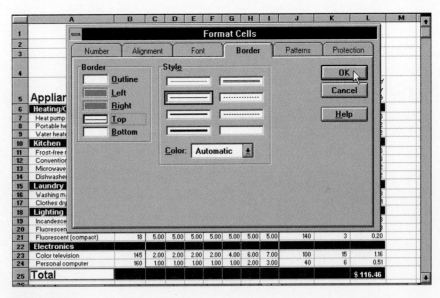

Figure 4.27

3 Select **OK** to apply the border.

To set an outline around the entire worksheet:

1 Select the entire functional area of the worksheet, A1:L25.

2 Choose **Cells** from the **Format** menu, select the **Border** tab, and set a Medium outline border for the worksheet. Medium is just under the Thin line style.

3 Turn cell gridlines off after completing the Border command. The worksheet should resemble Figure 4.28.

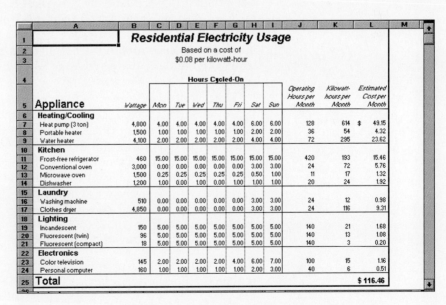

Figure 4.28

4 Turn cell gridlines back on.

5 Switch out of full-screen view and display the Formatting toolbar.

6 Save the workbook.

PRINTING AND MAKING FINAL MODIFICATIONS

In the steps that follow, you will learn how to suppress cell gridlines on the printout only (and keep gridlines on the screen). After printing the worksheet and examining the printout, you will notice areas that require adjustments. You will then print the worksheet again.

To suppress cell gridlines on a printout:

1 Make sure the printer is powered on and is online.

2 Choose **File** and then **Print.**

3 Select **Page Setup** in the Print dialog box.

4 Click the **Sheet** tab, clear the **Gridlines** checkbox, and then select **OK.**

5 Select **OK** in the Print dialog box.
The worksheet prints on two pages on most printers.

6 Zoom to 25 percent magnification.
If you examine the worksheet on-screen, you will see horizontal and vertical dashed lines placed by Excel at page breaks for your reference.

7 Zoom to 75 percent magnification.

Changing the Orientation of a Printout

Because the worksheet is printed on two pages, you would need to trim one of the sheets and tape the two pages together to have a single printed image of the worksheet. If you want this worksheet to fit on a single page, you can change the *scaling* (reducing it to fit) and you can flip the printout from *portrait orientation* (the default) to *landscape orientation.* Both the scaling and the orientation controls are in the Page tab of the Page Setup dialog box.

The text of a landscape printout reads along the long dimension of the paper. The terms *portrait* and *landscape* derive from the world of art, where portrait paintings are usually oriented with the long side on the vertical and landscape paintings with the long side on the horizontal.

You will also notice that the days of the week might look better if they were aligned in the centers of their cells, rather than aligned to the right. In the following steps, you will modify the alignment of the weekday names, and instruct Excel to produce a landscape printout centered on the page.

To adjust and reprint the worksheet:

1 Select the weekday names, *Mon* through *Sun,* and select the **Center** tool on the Formatting toolbar.

Reminder The Center tool has the same effect as choosing Center in the Alignment dialog box. It means to center each entry within its cell, and is not the same as centering an entry across columns.

2 Save the worksheet.

3 Choose **File, Print,** and then select **Page Setup.**

4 Click the **Page** tab.
The Page tab appears.

5 Select the **Landscape** option under **Orientation.**

6 Click the **Margins** tab.
The Margins tab appears.

7 Click the check boxes to center the printout horizontally and vertically, and then select **OK.**

8 Select **OK** in the Print dialog box to print the worksheet.
The completed landscape printout should resemble Figure 4.1.

Defining Named Ranges

Earlier in this project, you saw how to define names for constants. You can also define names for cells or larger ranges on the worksheet. You can then use the name as you enter new formulas. If formulas that refer to the named range already exist in the worksheet, you must *apply* the name to those formulas before the name will show up within the formulas.

Consider the formula for estimated cost per month in cell L7. It currently reads = $A$3*K7. The same reference, $A$3, is used in every one of the estimated cost formulas. The formula would be a little more understandable if it looked like this: = CostPerKilowattHour*K7. In the following steps, you will define the name *CostPerKilowattHour* to refer to cell $A$3. You will then apply the name to the cells containing the estimated cost formulas.

A quick way to define names that refer to ranges on the worksheet is to use the Name box in the formula bar.

To define and apply a named range:

1 Select cell A3, which contains *0.08*, the cost per kilowatt-hour.

2 Click in the Name box in the formula bar.

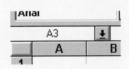

3 Type **CostPerKilowattHour** in the Name box and press (ENTER)
Remember to type the name as a single word with mixed upper- and lowercase letters.

4 Select cell L7, the estimated cost per month for the heat pump.
Notice that the formula still reads = $A$3*K7.

5 Select L7:L24, the range containing the formulas for estimated cost per month.

6 Choose **Insert, Name,** and then select **Apply.**
The Apply Names dialog box appears.

7 Select **OK** to apply the name *CostPerKilowattHour*, as shown in Figure 4.29.

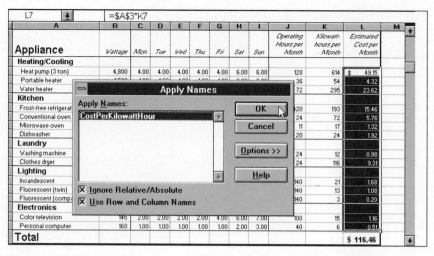

Figure 4.29

If you examine any of the formulas for estimated cost, you will discover that the name *CostPerKilowattHour* is now used instead of *$A$3*.

8 Save the workbook.

The dictionary of defined names is part of the workbook. Because the dictionary has changed, you should save the workbook.

THE NEXT STEP

Many of the commands you used in this project will help in constructing and managing larger worksheets. When the functional part of a worksheet grows to encompass thousands of cells, the increased complexity can be tamed somewhat by spending time initially on design, using named ranges, and using the Zoom Control command to view the worksheet from afar.

You have also worked with several sophisticated formatting features. Remember that the important thing about any worksheet is its results—usually numerical values resulting from formulas. Fonts, font styles, borders, and so on enhance the legibility of the worksheet and should not in themselves become a distraction to the person who reads the worksheet.

Perhaps one of the best ways to make the results of worksheets more legible is to present the information in pictures using Excel's superb charting capability. That is the subject of the next project.

This concludes Project 4. You can either exit Excel, or go on to work the Study Questions, Review Exercises, and Assignments.

SUMMARY AND EXERCISES

Summary

- Customized number formats allow you to attach special abbreviations and other text to a numeric entry.
- You can use the Zoom Control to magnify or reduce the view of the worksheet. Smaller magnifications are especially helpful for comprehending the arrangement of a large worksheet. Selecting full-screen view temporarily removes the toolbars and status bar to allow more room for the worksheet on-screen.
- You can use series fill to automatically fill a range that begins with a standard sequence or series.
- You can change the horizontal and vertical alignment of cell entries; titles above columns of numbers are usually easiest to read if they are aligned at the right or center. You can also make the text in cells wrap onto several lines.
- You can assign names to constants and to cells and ranges. Defined names make formulas more intelligible by eliminating constant numbers typed into formulas.
- You can copy to nonadjacent selections; this often saves you from using the Copy command repeatedly.
- Absolute cell references are usually necessary when you are copying a formula that contains a reference to a single cell in the worksheet.
- The font size (measured in points) and style (regular, italic, bold, underline, or bold italic) can be changed in selected cells or in a named cell style.
- Borders in a variety of thicknesses can be applied to cells and to larger selections.

Key Terms and Operations

Key Terms
absolute reference
AutoFill
border
customized format
defined name
fonts
font style
full-screen view
landscape orientation
points

portrait orientation
scaling
wrapping

Operations
Apply a style
Boldface text
Center across columns
Define a name
Format a cell
Italicize text
Zoom out or in

Study Questions

Multiple Choice

1. Excel displays number signs (#) in a cell when:
   a. A formatted number is too long to fit in the column.
   b. There is an error in a formula.
   c. A text entry is too long to fit in the column.
   d. An absolute cell address is required in a formula.
   e. The cell has an invalid customized format.

2. To conveniently enter a single value into a selected range, type the value in a cell within the selected range and then press:
   a. ENTER
   b. SHIFT + ENTER
   c. TAB
   d. CTRL + ENTER
   e. SHIFT + TAB

3. In the formula =SUM(G3:G12)*0.12115, *0.12115* is called a(n):
   a. defined name.
   b. number constant.
   c. absolute address.
   d. formula modifier.
   e. relative address.

4. In the formula =SUM(G3:G12)*ExpenseFactor, *ExpenseFactor* is a(n):
   a. text constant.
   b. manifest constant.
   c. hidden number.
   d. absolute address.
   e. defined name.

5. In the formula =$A$3*K7, *$A$3* is called a(n):
   a. defined constant.
   b. defined name.
   c. absolute cell address.
   d. relative cell address.
   e. manifest constant.

6. If the formula =A1+$A$2 were entered in cell A3 and then copied to cell B3, the copy in cell B3 would read:
   a. =B1+$A$2
   b. =A1+$A$2
   c. =A1+$B$2
   d. =B1+b2
   e. =B1+B2

7. Bold and Italic are examples of:
   a. font styles.
   b. patterns.
   c. alignments.
   d. font names.
   e. cell styles.

8. When adding several levels of borders to a worksheet, it is best to:
   a. Start from the innermost level and work outward.
   b. Start with the overall outline and work in.
   c. Proceed column by column.
   d. Zoom to a high magnification.
   e. Print with cell grid lines on.

9. Printing that is oriented along the long dimension of the paper is referred to as:
   a. portrait orientation.
   b. panoramic orientation.
   c. wide-angle printing.
   d. anisotopic mapping.
   e. landscape orientation.

10. Writing an incorrect formula that attempts to perform math by referring to a text entry causes Excel to display what in the formula's cell?
    a. ERROR
    b. 0
    c. #####
    d. #VALUE!
    e. !!!!!

Short Answer

1. How can you adjust the magnification of the worksheet so the selected range occupies the entire worksheet area?

2. What term is used to describe breaking a long text entry into several lines within its cell?

3. What type of format should be used when a numeric entry, such as 45, needs to appear in a single cell with text (for example, 45 degrees)?

4. What is the easiest way to enter the month names *Jan*, *Feb*, *Mar*, and so on in a range of cells?

5. Arial and Times New Roman are examples of what?

6. What unit of measurement is used when referring to the size of characters in a font?

7. If a formula refers to a specific, single cell, and the formula will be copied to other cells, how should the reference to the single cell appear in the formula?

8. If you want a border line to appear around all four sides of a selection, what command should you use?

9. How is a text entry normally aligned when it is entered into a cell?

10. How will numbers appear if they are formatted using the Comma Style tool?

For Discussion

1. What is the difference between using a style and applying a numeric format directly? What are the advantages of using styles?

2. What is the difference between relative and absolute cell addressing? Under what circumstances should a formula contain an absolute cell reference?

3. Explain the difference between portrait and landscape orientation. When is landscape printing appropriate?

4. In general, what steps are required to suppress gridlines on a printout, yet maintain them on the screen?

Review Exercises

Projecting Coffee House Income

Follow the steps below to construct a worksheet similar to Figure 4.30. The question marks in the figure indicate cells that will contain formulas.

Begin by entering all of the text constants (use AutoFill to enter the month names), and then enter the numbers for cost and price, and all the values for number sold. Enter the formula for income per cup as selling price per cup minus our cost per cup. Calculate the income for January by multiplying the number sold by the income per cup. Remember, the reference to income per cup should be absolute. Copy the formula to the other months.

	A	B	C	D	E	F	G	H	I
1			Clem's Coffee Clutch						
2			*Projected Income from Cappuccino Sales*						
3	Coffee	Our Cost per Cup	Selling Price per Cup	Income per Cup					
4	Cappuccino	$ 0.74	$ 1.50	?					
5									
6		*Jan*	*Feb*	*Mar*	*Apr*	*May*	*Jun*	*Total*	
7	Number Sold	440	350	370	340	290	220	?	
8	*Income*	?	?	?	?	?	?	?	
9									

Figure 4.30

Create formulas (using the SUM function) for total number sold and total income. Style in bold and center across columns the title and subtitle. Make the title a slightly larger size than the subtitle and make the subtitle italic. Format the column headings for our cost, selling price, and income per cup as bold, aligned to the right, and set to wrap. Format the month names and *Total* as bold, italic, and aligned to the right.

Apply the Currency style to the cost, price, and income per cup cells. Apply Currency style with no decimal places to the monthly income formulas and Comma style with no decimal places to the values for number sold each month. Adjust column widths and row heights as necessary, turn off cell gridlines, and apply borders so the worksheet resembles Figure 4.30. Save the workbook as COFFEE41, and then print the worksheet.

Computing Coffee Brand Income as Percent of Total Income

Figure 4.31 shows an enhanced version of the COFFEE3 worksheet from Assignment 2 in Project 3. A column has been added to show the income from each flavor of coffee expressed as a percent of the total income. For a particular flavor of coffee, this value is calculated by dividing its income amount by the total income. If such a formula is to be successfully copied to all the cells in the Percent of Total Income column, the reference to the total income must be absolute. The worksheet is also formatted with various alignments, borders, cell styles, and font styles.

	A	B	C	D	E	F	G	H
1	Coffee	Cost	Selling Price	No. Sold	Income	Percent of Total Income		
2	House Blend	$ 0.39	$ 0.95	60	$ 33.60	?		
3	Espresso	0.61	1.25	12	7.68	?		
4	Cappuccino	0.74	1.50	22	16.72	?		
5	Cafe Mocha	0.55	1.45	35	31.50	?		
6	Cafe Royale	0.68	1.85	55	64.35	?		
7	*Total*			184	$ 153.85	?		
8								

Figure 4.31

Refer to Figure 4.31 and build a similar worksheet. Add the new column first, and then proceed with formatting and borders. Apply the Currency and Comma cell styles as indicated in the figure. Use the Percent style for the new column of formulas.

Define the name *TotalIncome* to refer to the cell containing the total income, and then apply the name to the new formulas. Save the workbook under the name COFFEE42.

Assignments

Developing Your Own Electricity Worksheet

Construct a worksheet to calculate your monthly consumption of electricity. If necessary, look up energy consumption figures for the appliances in your home, apartment, or dorm room. Is there any appliance whose usage you can affect to such an extent that substantial amounts of electricity are saved? Save the workbook under the name MYENERGY.

Enhancing the Municipal Waste Worksheet

Figure 4.32 shows an enhanced version of the EPA2 workbook from the first Review Exercise in Project 3. The formula that computes the percent of the total for a particular category takes the 1990 value and divides it by the 1990 grand total (this is similar to the second review exercise in this project). Note that the borders have been customized, titles have been added, and numeric formatting has been adjusted.

A	B	C	D	E	F	G	H
Municipal Waste Trends							
in pounds per day per person					Percent of Grand Total (for		
Category	1960	1970	1980	1990	1990)		
Nonfood Wastes							
Paper	0.91	1.19	1.32	1.60	?		
Glass	0.20	0.34	0.36	0.28	?		
Plastics	0.01	0.08	0.19	0.32	?		
Metals	0.32	0.38	0.35	0.34	?		
Total Nonfood	1.44	1.99	2.22	2.54	?		
Other							
Food	0.37	0.34	0.32	0.29	?		
Yard	0.61	0.62	0.66	0.70	?		
Total Other	0.98	0.96	0.98	0.99	?		
Grand Total	2.42	2.95	3.20	3.53	?		

Figure 4.32

Build the new formulas and adjust the formatting as necessary to create a completed worksheet similar to Figure 4.32. Use Percent cell style for the new formulas. Save the modified workbook under the name EPA3.

Adapting to Off-Hours Discounts

Some electric utilities offer energy-savings time, a two-tier residential-electricity rate system, where customers who use electricity during off-peak hours receive a special reduced rate (for example, $0.05 per kilowatt-hour) and have to pay a premium rate (for example, $0.15 per kilowatt-hour) for electricity used during peak-demand hours. In the summer and fall, off-peak hours are usually from 9:00 p.m. to noon on weekdays and all day on weekends; in the winter and spring, off-peak hours are usually from 9:00 a.m. to 5:00 p.m. on weekdays and all day on weekends.

Adapt the ENERGY1 worksheet to accommodate a two-tier electricity price schedule. Save the workbook under the name ENERGYDL.

PROJECT 5: VISUALIZING INFORMATION WITH CHARTS

Objectives

After completing this project, you should be able to:

▶ Translate a verbal description and a sketch of a chart into a completed Excel chart

▶ Identify the major components of a chart

▶ Create column charts, pie charts, and 3-D perspective column charts

▶ Create both embedded charts and chart sheets

▶ Resize, position, and customize charts

▶ Link chart text to the worksheet

▶ Print charts

CASE STUDY: COMPARING PRIME-TIME TV SHOWS

Television has reigned as the predominant communications medium in the United States since shortly after the end of the Second World War. Figure 5.1 is a worksheet that shows the popularity of various kinds of prime-time TV shows in the United States from 1950 through 1990. This information is a snapshot of mid- to late twentieth-century U.S. popular culture.

The Most Popular Prime Time TV Shows
Genre by Decade (1950–1990)

Genre	1950s	1960s	1970s	1980s
Crime	8	4	13	16
Drama	10	7	8	14
Variety	20	14	2	0
Western	21	16	2	0
SitCom	23	48	61	54
Other	18	11	14	16
Total	100	100	100	100

Figure 5.1

For purposes of the worksheet, a television program is considered popular if it was among the ten most-watched *prime-time* (evening) programs each year. For each decade, there were 100 top programs. The worksheet condenses the data by considering whole decades and by classifying television shows by genre—or category—of show.

It's possible to see patterns in this table of numbers, but for most people, the best way to identify trends and interrelationships in data is to present the data visually as a ***chart,*** using lines, bars, geometric symbols, and colors.

In this project, you will construct several types of charts to display the information shown in Figure 5.1. Each type of chart emphasizes a certain aspect of the data or lends itself to a certain way of viewing or interpreting the information. Excel offers many more chart types than are needed for this project. Table 5.1 lists a few of the chart types you are likely to use for most of your charting needs.

Table 5.1

Chart Type	Description	Application
Bar	Compares individual values at a specific time. Emphasizes comparison rather than time flow.	Product launch, budget
Column	Similar to bar, but emphasizes variation over a period of time.	Quarterly sales forecast
Pie	Shows relationship between portions of a whole.	Sales levels in various cities
Line	Shows trends or changes over time. Emphasizes time flow and the rate of change rather than the amount of change.	Price index

Designing the Solution

If you want to build a chart, first decide what it is that you want to display in the chart and the type of chart that is most appropriate for the data you will plot. You can then figure out how the various aspects of the planned chart translate into Excel commands and charting options.

Suppose you want to show how the popularity of crime and drama shows changed between 1950 and 1990, and you want your chart to resemble Figure 5.2. Crime show popularity and drama show popularity are the variables that make up the *data series* that you wish to plot as a chart. A ***data series*** is a set of related values appearing in either a column or a row. A column chart like the one in Figure 5.2 is one way to view this kind of information.

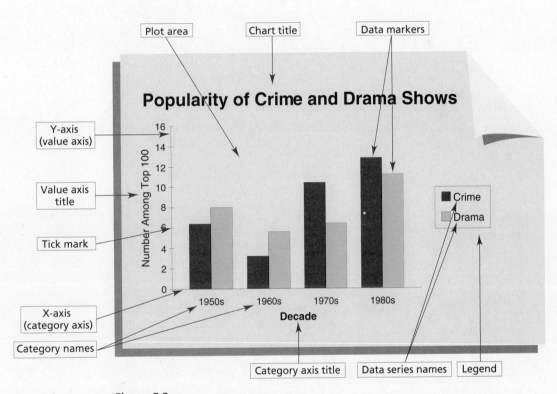

Figure 5.2

The labels along the bottom edge of the chart often correspond to worksheet column headings to tell you what the ***chart categories*** are. For example, the Drama data series has the value 7 in the 1960s category.

The graphic elements of the plot area include axes and the ***data markers*** that represent data points. Depending on the chart type, data markers can take the form of bars, lines, pictures, pie wedges, or other symbols. Each data series is graphically distinguished by the same pattern, color, or symbol. Each category, scale, or data series is marked off on the axis with a tick mark. There are generally two axes that act as the major frame for plotting. The horizontal or category axis—also referred to as the ***X-axis***—plots categories of the data series. The vertical or value axis—also called the ***Y-axis***—is the ruler for plotting data values. In addition to the graphical elements of the chart, text such as titles, a legend, and labels help to convey the interpretation of the data you are plotting.

In the worksheet, categories correspond to rows or columns, usually with titles that become the chart ***category names,*** used as labels along the axes. As shown in Figure 5.3, the categories for the example chart are 1950s, 1960s, 1970s, and 1980s.

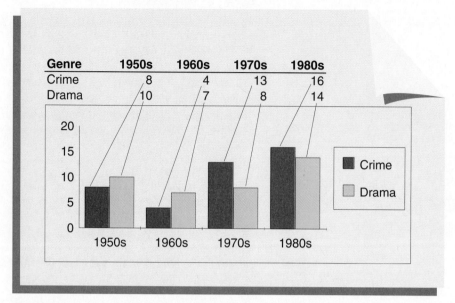

Figure 5.3

Figure 5.3 shows the relationship between a worksheet and a chart created from the worksheet. Each bar in the chart is a data marker. There are two data series: one for crime shows (represented by the red bars on the chart and the numbers 8, 4, 13, and 16 in the worksheet) and the other for drama shows (the green bars on the chart, and the numbers 10, 7, 8, and 14 in the worksheet). In a worksheet, you can often identify the data series as a group of values, in a column or a row, that *change over time*.

If a data series is a row, as is the number of shows each decade, then the chart categories of that data series—the decades—are represented in columns. Alternatively, if a data series is presented in a column, its chart categories are shown in rows. Figure 5.4 shows what the graph would look like if you switched the chart categories used in Figure 5.2 to data series, and the data series to chart categories. Whether you make the chart categories rows or columns depends entirely on the focus of the chart.

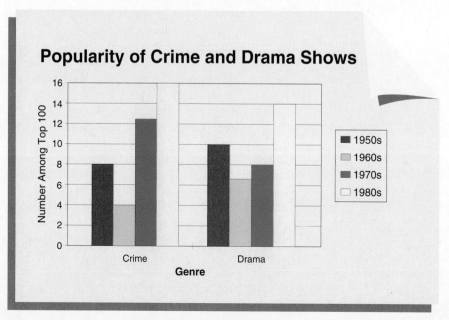

Figure 5.4

CREATING THE UNDERLYING WORKSHEET

In this section, you will make a worksheet similar to the one shown in Figure 5.1 and use that worksheet to create charts in the remainder of this project. You can refer to Figure 5.5 (which has been zoomed to 150 percent magnification) while typing the worksheet. The worksheet contains only four formulas, which compute totals for each column; their primary purpose is to help you check that you correctly typed the number constants.

	A	B	C	D	E	F
1	*The Most Popular Prime Time TV Shows*					
2	**Genre by Decade (1950-1990)**					
3	**Genre**	**1950s**	**1960s**	**1970s**	**1980s**	
4	Crime	8	4	13	16	
5	Drama	10	7	8	14	
6	Variety	20	14	2	0	
7	Western	21	16	2	0	
8	SitCom	23	48	61	54	
9	Other	18	11	14	16	
10	Total	100	100	100	100	

Figure 5.5

To build the basic worksheet:

1 Enter the title `The Most Popular Prime Time TV Shows` in cell A1.

2 Make the title in cell A1 11-point bold italic.

3 Enter the subtitle `Genre by Decade (1950-1990)` in cell A2, and make the subtitle bold.

4 Change the height of row 3 to about 28 points.

5 Referring to Figure 5.5, enter the column titles (*Genre* in A3 through *1980s* in E3), and make the titles bold.

6 Use the **Align Right** tool to adjust the column headings from *1950s* to *1980s*.

7 Refer to Figure 5.5 and enter the row titles (*Crime* in A4 through *Other* in A9) and the number constants (in the range B4:E9).

8 Enter `Total` in cell A10, and make the word bold.

9 Use the **AutoSum** tool to create total formulas where they are required in row 10.

10 Select A1:E2, and click the **Center Across Columns** tool.

Using a Tear-Off Palette

The Borders tool on the Formatting toolbar contains a group or *palette* of buttons that represent various commonly used border styles. If you want to keep the palette visible for repeated uses, you can "tear off" the palette and use it like a small floating toolbar. In the steps below, you will tear off the Borders palette and then apply a thin bottom border to the column headings, as well as a thin top and double bottom border to the totals row.

To tear off the Borders palette:

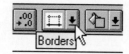

1 Click the arrow part of the **Borders** tool.
The Borders palette opens.

2 Click inside the **Borders** palette, drag its outline to the center right of the window, and then release the mouse button.

To apply borders using the Borders palette:

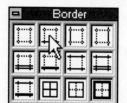

1 Select the column headings in the range A3:E3.

2 Click on the button for a thin bottom border in the **Borders** palette.

3 Select the range A10:E10, the totals row.

4 Click on the button for a thin top border and double-line bottom border.

5 Close the **Borders** palette.

6 Rename the Sheet1 tab to **TV Data**

7 Save the workbook as TV1.

BUILDING A COLUMN CHART WITH CHARTWIZARD

The easiest way to build basic charts is to use *ChartWizard,* a special command accessible only as a toolbar tool. In this section, you will build a column chart based on the plan in Figure 5.2. This first chart will be an *embedded chart;* that is, it will exist as an object embedded within the TV Data worksheet. Later you will create charts as separate *chart sheets.*

When working with embedded charts, you will usually need to see a large area of the worksheet. In the steps that follow, you will change the view of the worksheet by reducing magnification to 75 percent and temporarily removing the status bar from the window.

To change the view of the worksheet:

1 Zoom the window to 75 percent magnification.

2 Remove the status bar, if it is visible, by choosing **View** and then **Status Bar.**
The status bar disappears from the window.

To specify the range to be charted:

1 Select the range A3:E5, as shown in Figure 5.6, which encompasses the data to be charted and the associated category and data series names. Excel will ignore the corner cell containing *Genre,* because it is neither a data series nor a chart category.

	A	B	C	D	E	F	G	H	I	J	K	L	M
1	The Most Popular Prime Time TV Shows												
2		Genre by Decade (1950-1990)											
3	Genre	1950s	1960s	1970s	1980s								
4	Crime	8	4	13	16								
5	Drama	10	7	8	14								
6	Variety	20	14	2	0								
7	Western	21	16	2	0								
8	SitCom	23	48	61	54								
9	Other	18	11	14	16								
10	Total	100	100	100	100								
11													

Figure 5.6

 2 Click the **ChartWizard** tool.
The pointer changes to crosshairs. You can drag the mouse to select a location and size for the chart.

3 Position the crosshairs in the middle of cell G3, then hold down the mouse button and drag to the middle of cell K12, as shown in Figure 5.7, and then release the mouse button.

	A	B	C	D	E	F	G	H	I	J	K	L	M
1	The Most Popular Prime Time TV Shows												
2		Genre by Decade (1950-1990)											
3	Genre	1950s	1960s	1970s	1980s								
4	Crime	8	4	13	16								
5	Drama	10	7	8	14								
6	Variety	20	14	2	0								
7	Western	21	16	2	0								
8	SitCom	23	48	61	54								
9	Other	18	11	14	16								
10	Total	100	100	100	100								
11													
12													
13													
14													
15													

Figure 5.7

The ChartWizard Step 1 dialog box appears. Because you have already specified the range to be charted, you do not need to change anything in this dialog box.

4 Select **Next** in the ChartWizard Step 1 dialog box.
The Step 2 dialog box appears to let you pick one of the 15 major chart types.

 ### To set the chart type and format:

1 Select the **Column** chart type if necessary, and then select **Next,** as shown in Figure 5.8.

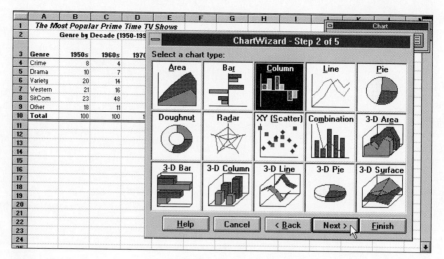

Figure 5.8

The Step 3 dialog box appears to let you pick the specific format for the chart type selected in the previous step.

2 Select chart format **1,** and then select **Next,** as shown in Figure 5.9.

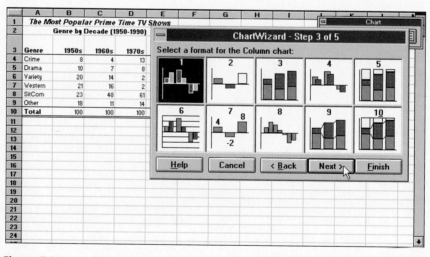

Figure 5.9

The Step 4 dialog box appears, as shown in Figure 5.10. You can use this dialog box to determine whether the data series will be in rows or columns and whether cells in the initially selected range should be used for data series and chart category names. Excel works on the assumption that you want fewer data series than chart categories, which means that for this worksheet, the data series are initially presented in rows.

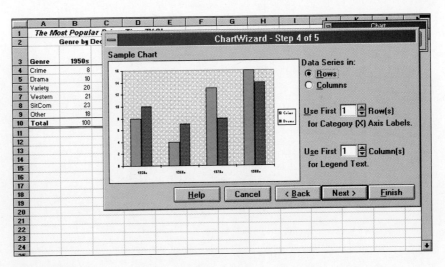

Figure 5.10

 To specify data series and chart categories:

1 Click the **Columns** button in the **Data Series in** section.
The screen should now resemble Figure 5.11; you can see what the chart
will look like if the data series is in columns rather than in rows. The other
sections of this dialog box concern whether the first row and/or column of
the range should be used for naming the chart categories and data series.
These settings are currently correct, because both column and row titles
are part of the selected range.

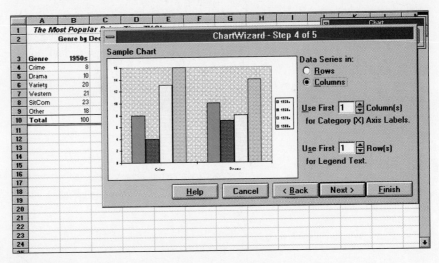

Figure 5.11

2 Click the **Rows** button.
The screen should once again resemble Figure 5.10; the data series are
again set up as rows.

3 Select **Next**.
The Step 5 dialog box appears, as shown in Figure 5.12. You can use this
dialog box to assign a legend and a title to the chart. A *legend* is a key that

lists what each color or symbol stands for. The default setting includes a legend but no title.

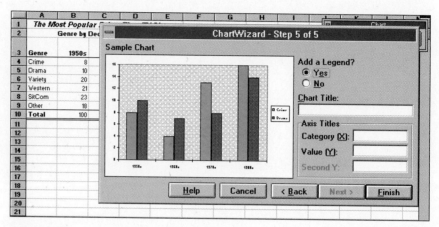

Figure 5.12

To a specify a legend and titles:

1 Select **No** in the **Add a Legend** section.
Now the chart appears without a legend. Column and bar charts are difficult to use without legends.

2 Select **Yes** in the **Add a Legend** section to restore the chart legend.

3 Click in the **Chart Title** box, and type `Popularity of Crime and Drama Shows`

4 Click in the **Category (X)** Axis Title box, and type `Decade`
Although it might seem obvious that the categories along the X-axis are decades, an axis title makes it even clearer.

5 Click in the **Value (Y)** Axis Title box, and type `Number Among Top 100`
Titles for the Y-axis are important, because they indicate what the units are—what the height of a bar stands for, for example. The screen should now resemble Figure 5.13.

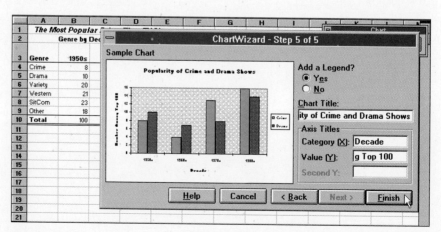

Figure 5.13

6 Select **Finish** to complete the chart.

The screen should resemble Figure 5.14. The completed chart appears, embedded in the worksheet, and a floating Chart toolbar also appears. If necessary, you can drag the Chart toolbar so that it does not obscure the worksheet or chart.

	A	B	C	D	E	F	G	H	I
1	The Most Popular Prime Time TV Shows								
2	Genre by Decade (1950-1990)								
3	Genre	1950s	1960s	1970s	1980s				
4	Crime	8	4	13	16				
5	Drama	10	7	8	14				
6	Variety	20	14	2	0				
7	Western	21	16	2	0				
8	SitCom	23	48	61	54				
9	Other	18	11	14	16				
10	Total	100	100	100	100				
11									
12									
13									
14									

Figure 5.14

Working with Embedded Charts

The embedded chart is part of the worksheet, but it does not fill any cells and it doesn't have a cell address. Instead, think of an embedded chart as existing in its own layer that floats on top of the worksheet cells. This means the chart can easily be moved and resized. Small black boxes, called **handles,** appear on the chart's corners and sides when the chart is selected. The Chart toolbar also may appear when a chart is selected. You can select a chart by clicking anywhere inside its rectangle. If you click in the chart and then drag the mouse, you can reposition the chart in the worksheet. If you click and drag one of the chart's handles, you can resize the chart window.

To reposition the embedded chart:

1 Select cell A1.

Notice that the Chart toolbar and the handles on the chart rectangle disappear—the chart is no longer selected.

2 Click once anywhere inside the chart rectangle.

The Chart toolbar and handles reappear, signaling that the chart is selected.

3 With the pointer positioned inside the chart rectangle, hold down the mouse button.

4 Drag the chart's outline so it is below the worksheet data (in rows 12 to 22), similar to Figure 5.15.

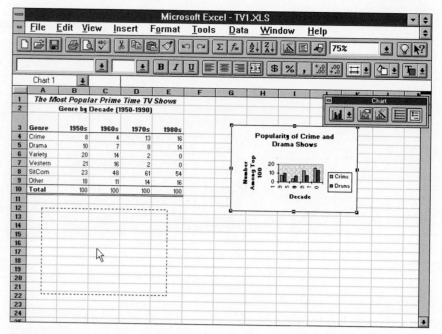

Figure 5.15

5 Release the mouse button.
The chart should now appear below the worksheet data.

The chart will be easier to read if you make it larger. You can change the width of the chart by dragging the middle handle of the left or right edge of the rectangle; change the height of the chart by dragging the middle handle at the top or bottom edge; and change both the width and the height of the chart simultaneously by dragging one of the corner handles.

It is often convenient to use the Print Preview command to see how the chart will appear on the printed page. After you use Print Preview, dotted lines will appear on the worksheet, showing you the boundaries of each printed page. You can then zoom out to 50 or even 25 percent and make adjustments to the chart location and size.

To preview the chart and worksheet printout:

1 Click the **Print Preview** tool on the Standard toolbar.
The Print Preview window appears, showing a simulated printout of the worksheet and chart. If you close the Print Preview window, you will still be able to see dotted reference lines showing page breaks.

2 Select **Close.**
The worksheet again appears, but with dotted reference lines.

3 Zoom to 25 percent magnification.
The placement of individual printout pages is more obvious if you zoom out.

To resize the embedded chart:

1 Zoom to 65 percent magnification.

2 Select the chart by clicking once in it.

3 Hold down the mouse button on the lower-right handle of the chart rectangle.

4 Drag the corner handle to the middle of cell G28, so the chart is wider and taller, similar to Figure 5.16.

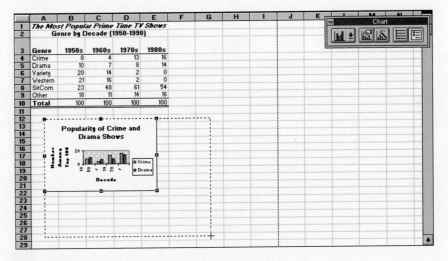

Figure 5.16

5 Release the mouse button.
The screen should now appear similar to Figure 5.17.

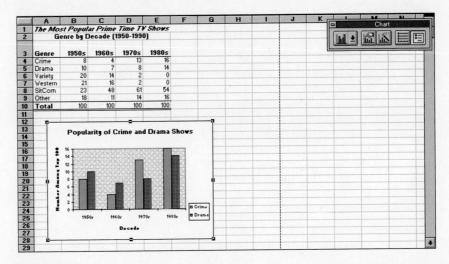

Figure 5.17

The chart you just created is **_linked_** to the worksheet: if the data upon which the chart depends changes, the chart will automatically update to reflect the change. In the following steps, you will change the value for crime shows in the 1960s to see the effect of this linkage. You will then use the Undo command to undo the entry and revert back to the original value.

To observe the effect of linkage:

1 Select cell C4, which contains *4*, the number of crime shows popular during the 1960s.
Note the bar on the chart that corresponds to this value.

2 Type **20** and press (ENTER)
The chart changes immediately to show the change in the worksheet.

3 Click the **Undo** tool on the Standard toolbar.

4 Save the workbook.

Reminder Undo, also available from the Edit menu, reverses the effect of the most recently issued command.

EXIT If necessary, you can quit Excel now and continue this project later.

Printing Embedded Charts

An embedded chart is part of the worksheet document and it will print with the surrounding worksheet data looking much as it does on-screen. The printing commands you have already learned will work with charts as well. In the following steps, you will use the Print Preview command to see a simulated printout on-screen; then you will print the worksheet. Print Preview is useful, because it allows you to detect problems with the printout without wasting paper, ink, or time.

To print the embedded chart with its worksheet:

1 Choose **File** and then **Print**.

2 Select **Print Preview**.
A simulated printout page appears. When the pointer is positioned over this page, the pointer shape changes to a magnifying glass; if you click the page, Excel will zoom in on the printout at the point you selected. Clicking again will zoom back out. You can also access other printing commands from the Print Preview window.

3 Position the pointer over the chart and click.
Excel zooms in at the point you clicked.

4 Click again to zoom out.
Notice that cell gridlines will appear on the printout, though it might look better without them.

5 Select **Setup**.
The Page Setup dialog box appears.

6 Select the **Sheet** tab.

7 Clear the **Gridlines** check box and then select **OK**.

8 Make sure the printer is ready, and then click the **Print** button.

Deleting Embedded Charts

You can have many different embedded charts in a worksheet. You can delete an embedded chart by selecting the chart and pressing (DEL) or choosing Clear from the Edit menu.

To delete the embedded chart:

1 Click within the chart to select it.

2 Press (DEL)

Plotting Nonadjacent Data

Suppose you wanted to make another column chart that showed the popularity of dramas and westerns for the 1950s and the 1970s only. This is *nonadjacent* information in the worksheet; that is, the ranges that contain the names and values are separated by cells that contain information that is not required for the chart.

Excel can easily make a chart from a nonadjacent selection, *provided that the pieces of the nonadjacent selection can be assembled into a rectangular range.* When you select the various ranges that comprise the nonadjacent selection, make sure the selections are each the same size and, if put together, that they form a rectangle. Any multicell ranges in the nonadjacent selection should be selected by dragging through the necessary cells, *not* by clicking each of the individual cells comprising the range. In the steps that follow, you will make a nonadjacent selection identical to Figure 5.18 (which is magnified for your reference), and then you will build a column chart based on that selection.

To make the nonadjacent selection:

1 Zoom to 75 percent magnification.

2 Select cell A3, which contains *Genre*, by clicking it. Keep the pointer in the middle of cell A3.

3 Hold down the mouse button and drag to the right to extend the selection to include cell B3, which contains *1950s*, and then release the mouse button.

4 Hold down (CTRL) and then click cell D3, which contains *1970s*.

5 Hold down (CTRL) and then click and drag to select A5:B5, which contains *Drama* and *10*.

6 Hold down (CTRL) and then click cell D5, which contains *8*.

7 Hold down (CTRL) and then click and drag to select A7:B7, which contains *Western* and *21*.

8 Hold down (CTRL) and then click cell D7, which contains *2*.
The completed nonadjacent selection should be identical to Figure 5.18.

Notice that the selection includes the names that should be used on the chart and that, if assembled, the nonadjacent parts would form a rectangle. As before, the upper-left cell (containing *Genre*) will not be used in the actual chart, but it is required if the combined selection is to be rectangular.

	A	B	C	D	E	F
1	*The Most Popular Prime Time TV Shows*					
2	Genre by Decade (1950-1990)					
3	Genre	1950s	1960s	1970s	1980s	
4	Crime	8	4	13	16	
5	Drama	10	7	8	14	
6	Variety	20	14	2	0	
7	Western	21	16	2	0	
8	SitCom	23	48	61	54	
9	Other	18	11	14	16	
10	Total	100	100	100	100	
11						

Figure 5.18

To build a column chart using the nonadjacent selection:

1 Select the **ChartWizard** button on the Standard toolbar.

2 Drag to select a chart area from about cell B12 to cell H23.

3 Select **Next** from the Step 1 dialog box.

4 Select the **Column** chart type and **Next** from the Step 2 dialog box.

5 Select chart format **1** and **Next** from the Step 3 dialog box.
The Step 4 dialog box appears.

6 Select **Next**.
The Step 5 dialog box appears.

7 Select **Finish** to create the chart.
You will not bother to add titles to this chart. The completed chart should resemble Figure 5.19.

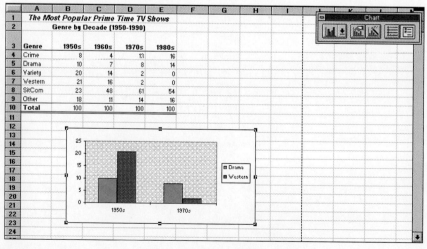

Figure 5.19

8 Delete the chart, and click on any single cell to cancel the selection.

BUILDING PIE CHARTS

A pie chart is different from most of the other chart types, because it shows just one data series. Pie charts are ideal for showing the relationship between a part and the whole—the relative share that each of the various categories represents.

In the following steps, you will create a pie chart showing the breakdown of different kinds of TV shows for the 1960s. This time, the data series will be in a column—the column for the 1960s—and the chart categories will be the different kinds of shows.

To build a pie chart:

1 Make a nonadjacent selection of the ranges A3:A9 and C3:C9, as shown in Figure 5.20. *Remember to drag to select multicell ranges.*

	A	B	C	D	E	F
1	*The Most Popular Prime Time TV Shows*					
2	**Genre by Decade (1950-1990)**					
3	**Genre**	**1950s**	**1960s**	**1970s**	**1980s**	
4	Crime	8	4	13	16	
5	Drama	10	7	8	14	
6	Variety	20	14	2	0	
7	Western	21	16	2	0	
8	SitCom	23	48	61	54	
9	Other	18	11	14	16	
10	**Total**	100	100	100	100	
11						

Figure 5.20

2 Click the ChartWizard button on the Standard toolbar.

3 Drag to select a chart area from about cell F2 to cell L23.

4 Select **Next** in the Step 1 dialog box.

5 Select the **Pie chart** type and then **Next** from the Step 2 dialog box.

6 Select chart format **5** and then **Next** from the Step 3 dialog box, as shown in Figure 5.21.

This pie chart format shows labels next to each slice of the pie.

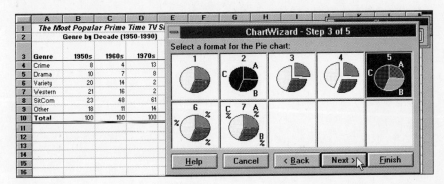

Figure 5.21

Note that the first column should be used for pie slice labels, and the first row for the chart title.

7 Select **Next** in the Step 4 dialog box, as shown in Figure 5.22. The Step 5 dialog box appears. A legend is not really necessary for this chart, because each slice is labeled.

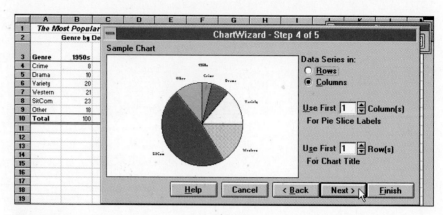

Figure 5.22

8 Select **Finish** in the Step 5 dialog box to create the chart.

9 Drag the Chart toolbar to the unused, lower-left part of the worksheet. The screen should resemble Figure 5.23.

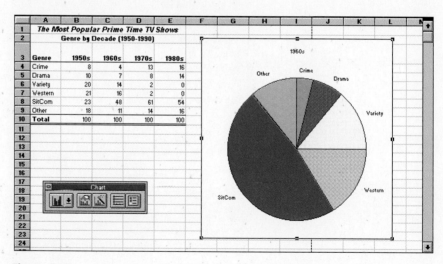

Figure 5.23

Editing an Embedded Chart

If you want to make extensive modifications to the text and graphic objects on a chart, you must first *activate* the chart for editing by *double-clicking* within the chart rectangle. In the following steps, you will activate and modify the pie chart.

Once a chart is activated, you can select an object within the chart by clicking that object. If several objects are in close proximity, you must pay close attention to which object is actually selected. Selected objects appear with handles that can be used to position or resize the object.

To modify an embedded chart:

1 Double-click in the pie chart.
The pie chart should now have a thick striped border, indicating that the chart is activated. Notice that the menu bar is different from the normal worksheet menu bar—it contains commands appropriate to working with charts.

2 Click once directly on the title *1960s*.
A box with handles appears around the text, indicating that the text is selected.

3 Type **Popular TV Shows in the 1960s** and press (ENTER)
The text you typed is used for the chart title.

4 Use the **Font Size** and **Bold** tools to make the title text 14-point bold.

5 Click once directly on the word *Variety*.
Notice that handles appear on all of the pie slice labels—the entire group of labels is selected.

6 Use the **Font Size** tool to change the size to 10 points.
All the pie slice labels are affected.

Suppose you wanted to emphasize or draw attention to the slice for the Western category. One way to do this is to *explode*—or pull out—that slice from the pie.

To explode a pie slice:

1 Position the pointer in the middle of the slice for Western and click.
Notice that all slices are selected.

2 Click again in the middle of the slice for Western.
Now the handles appear just on that slice.

3 Hold down the mouse button on the slice for Western and drag slightly to the right, as shown in Figure 5.24.

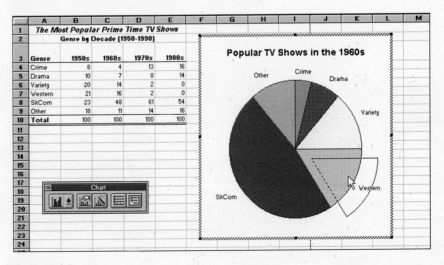

Figure 5.24

The slice for Western should now be pulled out from the pie. Once the mouse button is released, handles once again appear on the slice, which means the slice is still selected within the chart. Do not be concerned if the slice label *Western* is partly cut off.

4 Clear the slice handles by pressing (ESC) once.

Changing the Chart Type

Perhaps a fancier pie chart—such as a 3-D pie chart—would look better. You can change the chart type by using the Chart toolbar or by choosing Chart Type from the Format menu.

To change the type of a chart:

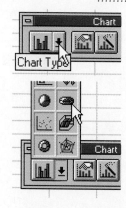

1 Click the list-box arrow on the **Chart Type** tool in the Chart toolbar.

2 Click the 3-D pie chart type.
The chart now appears as a 3-D pie chart. The slice for Western would appear more prominent if the chart were rotated clockwise.

3 Choose **Format** and then **3-D View.**

4 Click the clockwise rotation button three times so the chart is rotated 30 degrees clockwise, and then select **OK,** as shown in Figure 5.25.

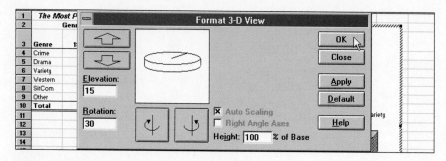

Figure 5.25

5 Click outside of the chart to deactivate it.

6 Close the Chart toolbar.

BUILDING A 3-D COLUMN CHART ON A SEPARATE CHART SHEET

What type of chart would help you to visualize the changing popularity of all the genres for the entire time span of the worksheet? A regular column chart would be cramped, as shown in Figure 5.26. A three-dimensional (3-D) column chart, which you can think of as a group of column charts seen in perspective, might be better.

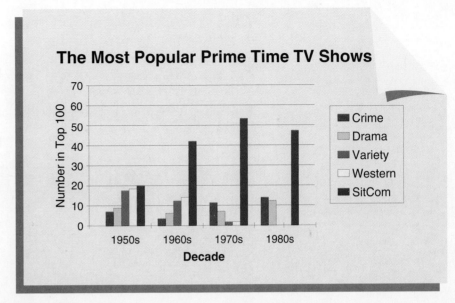

Figure 5.26

In this section, you will create a 3-D perspective column chart on a separate *chart sheet* within the workbook. Like embedded charts, charts in separate chart sheets are still linked to worksheet data. The primary advantage of having separate sheets for various charts is to organize your work and prevent having a single sheet cluttered with a variety of different charts.

To create a chart in a separate chart sheet:

1 Select A3:E8, as shown in Figure 5.27. *Do not include the Other category.*

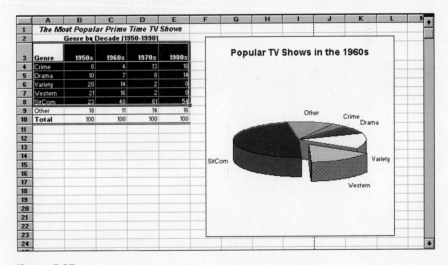

Figure 5.27

2 Choose **Insert, Chart,** and then **As New Sheet.**
The ChartWizard Step 1 dialog box appears.

3 Select **Next** in the Step 1 dialog box.

4 Select the **3-D Column** chart type and then **Next** from the Step 2 dialog box.

5 Select chart format **6** and then **Next** from the Step 3 dialog box. The Step 4 dialog box appears. It will be easier to see the various columns of the chart if the data series is in rows, rather than in columns.

6 Select **Rows** from the Step 4 dialog box, and then **Next**, as shown in Figure 5.28.

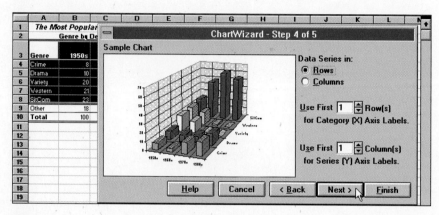

Figure 5.28

The Step 5 dialog box appears.

7 Select **Finish** to create the chart.
The chart appears in its own sheet, whose tab is named Chart1.

8 Double-click the **Chart1** sheet tab and rename it `3-D Column`

9 Drag the 3-D Column sheet tab so the chart sheet is layered after the TV Data worksheet.
The screen should resemble Figure 5.29.

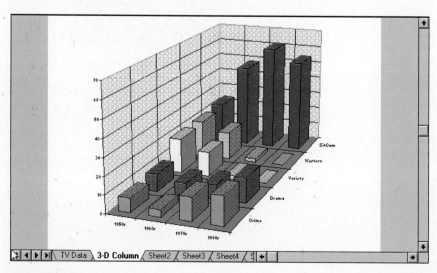

Figure 5.29

Changing the View of a 3-D Chart

The columns of the chart would be a little easier to see if the chart were viewed from a "higher" vantage point and if it were rotated clockwise slightly. It might also look better if the perspective—the three-dimensional effect—were exaggerated. The 3-D View command from the chart sheet's Format menu allows you to experiment with and set different viewing angles and perspectives.

To change the view of the 3-D chart:

1 Choose **Format** and then **3-D View.**

2 Move the pointer to the title bar of the 3-D View dialog box, and drag the dialog box to the upper-left area of the screen so most of the chart is visible, as shown in Figure 5.30.

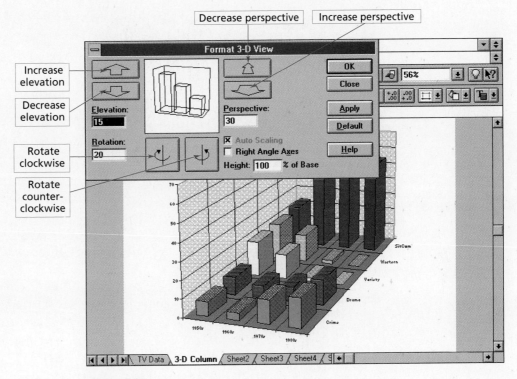

Figure 5.30

3 Use the **Increase Elevation** button to increase the degrees of elevation to 25.
Notice that the small wire-frame example chart in the dialog box changes slightly.

4 Select **Apply** to see the 3-D view settings applied to the actual chart.

5 Click the **Rotate Clockwise** button twice, until the chart is rotated to 40 degrees, and then select **Apply.**

6 Change the perspective to 40 degrees, and then select **OK,** as shown in Figure 5.31.

Selecting OK automatically applies the new 3-D view settings.

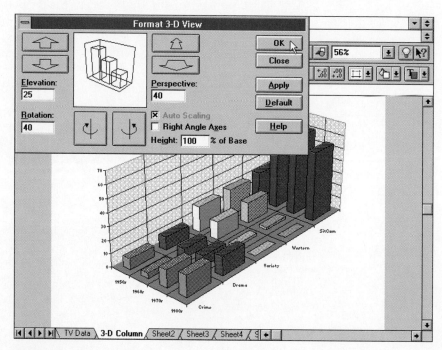

Figure 5.31

Attaching Titles to a Chart

In the following steps, you will add a main chart title that is linked to the worksheet. You will also enter titles for each of the axes.

To attach text to a chart:

1 Make sure the 3-D Column chart sheet is selected (click its tab, if necessary).

2 Zoom to 50 percent magnification; if the chart is not centered on-screen, use the scroll bars to center the chart.

3 Choose **Insert** and then **Titles.**
The Titles dialog box appears.

4 Click all of the check boxes: **Chart Title, Value (Z) Axis, Category (X) Axis,** and **Series (Y) Axis.**

5 Select **OK.**
The word *Title* appears above the chart; the letters *X*, *Y*, and *Z* label their respective axes.

6 Click on the word *Title* at the top of the chart.

7 Type =

8 Click on the **TV Data** sheet tab, and then select cell A1 (which contains the title text), as shown in Figure 5.32.

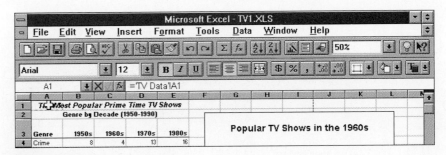

Figure 5.32

9 Press (ENTER) or click the **Enter** box on the formula bar.
The formula ='TV Data'!$A$1 means "get the contents of cell A1 from the sheet named TV Data."

10 Use the Formatting toolbar to change the main title font to Times New Roman 24-point bold italic.

To enter the other chart titles:

1 Click the label *Z*.
The Z-axis in a 3-D chart is marked with the measurement units of the data.

2 Type **Number in Top 100** and press (ENTER)

3 Change the font to Times New Roman 14-point bold italic.

4 Click the label *Y*.
The Y-axis is composed of the data series.

5 Type **Genre** and press (ENTER)

6 Change the font to Times New Roman 14-point bold italic.

7 Click the label *X*.
The X-axis is composed of the chart categories.

8 Type **Decade** and press (ENTER)

9 Change the font to Times New Roman 14-point bold italic.

To print the chart:

1 Choose **File** and then **Print Preview.**
A simulated printout appears. Notice that it includes a header and a footer—information at the top and bottom of the page. (In the next project, you will learn how to specify your own header and footer.) In this case, the header and footer are not necessary and reduce the space available for the chart itself, so they should be removed.

2 Select **Setup.**
The Page Setup dialog box appears.

3 Click the **Header/Footer** tab.

4 Scroll to the top of the **Header** list box and select **(none).**

5 Scroll to the top of the **Footer** list box and select **(none).**

6 Select **OK** in the Page Setup dialog box.

7 Select **Print** in the Print Preview window.
The Print dialog box appears.

8 Click **OK** to print the chart.
The printout should resemble Figure 5.33.

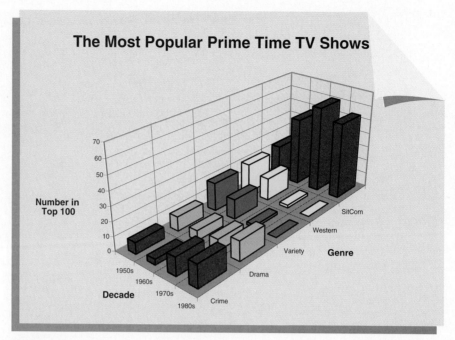

Figure 5.33

9 Save the workbook.

10 Exit Excel.

> *Tip* If a color or shade that Excel uses in a pie slice or bar on the printout is unacceptable (for example, too dark to show detail), double-click the specific object whose color you want to change, and select a different color and pattern from the Patterns tab of the Format Data Series dialog box.

The 3-D column chart conveys information more effectively than does the original table of numbers. If you follow a group of bars of a single color, you are tracing through time, following the changing popularity of a particular genre of TV show. If you read from lower left to upper right across the chart, you can examine the relative popularity of different kinds of shows for a particular decade.

THE NEXT STEP

Charts can help you analyze information, and they can also help you convey worksheet information more effectively to other people. If you are building a worksheet to make a point—to convince or educate other people about some conclusion or decision— charting can be a powerful tool.

However, you will encounter some worksheets, such as the one in the next project, for which a chart would not be of primary value. Use charting as you would use fonts and formatting: to support the understanding of information in worksheets, and not to distract or confuse.

This concludes Project 5. You can either exit Excel, or go on to work the Study Questions, Review Exercises, and Assignments.

SUMMARY AND EXERCISES

Summary

- Charting makes it easier to visualize and identify patterns in a table of numbers.
- Excel has 14 major types of charts, and many variations can be made of each type.
- The data you want to plot (display) in a chart is called a data series; each member of the data series corresponds to a chart category.
- If data series are in columns on the worksheet, their chart categories are in rows, and vice versa.
- Chart-category names appear along the horizontal (X) axis of a chart. The vertical axis is called the Y-axis.
- The symbols used to plot a value—such as the columns of a column chart—are called data markers.
- Using the ChartWizard tool is the quickest way to build a basic chart. You begin by selecting the range you want to chart, including any names that you want to appear on the chart.
- An embedded chart is a chart within a worksheet; a chart sheet exists in a workbook and is accessed using a worksheet tab.
- Charts are linked to the worksheets upon which they are based; if the worksheet data changes, the chart changes.
- Nonadjacent worksheet selections can be charted, provided the selections can be assembled into a rectangle.
- Embedded charts can be repositioned and resized in the worksheet and will print along with surrounding worksheet data.

Key Terms and Operations

Key Terms
category name
chart
chart category
chart sheet
ChartWizard
data marker
data series
embedded chart
explode

handle
legend
linked (chart)
palette
X-axis
Y-axis

Operations
Format a chart
Insert a chart
Insert titles

Study Questions

Multiple Choice

1. The labels that appear along the bottom edge of a chart are known as the chart:
   a. series.
   b. variables.
   c. categories
   d. data markers.
   e. data points.

2. A chart that appears within a worksheet is referred to as a(n):
   a. bar chart.
   b. column chart.
   c. category chart.
   d. worksheet chart.
   e. embedded chart.

3. How many major chart types are there in Excel?
   a. 1
   b. 2
   c. 3
   d. 4
   e. 14

4. On a chart, what is used to indicate what each color or symbol stands for?
   a. the X-axis
   b. a legend
   c. a data series
   d. a category
   e. a title

5. Line charts are most appropriate for:
   a. showing trends or changes over time.
   b. comparing individual values at specific times.
   c. showing relationships among portions of a whole.
   d. All of the above.
   e. None of the above.

6. Column charts are most appropriate for:
   a. showing trends or changes over time.
   b. comparing individual values at specific times.
   c. showing relationships among portions of a whole.
   d. All of the above.
   e. None of the above.

7. Pie charts are most appropriate for:
   a. showing trends or changes over time.
   b. comparing individual values at specific times.
   c. showing relationships among portions of a whole.
   d. All of the above.
   e. None of the above.

8. A nonadjacent range to be charted should:
   a. assemble into a rectangle.
   b. contain only text.
   c. contain only values.
   d. contain more chart categories than data series.
   e. contain more data series than chart categories.

9. If you want to modify an embedded chart, you must:
   a. Double-click it.
   b. Choose Edit from the Chart menu.
   c. Choose Chart from the Edit menu.
   d. Insert the chart into a chart sheet.
   e. Link the chart to an empty cell.

10. Embedded charts are especially useful when:
   a. The chart is to be displayed or printed along with the worksheet itself.
   b. Several charts are needed, all based on the same worksheet.
   c. A chart should exist in a separate chart sheet.
   d. The worksheet contains a large number of formulas (rather than number constants).
   e. The worksheet contains a large number of number constants (rather than formulas).

Short Answer

1. What is often the best way to identify trends and interrelationships in data?

2. If the data series is horizontal (in rows) in a worksheet, how are the chart categories arranged?

3. Which axis is the X-axis? Which is the Y-axis?

4. What are chart handles used for?

5. How is a pie chart different from most of the other chart types?

6. What term is used to describe a pie slice that has been pulled out of the pie for emphasis?

7. What type of chart would be most appropriate for showing month-by-month profits for a 48-month series?

8. What type of chart would be most appropriate for showing the relative market share of various brands of automobiles?

9. How do you modify an embedded chart? How do you delete an embedded chart?

10. Can chart sheets change if the worksheets upon which they were originally built change?

For Discussion

1. In what ways might a column chart provide a deceptive view of data? What about a 3-D perspective column chart? What do certain charts imply that may not really be present in the data?

2. When is a pie chart an appropriate chart type? When is a column chart appropriate?

3. What is a chart legend, and why is it usually important?

Review Exercises

Creating a Column Chart of Audio Sales for 1975–1990

Open the AUDIO2 workbook that you completed in Project 3. Using the ChartWizard tool and making nonadjacent selections, construct an embedded column chart that shows how sales of total records and total tapes changed over the time period of 1975 through 1990. The data series for this chart are in rows. The chart should resemble Figure 5.34. Print the embedded chart along with the worksheet. Save the workbook.

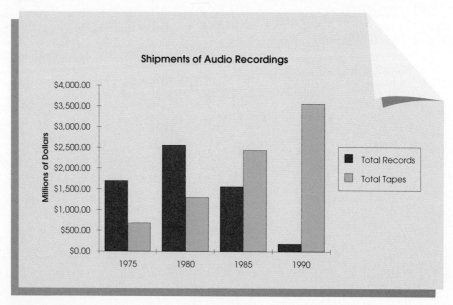

Figure 5.34

Creating a 3-D Pie Chart of Audio Sales for 1985

Open the AUDIO2 workbook that you completed in Project 3. Using the ChartWizard tool and making nonadjacent selections, construct a chart sheet that contains a 3-D pie chart that shows sales of total tapes, total records, and total CDs for 1985. Rotate the chart so the Total CD slice is in front. Explode the Total CD slice. Name the sheet AUDIOPIE. Print the chart. Save the workbook.

Assignments

Creating a 3-D Column Chart of Audio Sales for 1975–1990

Open the AUDIO2 workbook from Project 3. In a separate chart sheet, construct a 3-D column chart showing sales of LP albums, singles, 8-tracks, cassettes, and regular CDs over the 1975 to 1990 time period. Rotate the chart as needed to provide a good view of the columns. Print the chart and save the workbook.

Creating a Pie Chart of Energy Usage of Home Appliances

Open the ENERGY1 workbook from Project 4. Construct a pie chart in a separate chart sheet, with a legend but without labels for each slice, showing the share of the total monthly energy bill for each appliance in the worksheet. Add appropriate titles to the chart. Make another pie chart that graphs only the major users of electricity. Print the charts and save the workbook.

Creating a 3-D Column Chart of Daily Appliance Usage

Using the ENERGY1 worksheet from Project 4, construct a chart sheet containing a 3-D perspective column chart that shows, for each day of the week, the number of hours the following appliances are used: conventional oven, microwave oven, dishwasher, and clothes dryer. Rotate and format the chart as needed. Print the chart and save the workbook.

Objectives

After completing this project, you should be able to:

▶ Create customized formats for serial numbers

▶ Work with calendar dates and date formats

▶ Build formulas that keep a running balance

▶ Use the IF and ISBLANK functions

▶ Use the Function Wizard

▶ Use mixed cell references

▶ Streamline the worksheet by hiding columns, assigning notes, setting protection, assigning patterns, and creating customized styles

▶ Freeze window panes

▶ Specify print area, headers, footers, and scaling

▶ Set up multiple worksheets in a workbook

▶ Reconcile a checking account

CASE STUDY: BALANCING A CHECKBOOK

In this project, you will build a worksheet that will enable you to balance a checkbook easily. Suppose you have a checking account. The record of checks and other transactions in your checkbook is called a *check register*. Figure 6.1 illustrates a small check register. The withdrawals category includes checks, automated teller machine (ATM) debits, electronic fund transfer (EFT) payments, charges, fees, and so on. The deposits category includes ordinary deposits, automatic payroll transfers, credits, and refunds. Note that round numbers will be used in this project to make it easier to follow the examples.

Number	Date	Description	Register	Match	Withdrawal	Deposit	Balance Forward
							300.00
101	11/06/95	Kang Xi Grocery Store			50.00		250.00
DEP	11/11/95	Paycheck				1,200.00	1,450.00
102	11/14/95	Metro Electric Power			100.00		1,350.00
103	11/14/95	Imperial Apartments			400.00		950.00
DEP	11/18/95	Lottery Winnings				50.00	1,000.00

Figure 6.1

The list of transactions—deposits, checks paid, charges, and so on—that the bank sends to you each month is called a *bank statement*. Figure 6.2 shows a typical bank statement.

```
       First Interdimensional Bank
           Checking Account Statement

Deposits/Credits

          Date   Description              Amount
         11/11/95 Deposit                1,200.00

Checks/Withdrawals/Fees

          Date   Description              Amount
         11/9/95  Check 101                 50.00
         11/16/95 Check 103                400.00
         11/17/95 Monthly Fee              10.00

Account Summary as of 11/17/95

         Beginning Balance                300.00
         Plus 1 Deposit/Credit          1,200.00
         Less 3 Checks/Withdrawals/Fees   460.00
         Ending Balance                 1,040.00
```

Figure 6.2

The bank statement informs you that you have a certain amount of money in your account—this is the statement's *ending balance*. Your check register also has its own balance—how much money *you* think you have in the account—and it's likely that the two balances are different.

Why are they different? First, there were probably checks you wrote that had not yet been presented to the bank for payment by the time the statement was printed and mailed. In the example, the check to Metro Electric Power is one of these. Your check register also probably lists transactions that you made *after* the bank printed the statement, such as the deposit of lottery winnings in the example.

Second, the bank statement probably shows transactions such as charges, fees, and automatic payments that you might not have known about and did not record in the register. And, of course, it's quite possible that you wrote a check or withdrew money from an ATM and forgot to record it in the register.

Reconciling the two balances—balancing the checkbook—means adjusting the register balance so it is updated about transactions appearing only in the bank statement, and adjusting the statement balance so it is updated about transactions appearing only in the register. There are several approaches to reconciling. The method you'll find described on the back of a bank statement is more suitable for pencil and paper than it is for electronic worksheets. The method you will implement in this project is one that uses an electronic worksheet (rather than a register booklet) as the actual check register. This method eliminates the need for a complete paper register.

Designing the Solution

The electronic check register will contain a record of all checking account transactions that you know of. When a new statement arrives, any transactions appearing in the statement but not in the register should be entered into the register. This is how you let the register "know" about transactions appearing only in the bank statement. For example, suppose you receive a statement and you see that you were charged a $10.00 monthly fee. You would record that fee in the register, as shown in Figure 6.3. Once you record transactions such as this in the check register, the register balance is updated or adjusted to reflect the information in the bank statement.

Number	Date	Description	Register Match	Withdrawal	Deposit	Balance Forward
						300.00
101	6-Nov-95	Kang Xi Grocery Store		50.00		250.00
DEP	11-Nov-95	Paycheck			1,200.00	1,450.00
102	14-Nov-95	Metro Electric Power		100.00		1,350.00
103	14-Nov-95	Imperial Apartments		400.00		950.00
DEP	18-Nov-95	Lottery Winnings			50.00	1,000.00
FEE	17-Nov-95	Monthly Fee		10.00		990.00

Figure 6.3

What about transactions that you made and recorded in the register *after* the bank printed its statement? How do you let the bank statement know about these? You don't modify the statement directly. Instead, you mark off in the register all withdrawals and deposits that also appear in the statement, as shown in Figure 6.4. Any unmarked entry is *unmatched*—it appears only in the register and not in the statement.

Number	Date	Description	Register Match	Withdrawal	Deposit	Balance Forward
						300.00
101	11/06/95	Kang Xi Grocery Store	X	50.00		250.00
DEP	11/11/95	Paycheck	X		1,200.00	1,450.00
102	11/14/95	Metro Electric Power		100.00		1,350.00
103	11/14/95	Imperial Apartments	X	400.00		950.00
DEP	11/18/95	Lottery Winnings	X		50.00	1,000.00
FEE	11/17/95	Monthly Fee		10.00		990.00

Figure 6.4

You then proceed to total all the unmatched entries—all the withdrawals and deposits that appear in the register but not in the statement. To produce an adjusted statement balance, you subtract the total withdrawals and add the total deposits to the bank statement's ending balance, as shown in Figure 6.5. The adjusted statement balance should equal the adjusted register balance.

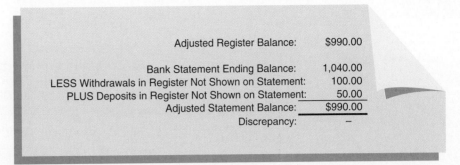

Adjusted Register Balance:	$990.00
Bank Statement Ending Balance:	1,040.00
LESS Withdrawals in Register Not Shown on Statement:	100.00
PLUS Deposits in Register Not Shown on Statement:	50.00
Adjusted Statement Balance:	$990.00
Discrepancy:	–

Figure 6.5

If the two adjusted balances agree, the checkbook is balanced. If not, there must be some transaction or a group of transactions that has not been correctly accounted for or that contains mistakes. The worksheet you will build in this project cannot automatically correct such recording errors, although it can be of some help in finding them.

In automating the task of balancing a checkbook, you will begin by constructing a check register similar to the one shown in Figure 6.1. The register will contain columns for check number, date, description, match, withdrawal, deposit, and balance forward. The only formula in these columns will be one to compute the balance forward. Once the check register is complete, you will proceed to construct formulas that reconcile the register with information derived from a bank statement.

BUILDING A CHECK REGISTER

You will now make the initial text entries for the check register, as shown in Figure 6.6. Notice that some space is being preserved at the top of the worksheet; later, you will place the balancing formulas there. It makes more sense to put those formulas near the top (or perhaps to the right), because the top section of the worksheet is easy to find. Also, as you make new entries in the register, the worksheet will spread downward, and it would be inconvenient to have something else in the way.

	A	B	C	D	E	F	G	H
1	Checkbook Balancing System							
2								
3								
4								
5								
6								
7								
8								
9								
10	Register						Balance Forward	
11	Number	Date	Description	Match	Withdrawal	Deposit		
12								
13								
14								
15								

Figure 6.6

The sample data that you enter in the check register will be based on Figure 6.1.

To prepare the worksheet and enter the main title:

1 Open a new, blank workbook, and select Sheet1.

2 In cell A1, enter `Checkbook Balancing System`

3 Make sure cell A1 is still selected, and change the font size and style to 14-point bold italic.

4 Enter `Register` in cell A10.

5 Use the **Format Painter** tool to copy the formatting of cell A1 to cell A10.

6 Save the workbook as CHKBAL1.

To enter the column titles:

1 Increase the height of row 11 to about 18 points.

2 Enter `Number` in cell A11.

3 Enter `Date` in cell B11.

4 Enter `Description` in cell C11.

5 Enter `Match` in cell D11.

6 Enter `Withdrawal` in cell E11.

7 Enter `Deposit` in cell F11.

8 Select cell G10 and enter `Balance Forward`
The screen should now resemble Figure 6.7.

	A	B	C	D	E	F	G	H	I
1	*Checkbook Balancing System*								
2									
3									
4									
5									
6									
7									
8									
9									
10	*Register*						Balance Forward		
11	Number	Date	Description	Match		Withdrawa	Deposit		
12									
13									

Figure 6.7

To format the column titles:

1 Set the format of *Balance Forward* in cell G10 to bold, right horizontal alignment, and wrap text.

2 Select the other column titles in the range A11:F11 and set the format to bold.

3 Set the horizontal alignment to center for the column titles in the range A11:F11.

4 Extend the selection to include G11 and set a medium bottom border, as shown in Figure 6.8.

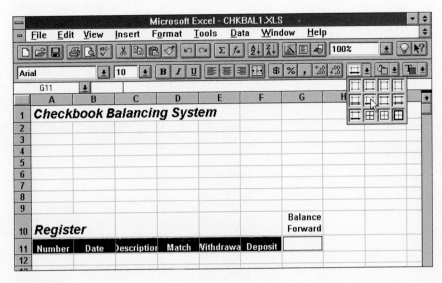

Figure 6.8

5 Widen the withdrawal, deposit, and balance forward columns (E:G) to 12.

6 Widen the description column (C) to 25.

7 Narrow the match column (D) to 7.

8 Widen the date column (B) to 10.

9 Choose **View** and then **Status Bar** to turn off the display of the status bar.

10 Zoom the window to a magnification of 85 percent.
The worksheet should now resemble Figure 6.6.

11 Save the workbook.

Using Custom Number Formats

In an earlier project, you saw that customized number formats could be used to attach abbreviations of special measurements or currency units. Customized number formats are also valuable in preserving special punctuation in entries such as telephone numbers, Social Security numbers, Zip codes, inventory part numbers, and serial numbers. For example, the number format (000) 000-0000 will cause the number 8005551212 to display as (800) 555-1212.

It is also important to preserve *leading zeros* in Zip codes and serial numbers. Normally, Excel removes leading zeros, because they have no mathematical significance; the number 0001 is normally displayed as 1. In this worksheet, you will assign a format code of 0000 to the check serial numbers so four digits are used, even if the number is less than 1000. For example, check number 101 will appear as 0101; this is how check serial numbers are traditionally printed.

To assign a customized format for the check numbers:

1 Enter **101** in cell A12.

2 Select all of column A.

3 Choose **Format** and then **Cells,** click the **Number** tab, and create a new format code of 0000, as shown in Figure 6.9.

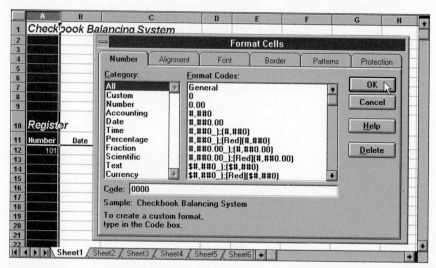

Figure 6.9

4 Select **OK** to complete the format.

Notice that the entry in cell A12 now appears as 0101. Any number entered in column A will now be subject to the customized format you just created and assigned.

Using Calendar Dates in Excel

Excel allows you to enter dates (and times) in a worksheet cell. A date is considered a special kind of number. Excel dates are useful in several respects.

You can perform *date arithmetic* with Excel, which means you can add days to a date, subtract days from a date, or subtract an earlier date from a later date (to determine the number of days between the two dates). Suppose the date *May 7, 1995,* is stored in cell A1 and the date *December 16, 1994,* is stored in cell A2. The formula =A1-A2 will result in 142, the number of days between the two dates.

Dates can also appear with a wide variety of specialized and customizable formats. Table 6.1 shows several format codes and how the date *May 7, 1995,* would appear with each.

Table 6.1

Format	Result
m/d/yy	5/7/95
d-mmm-yy	7-May-95
d-mmm	7-May
mmm-yy	May-95
dddd	Sunday
ddd dd-mmm-yy	Sun 07-May-95
dddd, mmm d, yyyy	Sunday, May 7, 1995

To enter a specific, constant date—such as *October 20, 1980*—into a cell, type the date directly. You could type 10/20/80 or 20 Oct 1980. Excel will convert your entry to a date serial number, and it will automatically assign a date format consistent with the way you entered the date.

If you want today's date—which changes each day—to appear in a cell, type the formula =NOW( ). The result of this function depends on whatever date the computer system is set to and will automatically update whenever the date changes. Excel has a number of functions designed to help with date calculations. Table 6.2 lists a few of these; the examples presume that cell A1 contains a valid date, such as 5/7/95, and that the current system time and date are 11:45 a.m., 10/20/1995.

Table 6.2

Task	Function	Result
To show the current date	=NOW( )	10/20/95 11:45
To extract the month (1 to 12) from a date in another cell	=MONTH(A1)	5
To extract the day of the month from a date in another cell	=DAY(A1)	7
To extract the year from a date in another cell	=YEAR(A1)	1995
To extract the day of the week (1 to 7, where 1 is Sunday) from a date in another cell	=WEEKDAY(A1)	1

In the following steps, you will enter a date for the first check and then assign the number format d-mmm-yy to the Date column of the check register.

 To enter and format a date:

1 Enter **11/6/95** in cell B12.
Notice that this entry appears in the formula bar as *11/6/1995*. Excel automatically interpreted the entry as a date and assigned a default format of m/d/y.

2 Select all of column B.

3 Choose **Format** and then **Cells.**

4 Click the **Number** tab.
The Number Format dialog box appears.

4 Select the **Date** category; select the Format Code **d-mmm-yy**, and then select **OK**, as shown in Figure 6.10.

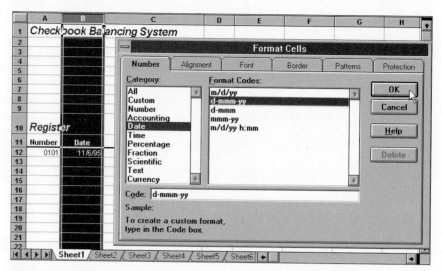

Figure 6.10

To enter the check description and withdrawal amount:

1 Enter `Kang Xi Grocery Store` in cell C12 as the description of this entry.
Note that the match column will be left blank for now.

2 Enter a withdrawal amount of **50** in cell E12.
A check is the most common kind of withdrawal from the account.

Using Comma Style

Values appearing in the withdrawal, deposit, and balance forward columns are dollar amounts and should appear consistently with two digits to the right of the decimal. In the following steps, you will assign the Comma cell style, which includes an appropriate numeric format, to these three columns.

To assign Comma style:

1 Select columns E, F, and G.

2 Click the **Comma Style** tool on the Formatting toolbar to apply the style.

Keeping a Running Balance

The balance forward column in the check register is a typical example of a *running balance*—a value that appears on each line of an account or register to show the current balance. The starting balance for this register will be entered in cell G11. Calculation of the balance for each line of the register will involve taking the previous balance, subtracting any withdrawals, and adding any deposits.

Such a formula uses relative cell references and can be copied to provide a running balance for each line of the register. In the steps that follow, you will copy the formula downward so ten rows of the worksheet will be ready to contain check-register entries.

Ten is an arbitrary number of rows: if new rows are later needed in the register, the formula can easily be copied to them. The advantage of copying the formula in advance to a large number of rows is that you won't have to remember to copy the formula each time the worksheet grows. The disadvantage is that the extra formulas (until they are needed) can use up memory and slow down the calculation of the worksheet.

To build the formula for balance forward:

1 Enter **300** for the starting balance in cell G11.

2 Select cell G12, which will contain a formula to compute the balance forward for the first line of the register.

3 Type **=**

4 Select the previous balance (300, in cell G11).

5 Type **-**

6 Select the withdrawal amount (50, in cell E12).

7 Type **+**

8 Select the deposit amount (cell F12, which is blank), and then press (ENTER)

9 Copy the formula down column G to cell G21.

The screen should look like Figure 6.11.

G12		=G11-E12+F12					
A	B	C	D	E	F	G	H
1 Checkbook Balancing System							
2							
3							
4							
5							
6							
7							
8							
9							Balance Forward
10 Register							
11 Number	Date	Description	Match	Withdrawal	Deposit	300.00	
12 0101	6-Nov-95	Kang Xi Grocery Store		50.00		250.00	
13						250.00	
14						250.00	
15						250.00	
16						250.00	
17						250.00	
18						250.00	
19						250.00	
20						250.00	
21							
22							

Sheet1 / Sheet2 / Sheet3 / Sheet4 / Sheet5 / Sheet6

Figure 6.11

The result of the formula is 250.00. This relative formula means, "Take what is one cell above the formula, subtract what is two cells to the left, and add what is one cell to the left." Because no further deposits or withdrawals are currently entered in later lines of the register, the balance forward is 250 in each remaining cell.

The first line of the register contains only a withdrawal—so why bother having the balance forward formula add the blank deposit cell? You should design formulas for flexibility; this single formula will work for either a deposit or a withdrawal entry in the register, and this flexibility allows the formula to be used in any line of the register without regard to the type of register entry.

Completing the Remaining Register Entries

In the following steps, you can refer to Figure 6.12 to complete the other four check-register entries.

	A	B	C	D	E	F	G	H
1	Checkbook Balancing System							
2								
3								
4								
5								
6								
7								
8								
9								
10	Register						Balance Forward	
11	Number	Date	Description	Match	Withdrawal	Deposit	300.00	
12	0101	6-Nov-95	Kang Xi Grocery Store		50.00		250.00	
13	DEP	11-Nov-95	Paycheck			1,200.00	1,450.00	
14	0102	14-Nov-95	Metro Electric Power		100.00		1,350.00	
15	0103	14-Nov-95	Imperial Apartments		400.00		950.00	
16	DEP	18-Nov-95	Lottery Winnings			50.00	1,000.00	
17							1,000.00	
18							1,000.00	
19							1,000.00	
20							1,000.00	
21							1,000.00	
22								

Sheet1 / Sheet2 / Sheet3 / Sheet4 / Sheet5 / Sheet6

Figure 6.12

To make the other check-register entries:

1 Enter **DEP** (an abbreviation for *deposit*) in cell A13.

2 Enter **11/11/95** for the date in cell B13.

3 Enter **Paycheck** for the description in cell C13.

4 Enter **1200** for the deposit amount in cell F13.

5 Enter the information for the other three lines of the check register, referring to Figure 6.12.
The screen should now resemble Figure 6.12.

6 Save the workbook.

BUILDING THE RECONCILIATION SYSTEM

How can the check register you've just completed be made to work as part of a checking account balancing system? Suppose a statement arrives from the bank, as illustrated in Figure 6.13. You will recall that the first step in reconciling the computerized check register is to include any entries to the register that appear only on the statement. This is simply a matter of entering some new lines of information in the register. In the case of the example statement, only one item, a $10.00 monthly fee, needs to be included in the register.

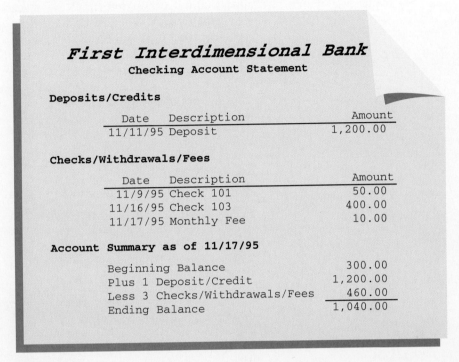

First Interdimensional Bank
Checking Account Statement

Deposits/Credits

Date	Description	Amount
11/11/95	Deposit	1,200.00

Checks/Withdrawals/Fees

Date	Description	Amount
11/9/95	Check 101	50.00
11/16/95	Check 103	400.00
11/17/95	Monthly Fee	10.00

Account Summary as of 11/17/95

Beginning Balance	300.00
Plus 1 Deposit/Credit	1,200.00
Less 3 Checks/Withdrawals/Fees	460.00
Ending Balance	1,040.00

Figure 6.13

To include entries to the register from the statement:

1 Enter FEE in cell A17.

2 Enter 11/17/95 in cell B17.

3 Enter Monthly Fee in cell C17.

4 Enter 10 in cell E17 (in the withdrawal column).

The screen should now resemble Figure 6.14.

	A	B	C	D	E	F	G	H
1	*Checkbook Balancing System*							
2								
3								
4								
5								
6								
7								
8								
9								Balance Forward
10	*Register*						300.00	
11	**Number**	**Date**	**Description**	**Match**	**Withdrawal**	**Deposit**		
12	0101	6-Nov-95	Kang Xi Grocery Store		50.00		250.00	
13	DEP	11-Nov-95	Paycheck			1,200.00	1,450.00	
14	0102	14-Nov-95	Metro Electric Power		100.00		1,350.00	
15	0103	14-Nov-95	Imperial Apartments		400.00		950.00	
16	DEP	18-Nov-95	Lottery Winnings			50.00	1,000.00	
17	FEE	17-Nov-95	Monthly Fee		10.00		990.00	
18							990.00	
19							990.00	
20							990.00	
21							990.00	
22								

Sheet1 / Sheet2 / Sheet3 / Sheet4 / Sheet5 / Sheet6

Figure 6.14

Setting Up the Match Column

You would repeat the procedure you just completed—adding items that appear only on the statement to the checkbook register—each time a new statement arrived. What about items that appear on the register but not on the statement? You will recall that entries that *do* appear on both the register and the statement should be checked off in the match column. Any unmatched entries identify those items that appear *only* in the register.

In this check register, a letter *X* will be used as the checkmark. In the steps that follow, you will format and then fill in the match column of the register.

To prepare the match column:

1 Select all of column D.

2 Set the horizontal alignment to center.

3 Refer to the sample bank statement in Figure 6.13 and mark off entries in the register that are matched on the statement. Use a capital *X* to mark matches.

The worksheet should now resemble Figure 6.15.

	A	B	C	D	E	F	G	H
1	*Checkbook Balancing System*							
2								
3								
4								
5								
6								
7								
8								
9								
10	*Register*						Balance Forward	
11	**Number**	**Date**	**Description**	**Match**	**Withdrawal**	**Deposit**	300.00	
12	0101	6-Nov-95	Kang Xi Grocery Store	X	50.00		250.00	
13	DEP	11-Nov-95	Paycheck	X		1,200.00	1,450.00	
14	0102	14-Nov-95	Metro Electric Power		100.00		1,350.00	
15	0103	14-Nov-95	Imperial Apartments	X	400.00		950.00	
16	DEP	18-Nov-95	Lottery Winnings			50.00	1,000.00	
17	FEE	17-Nov-95	Monthly Fee	X	10.00		990.00	
18							990.00	
19							990.00	
20							990.00	
21							990.00	
22								

Sheet1 / Sheet2 / Sheet3 / Sheet4 / Sheet5 / Sheet6

Figure 6.15

4 Save the workbook.

Setting Up the Columns for Unmatched Entries

To reconcile the account, you will need to know the total of withdrawals shown on the register but not on the statement, as well as the total of deposits shown on the register but not on the statement. In other words, you somehow need to identify and total the unmatched withdrawals and the unmatched deposits.

In the steps that follow, you will set up two special columns to the right of the register. One column will contain unmatched withdrawals, and the other will contain unmatched deposits. Note that the titles for these columns will be placed a couple of cells above the top of the main register area.

To set up the reconciliation columns:

1 Set the magnification of the window to 70 percent.

2 In cell H9, enter `Withdrawals in Register Unmatched on Statement`

3 In cell I9, enter `Deposits in Register Unmatched on Statement`

4 Widen columns H and I to about 12.

5 Set the format of cells H9:I9 to align to the right with wrapped text.

6 Increase the height of row 9 to about 57.

The screen should resemble Figure 6.16.

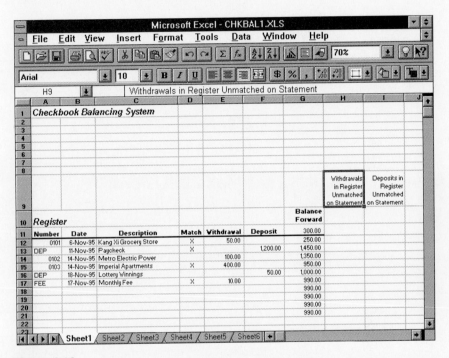

Figure 6.16

7 Select the two-cell range H10:I10, type `Total:` and then press
CTRL + ENTER

8 Set the horizontal alignment of H10:I10 to align to the right.

9 Select all of columns H and I, and assign the Comma style.

10 Set a medium bottom border to cells H11 and I11 (you can use the Format Painter tool to copy the format of cell G11).

The worksheet should resemble Figure 6.17.

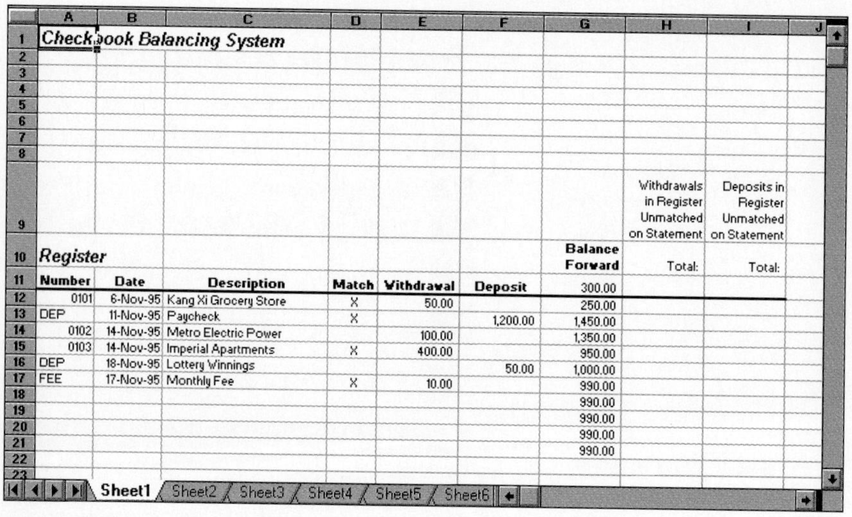

	A	B	C	D	E	F	G	H	I	J
1	Checkbook Balancing System									
2										
3										
4										
5										
6										
7										
8										
9									Withdrawals in Register Unmatched on Statement	Deposits in Register Unmatched on Statement	
10	Register						Balance Forward			
11	Number	Date	Description	Match	Withdrawal	Deposit	300.00	Total:	Total:	
12	0101	6-Nov-95	Kang Xi Grocery Store	X	50.00		250.00			
13	DEP	11-Nov-95	Paycheck	X		1,200.00	1,450.00			
14	0102	14-Nov-95	Metro Electric Power		100.00		1,350.00			
15	0103	14-Nov-95	Imperial Apartments	X	400.00		950.00			
16	DEP	18-Nov-95	Lottery Winnings			50.00	1,000.00			
17	FEE	17-Nov-95	Monthly Fee	X	10.00		990.00			
18							990.00			
19							990.00			
20							990.00			
21							990.00			
22										
23										

Sheet1 / Sheet2 / Sheet3 / Sheet4 / Sheet5 / Sheet6

Figure 6.17

11 Spell-check the worksheet.

12 Save the workbook.

Creating Formulas That Make Decisions

Consider how the new column for unmatched withdrawals should work. If a particular withdrawal in the register is not matched on the statement (that is, if there is no X in the match cell), that amount should appear in the unmatched withdrawals column. In the small example register you have built, there is only one place in the unmatched withdrawals column where a nonzero number should appear: 100 should display in cell H14, because Metro Electric Power had not presented the check for payment before the bank printed the statement.

If the task of identifying unmatched entries is going to be automated, a special formula is required for each cell in the unmatched withdrawals column. The formula must be capable of performing a simple test: "If the match cell in this row contains an X, then show a zero; otherwise, show the withdrawal amount."

Using the IF Function

In Excel, the IF function provides the capability to automate simple decisions. The syntax of the IF function is described in this way:

IF(*logical_test, value_if_true, value_if_false*)

This means the IF function takes three arguments: the first argument expresses some sort of test or question; the second argument expresses what to do if the test result is true; the third argument expresses what to do if the test result is false.

There are several ways you can apply the IF function to solve the problem of identifying unmatched entries. In the following sections, you will try two approaches. The first version will produce a formula that can be understood this way: "If there is an X in the match cell, then show a zero; otherwise, show the withdrawal amount."

To build the IF formula for unmatched withdrawals (version 1):

1 Select cell H12, the first cell in the unmatched withdrawals column.

2 Type `=if(`

3 Select the match cell, D12.

4 Type `="X",0,`
Note that the *X* is uppercase.

5 Select the withdrawal cell, E12.

6 Type `)` and press (ENTER)

The completed formula in cell H12 is $=IF(D12="X",0,E12)$. The result appears as a hyphen rather than a zero, because you assigned the Comma style to the cells in column H. The hyphen means zero, though.

Ignoring relative cell reference terminology for the moment, this formula can be interpreted as meaning "If what's in cell D12 equals an *X*, then result in a 0; otherwise result in what's in cell E12." The *X* appears in quotation marks because it is a *text string*—a sequence of one or more characters to be taken literally—and not a defined name or the name of a function.

Because the match cell contains an *X*, the result of the formula is 0.00. This formula is straightforward, but it is also *brittle*—it is sensitive to slight variations in the tested condition and could give unwanted results to an unsuspecting or careless computer user. In the steps that follow, you will test the formula to see how it responds to other kinds of entries in the match cell.

To test the first IF formula:

1 Select the first match cell, D12.

2 Type `x` and press (ENTER)
Make sure you enter a lowercase character. The result of the IF formula is still zero, which is correct. You can conclude that the formula is not *case-sensitive*—that is, it doesn't care whether a letter is entered in uppercase or lowercase. But suppose someone used an *m* to mark matching entries.

3 In cell D12, type `m` and press (ENTER)
The result of the IF formula is now 50.00, which is wrong. The problem is that the tested condition is too particular: this would be a more robust formula if it tested simply whether the match cell was blank. Excel provides a special function to do this: ISBLANK(D12) will return (result in) TRUE if cell D12 is blank, and FALSE otherwise.

To build the IF formula for unmatched withdrawals (version 2):

1 Select cell H12, the first cell in the unmatched withdrawals column.

2 Type `=if(isblank(`

3 Select the match cell, D12.

4 Type `),`

5 Select the withdrawal cell, E12.

6 Type `,0)` and press (ENTER)

The screen should resemble Figure 6.18. The formula is
=IF(ISBLANK(D12),E12,0). Its result is zero, which is correct, even
though an *m* was used in the match cell, rather than an *X*.

	H12	↓		=IF(ISBLANK(D12),E12,0)						
	A	B	C	D	E	F	G	H	I	J
1	*Checkbook Balancing System*									
2										
3										
4										
5										
6										
7										
8										
9								Withdrawals in Register Unmatched on Statement	Deposits in Register Unmatched on Statement	
10	*Register*						Balance Forward			
11	Number	Date	Description	Match	Withdrawal	Deposit		Total:	Total:	
12	0101	6-Nov-95	Kang Xi Grocery Store	m	50.00		300.00			
13	DEP	11-Nov-95	Paycheck	X		1,200.00	250.00			
14	0102	14-Nov-95	Metro Electric Power		100.00		1,450.00			
15	0103	14-Nov-95	Imperial Apartments	X	400.00		1,350.00			
16	DEP	18-Nov-95	Lottery Winnings			50.00	950.00			
17	FEE	17-Nov-95	Monthly Fee	X	10.00		1,000.00			
18							990.00			
19							990.00			
20							990.00			
21							990.00			
22										
23										

Sheet1 / Sheet2 / Sheet3 / Sheet4 / Sheet5 / Sheet6

Figure 6.18

7 Enter **X** in cell D12.

Note that the logical sense of the new IF formula is reversed: the earlier
formula means "If there's an *X* in the match cell, then display 0; otherwise
display the withdrawal amount." The new formula is "If the match cell is
blank, then display the withdrawal amount; otherwise display 0."

Using Mixed Cell References

The IF formula uses relative cell references and should work without a
problem for the other cells in the unmatched withdrawals column. It might
seem as though this formula would work for the unmatched deposits
column as well, because the same basic IF test is needed. The best way to
understand why the formula won't correctly duplicate in its present form is
to copy the formula and examine the results.

In the steps that follow, you will copy the formula across to the first
unmatched deposits cell. You will then copy two cells at once down columns
H and I and study the resulting formulas.

To copy a range of cells:

1 Copy the IF formula in cell H12 to cell I12.

2 Select the range H12:I12.

3 Position the pointer at the lower-right area of the selection, and drag
the fill handle down to row 21.

4 Clear the selection by selecting any single cell.

The screen should resemble Figure 6.19.

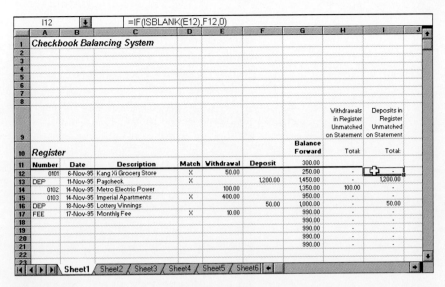

Figure 6.19

5 Display the Auditing toolbar, and position the toolbar so it does not obscure any worksheet contents or column headings.

6 Select the first match cell, D12.

7 Click the **Trace Dependents** tool on the Auditing toolbar.

8 Select cell I12.

The screen should resemble Figure 6.20. The formulas for both the unmatched withdrawals and the unmatched deposits should depend on cell D12, but only the original formula in cell H12 is a dependent.

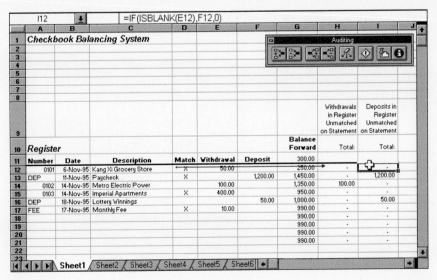

Figure 6.20

The formula in cell I12 reads =IF(ISBLANK(E12),F12,0), which can be read as "If the cell four columns to the left is blank, then display the value in the cell three columns to the left; otherwise, display zero."

The cell that *should* be tested by ISBLANK is D12, not E12. It is correct, however, that the formula displays the value of F12 if the match cell is blank. The relative cell reference to F12 in this formula is correct, but a relative reference does not work for the cell being tested by ISBLANK.

If you look at the results in the unmatched deposits column, you will see that they are incorrect. Will a fully absolute reference to D12 solve the problem? In the following steps, you will modify and recopy the IF formula to find out whether it will.

To modify the IF formula (using fully absolute cell references):

1 Click the **Remove All Arrows** tool on the Auditing toolbar.

2 Select cell H12, which contains the original IF formula.

3 Click the text *D12* in the formula bar.

4 Press (F4) to make the reference fully absolute. The formula now reads = IF(ISBLANK($D$12),E12,0)

5 Press (ENTER)

6 Copy the formula in H12 across and down to replace the old IF formulas in the range H12:I21.

7 Select the first match cell, D12.

8 Click the **Trace Dependents** tool on the Auditing toolbar.

9 Select cell I17.
The screen should look like Figure 6.21.

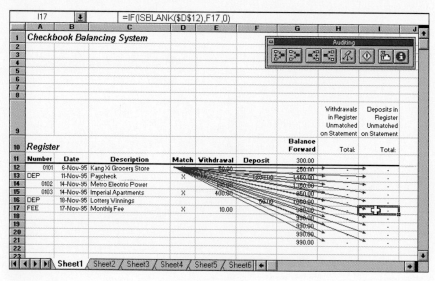

Figure 6.21

Now the formula has trouble in both the unmatched withdrawals and the unmatched deposits columns: *all* the formulas depend on the original match cell, D12. Consider the formula in cell I17, which reads = IF(ISBLANK($D$12),F17,0). The ISBLANK part of this formula, like all of the other new IF formulas, tests cell D12. It should be testing D17, the match cell in its own row.

Now consider the original formula in cell H12:

```
=IF(ISBLANK($D$12),E12,0)
```

You will recall that any time you are referring to a cell while building a formula and that cell *alone* provides the required information for the formula and for future copies of the formula, the reference to the cell should be absolute. In this case, it is not only cell D12 that all the copied formulas will need to refer to.

What can be said about the copied formulas? Each one will have to refer to the cell in the match column (D) of its own row. In other words, the cell tested by ISBLANK will always be D*something*. Only the *column* part of the cell reference should be absolute. The row should be allowed to adjust as the formula is copied. This is an example of a ***mixed cell reference***— a cell reference in which only the column or only the row is static. Only one dollar sign appears in a mixed reference, such as, $D12 or F$3. In the steps that follow, you will rebuild and recopy the formula once again, this time using a mixed cell reference where appropriate.

To modify the IF formula:

1 Click the **Remove All Arrows** tool on the Auditing toolbar.

2 Select cell H12, which contains the original IF formula.

3 Click within the text *$D$12* in the formula bar.

4 Press (F4) repeatedly until the mixed reference $D12 appears.
The formula now reads =IF(ISBLANK($D12),E12,0). The $D12 in the new formula can be interpreted as "column D, current row."

5 Press (ENTER)

6 Copy the formula in H12 across and down to replace all the old IF formulas in the range H12:I21.

7 Close the Auditing toolbar.
The screen should resemble Figure 6.22.

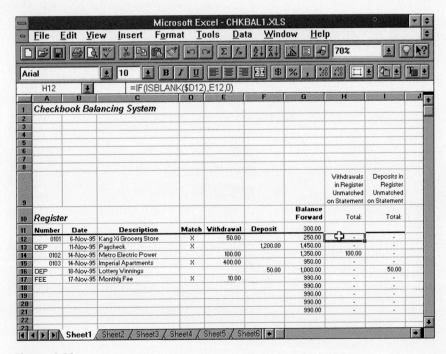

Figure 6.22

8 Save the workbook.

> **Tip** The general rule is to use an ordinary, fully relative cell reference. If, when you copy a formula, you get incorrect results from the duplicated formulas, follow these guidelines to rebuild and recopy the original formula:
>
> - Any time you are pointing to a cell while building a formula, and that cell alone provides the required information for the formula (and for future copies of the formula), the reference to the cell should be fully absolute.
> - If the required information is all in one column, make only the column reference absolute.
> - If the required information is all in one row, make only the row reference absolute.

Calculating the Total Unmatched Withdrawals and Deposits

The totals of unmatched withdrawals and deposits are required to balance the checkbook. In the following steps, you will build a SUM formula, first using a keyboard shortcut called *tracking* to speed the selection of the range to be summed. When tracking, Excel moves along adjacent nonempty cells until it finds an empty cell; it will stop immediately before the empty cell.

To use tracking when building a formula:

1 Turn off (NUM LOCK) if it is activated on the keyboard.
On some systems, tracking works only on the numeric keypad arrow keys.

2 Select cell H11, which will contain the total unmatched withdrawals.

3 Type =sum(

4 Press ⬇ and then press (CTRL)+(SHFT)+⬇
Excel automatically finds the bottom of the block of nonempty cells and extends the selection to that point.

5 Type) and press (ENTER)
The formula is =SUM(H12:H21) and its current result is 100.

Although this formula could be copied to calculate the total unmatched deposits, you will instead use another shortcut selection technique.

To use quick selection when building a formula:

1 Select cell I11, which will contain the total unmatched deposits.

2 Type =sum(

3 Click in cell I12. Position (do not drag) the pointer to cell I21, hold down (SHIFT) and click the mouse button, and then type)

4 Press (ENTER)
The formula reads =SUM(I12:I21) and its current result is 50.

5 Save the workbook.

In the steps that follow, you will see how to use tracking for moving around the worksheet and for making selections.

To use tracking to position the active cell:

1 Select cell G10, which contains *Balance Forward.*

2 Position the pointer so it appears as an arrow just touching the bottom edge of the active cell, and then double-click.
The active cell positions to G21, the bottom of the group.

3 Position the pointer so it forms an arrow just touching the right edge of the active cell, and then double-click.
The active cell positions to I21, the right of the group.

You can also use tracking techniques to make selections; Excel calls this the **AutoSelect** feature.

To use tracking to make selections:

1 Select cell G10, which contains *Balance Forward.*

2 Position the pointer so it appears as an arrow just touching the bottom edge of the active cell, hold down (SHIFT) and then double-click.
The group G10:G21 is selected.

3 Position the pointer so it forms an arrow just touching the right edge of the selected area, hold down (SHIFT) and then double-click.
The selected range grows to G10:I21.

4 Select any single cell to cancel the selection.

Building the Balance Reconciliation Formulas

The formulas to perform the calculations that balance the account will be placed in the top section of the worksheet. The method used will be the same as the one discussed at the beginning of this project. The register balance is already adjusted, because items that appeared at first only on the statement were later included in the register. Now you will create formulas to adjust the statement balance to reflect unmatched withdrawals and deposits.

To enter the row titles:

1 Enter `Adjusted Register Balance` in cell D2.

2 Enter `Bank Statement Ending Balance` in cell D3.

3 Enter `LESS Withdrawals in Register Not Shown on Statement` in cell D4.

4 Enter `PLUS Deposits in Register Not Shown on Statement` in D5.

5 Enter `Adjusted Statement Balance` in D6.

6 Enter `Discrepancy` in D7.

7 Align to the right the text you just entered in D2:D7.

8 Increase the height of row 1 to 30 points.

9 Select cell A1. Choose **Format** and then **Cells.**

10 Click the **Alignment** tab, change the *vertical* alignment to **Top**, and then select **OK**.

11 Center the main worksheet title, *Checkbook Balancing System*, across the selection A1:G1.

12 Increase the height of row 3 to about 25 points.
The screen should resemble Figure 6.23.

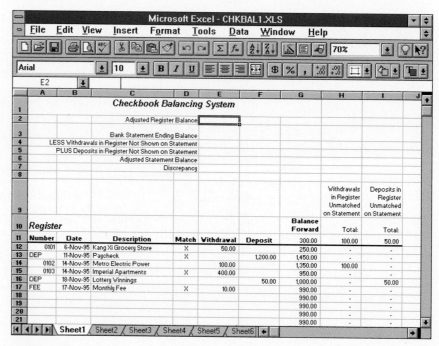

Figure 6.23

13 Spell-check the worksheet and save the workbook.

The adjusted register balance is the current balance shown in the register. The very short formula to calculate this, =G21, will simply take the value of the bottom cell (G21) of the balance forward section of the register. If new rows are inserted within the register, they will push the bottom cell downward, and Excel will adjust the formula so it still refers to the bottom cell.

To calculate the adjusted register balance:

1 Select cell E2.

2 Type =

3 Select the last entry in the balance forward column, G21.

4 Press (ENTER)

The formula reads =G21, and its result is 990.00.

The bank statement's ending balance is not a formula; it is a value specified on the bank statement. Refer to Figure 6.13 or 6.2 to obtain this number.

To enter the bank statement ending balance:

1 Select cell E3.

2 Enter **1040**

The totals of unmatched withdrawals and deposits are already calculated by the SUM formulas in cells H11 and I11. The formulas in the reconciliation section will refer to these cells.

To show unmatched withdrawals and deposits:

1 Select cell E4 (which will contain the total of withdrawals recorded in the register but not shown on the statement).

2 Type =

3 Select the total unmatched withdrawals (cell H11) and then press **ENTER**
The completed formula is =H11, and its result is 100.00.

4 Select cell E5 (which will contain the total of deposits recorded in the register but not shown on the statement).

5 Type =

6 Select the total unmatched deposits (cell I11) and then press **ENTER**
The completed formula is =I11, and its result is 50.00.

The adjusted statement balance is computed by taking the bank statement ending balance, subtracting unmatched withdrawals, and adding unmatched deposits.

To compute the adjusted statement balance:

1 Select cell E6, which will contain a formula to compute the adjusted statement balance.

2 Type =

3 Select the bank statement ending balance in cell E3, and then type -

4 Select the withdrawals in the register not shown on the statement in cell E4, and then type +

5 Select the deposits in the register not shown on the statement in cell E5, and then press **ENTER**
The completed formula is =E3-E4+E5, and its result is 990.00.

The discrepancy is the difference between the adjusted register balance and the adjusted statement balance. If the discrepancy is zero (which displays as a hyphen in the Accounting number formats), the account is balanced.

To calculate the discrepancy:

1 Select cell E7 and type =

2 Select the adjusted register balance in cell E2 and type -

3 Select the adjusted statement balance in cell E6 and press **ENTER**
The formula is =E2-E6, and its result is 0; the account balances.

4 Assign the Currency cell style to the adjusted register and statement balances in cells E2 and E6.

5 Set a thin top border and a medium bottom border for the adjusted statement balance in cell E6.
The worksheet should resemble Figure 6.24.

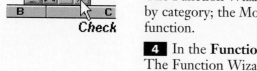

						Balance Forward	Withdrawals in Register Unmatched on Statement	Deposits in Register Unmatched on Statement
Checkbook Balancing System								
Adjusted Register Balance	$	990.00						
Bank Statement Ending Balance		1,040.00						
LESS Withdrawals in Register Not Shown on Statement		100.00						
PLUS Deposits in Register Not Shown on Statement		50.00						
Adjusted Statement Balance	$	990.00						
Discrepancy		-						
Register							Total:	Total:
Number	**Date**	**Description**	**Match**	**Withdrawal**	**Deposit**	300.00	100.00	50.00
0101	6-Nov-95	Kang Xi Grocery Store	X	50.00		250.00	-	-
DEP	11-Nov-95	Paycheck	X		1,200.00	1,450.00	-	-
0102	14-Nov-95	Metro Electric Power		100.00		1,350.00	100.00	-
0103	14-Nov-95	Imperial Apartments	X	400.00		950.00	-	-
DEP	18-Nov-95	Lottery Winnings			50.00	1,000.00	-	50.00
FEE	17-Nov-95	Monthly Fee	X	10.00		990.00	-	-
						990.00	-	-
						990.00	-	-
						990.00	-	-
						990.00	-	-

Sheet1 / Sheet2 / Sheet3 / Sheet4 / Sheet5 / Sheet6

Figure 6.24

6 Save the workbook.

Now that you have learned about the IF function, you can create a formula that displays a message about whether the account balances. If the discrepancy is zero, then the IF function should display a message such as, *The account balances!* If the discrepancy is not zero, then the message should be *The account does NOT balance!*

Using the Function Wizard

Rather than build a new IF formula by hand, you can use a tool called the *Function Wizard.* This series of dialog boxes steps you through building an Excel function. This process is useful because it helps remind you of the purpose of the various arguments to a function.

To build an IF formula for the balancing message:

1 Select cell C9.

2 Type =

3 Click the **Function Wizard** tool in the formula bar.
The Function Wizard Step 1 dialog box appears. Functions are organized by category; the Most Recently Used category already contains the IF function.

4 In the **Function Name** box, select **IF,** and then select **Next.**
The Function Wizard Step 2 dialog box appears. The three boxes correspond to the three arguments to an IF function. In a later step, you will want to point to the discrepancy amount, so you may need to reposition the dialog box to make this cell visible.

5 Drag the Function Wizard dialog box to the lower right of the screen, as shown in Figure 6.25.

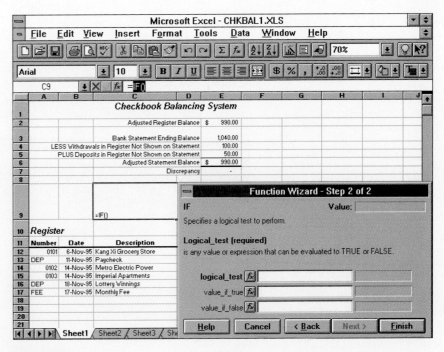

Figure 6.25

6 Click in the **logical_test** box, select the discrepancy cell (E7), and then type **=0**

7 Click in the **value_if_true** box, and then type **"The account balances!"**

8 Click in the **value_if_false** box, and then type **"The account does NOT balance!"**
The screen should resemble Figure 6.26.

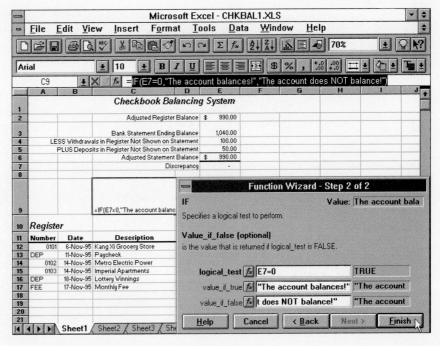

Figure 6.26

9 Select **Finish.**

10 Press (ENTER) to complete the function.

11 Set the format of cell C9 to bold, with left horizontal alignment, wrapped text, and top vertical alignment.
The screen should resemble Figure 6.27.

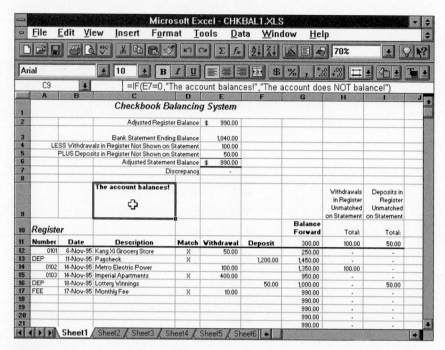

Figure 6.27

12 Rename the Sheet1 tab to **Checking** and save the workbook.

> **Tip** Notice in the Function Wizard Step 2 dialog box in Figure 6.25 that each argument box is preceded by a small Function Wizard button. These can be used to "nest" functions within functions. For example, earlier in this project the ISBLANK function was nested within the IF function used to calculate unmatched withdrawals and deposits.
>
> The Function Wizard button is also available on the Standard toolbar; if you use the Function Wizard from there, you won't need to type an equal sign to start a formula or press (ENTER) to end one.

EXIT   If necessary, you can quit Excel now and continue this project later.

STREAMLINING A WORKSHEET

The worksheet is now fully functional, but several improvements are possible. You should give some consideration to making a worksheet easy to use and error-resistant. This is especially true if the worksheet might be used by people other than its creator.

Hiding Columns

Certain parts of this worksheet, such as the columns for calculating the unmatched totals, hold little interest for someone who just wants to know whether an account balances. In the following steps, you will learn how to hide columns on the worksheet so these columns are not distractions.

To hide selected columns:

1 Select columns H and I.

2 Choose **Format** and then **Column.**

3 Choose **Hide.**
Columns H and I are no longer visible, but they still exist and cells within them can be referred to by formulas in the worksheet.

4 Select any single cell.
Notice that a thick line appears between column headings G and J; this is a reminder that one or more hidden columns are present.

5 Increase the window magnification to 90 percent.

> **Tip** You can disclose hidden columns by selecting a column range spanning the hidden columns, choosing Column Width from the Format menu, and then selecting Unhide.

Attaching Notes to Cells

You can document your worksheet by attaching text notes to a cell. *Cell notes* serve to remind you and inform other users about the design logic of your worksheet. You can also attach sound (audio) notes. Sound notes require that you have a microphone and an audio board installed for use with Windows. Once a note is attached to a cell, a small dot appears in the upper-right corner of the cell. If the user then selects the Attach Note button, the note is displayed (or played, in the case of sound notes).

> **Tip** Be brief and selective when recording sound notes; they consume large amounts of storage and will significantly increase the size of a workbook file.
>
> You can also use the Text Box tool on the Standard toolbar to post a rectangular note box directly over the worksheet. Such a note is not stored in a cell, but instead "floats" in its own layer above the worksheet cells.

Many cells could be documented in this worksheet; here you will create just one note that will explain how to use the match column.

To create and display a text note:

1 Display the Auditing toolbar.

2 Select cell D11, which contains the column title *Match*.

3 Click the **Attach Note** tool on the Auditing toolbar.
The Cell Note dialog box appears.

4 In the **Text Note** box, type `Place an X in this column if the register entry also appears on the bank statement.`

5 Select **OK** to attach the note.
Observe the small dot in the upper-right corner of the cell, reminding you that a note is attached.

6 Click the **Attach Note** tool on the Auditing toolbar.
The note appears.

7 Select **Close** and then close the Auditing toolbar.

Protecting Cells

With so many formulas on the worksheet, a user could easily wipe out a formula by accidentally entering something else in its cell. For this reason the user should be allowed to change only certain cells. In the following steps, you will learn how to *protect* the entire worksheet, and *unlock* only the cells for which changes are allowed.

By default, all cells are initially locked, but locked and unlocked settings have no effect until the protection system is activated. In using cell protection, you designate the cells that the user is allowed to change as being unlocked, and then activate the worksheet protection system.

One cell that should be unlocked is E3, the bank statement ending balance. The user must be allowed to make entries in this cell.

To unlock a cell:

1 Select cell E3, which contains the bank statement ending balance.

2 Choose **Format** and then **Cells.**

3 Select the **Protection** tab.

4 Clear the **Locked** checkbox and select **OK**, as shown in Figure 6.28.

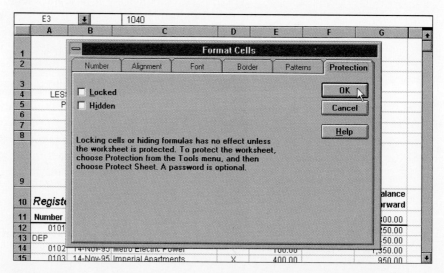

Figure 6.28

This cell is now the only unlocked cell on the worksheet, but this setting will have no effect until the protection system is activated.

To protect a document:

1 Choose **Tools** and then **Protection.**

2 Choose **Protect Sheet.**
The Protect Sheet dialog box appears.

3 Select **OK** to protect the worksheet.

4 Select cell G11, the starting balance forward, and type **350**
You are not able to enter anything into G11, because this and all other cells on the worksheet, except E3, are locked.

5 Select **OK** to clear the message box.

6 Select cell E3, type **1030** and press (ENTER)
Observe that changes *can* be made to the unlocked cell.

7 Click the **Undo** tool on the Standard toolbar.
The protection system must now be turned off so you can make further modifications to the worksheet.

8 Choose **Tools** and then **Protection.**

9 Choose **Unprotect Sheet.**

Assigning Cell Patterns

The worksheet would be easier to use if unlocked cells that required or allowed entry were clearly marked. In the steps that follow, you will assign a hairline outline border and a *cell pattern* to cell E3. A pattern describes how a cell should be shaded or colored.

To assign a cell border and a cell pattern:

1 Choose **Tools** and then **Options,** click the **View** tab, clear the **Gridlines** checkbox, and then select **OK.**

2 Set the worksheet magnification to 70 percent.

3 Select cell E3, the bank statement ending balance.

4 Choose **Format** and then **Cells,** click the **Border** tab, set a hairline outline border, and then select **OK.**

5 Select the list-box arrow of the **Color** tool on the Formatting toolbar.
A palette of colors appears.

6 Select a bright color (such as yellow) or a light shade (if you use a monochrome monitor).
As shown in Figure 6.29, the cell now appears with an outline border and in a different color or shade.

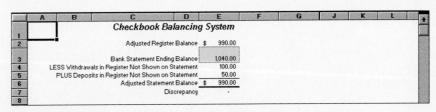

Figure 6.29

Tip The Font Color tool, next to the Color tool on the Formatting toolbar, provides a similar palette for choosing the color of text or values displayed in a cell. Both palettes can be "torn off."

Creating Customized Cell Styles

Other cells on the worksheet, such as the starting balance forward cell and all the rows of the register itself, also should have the combination of protection settings, patterns, and borders that you have just assigned to cell E3. You will recall from Project 3 that cell styles allow a collection of format settings to be named and applied in a single command. In the following steps, you will create a style called *UserInput*, which you can apply to any cell in which user input is allowed.

To create a customized cell style:

1 Select cell E3, the bank statement ending balance.
Excel automatically uses the active cell as a model for a new cell style.

2 Choose **Format** and then **Style**.
The Style dialog box appears.

3 In the **Style Name** box, type `UserInput`

4 In the **Style Includes** group, clear the check boxes for **Number, Font,** and **Alignment.**
The new style should include only border, patterns, and protection settings.

5 Select **OK** to establish the style, as shown in Figure 6.30.

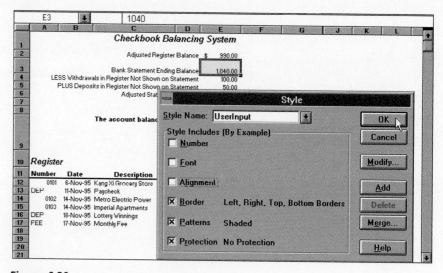

Figure 6.30

Now you can apply the UserInput style to other cells.

To apply the customized style:

1 Select the nonadjacent cells that comprise the starting balance forward (cell G11) and the data entry area of the check register (A12:F21).

2 Choose **Format** and then **Style.**

3 Open the **Style Name** list box, and then select **UserInput.**

4 Select **OK** to apply the style, as shown in Figure 6.31.

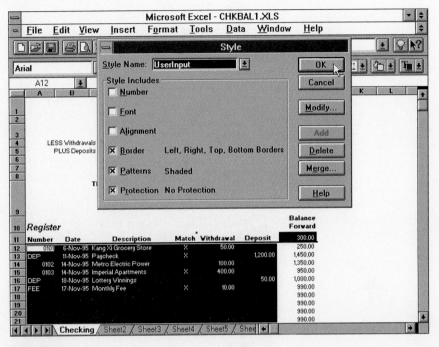

Figure 6.31

5 Click any single cell to cancel the selection.

6 Save the workbook.

Style

Tip The Style tool provides a drop-down list box that can be used to easily apply styles. To add this tool to a toolbar, choose Toolbars from the View menu, select Customize, select the Formatting category, and drag the tool to an on-screen toolbar. The Toolbars dialog box can also be used to reset a toolbar to its default set of buttons.

Moving among Unlocked Cells

When worksheet protection is activated, you can use (TAB) and (SHIFT) + (TAB) to skip forward and backward from one unlocked cell to another. This process can make data entry easier, because unlocked cells are normally those that require user input. Now that the UserInput style, which includes unlocked protection, has been applied to several cells, you can experiment with (TAB) and (SHIFT) + (TAB).

To move among unlocked cells:

1 Choose **Tools** and then **Protection,** choose **Protect Sheet,** and then click **OK.**

2 Press (CTRL) + (HOME) to position to the top-left corner of the worksheet.

3 Press (TAB) five times; press (SHIFT) + (TAB) five times.

Observe that (TAB) and (SHIFT) + (TAB) can be used to skip from one unlocked cell to another in the worksheet.

4 Choose **Tools** and then **Protection.**

5 Choose **Unprotect Sheet.**

6 Set the window magnification to 90 percent.

Freezing Part of a Window

If you scroll down the worksheet, you will notice that the account reconciliation section disappears from view. It would be nice for the top section of the worksheet to be visible for reference at all times, especially when the number of register entries increases beyond one screen.

Excel is capable of freezing rows and/or columns so these rows or columns always remain visible, even as the worksheet is scrolled. You use this feature by first positioning the active-cell rectangle so the rectangle is just below and to the right of any rows or columns that you want to remain visible. Then you use the Freeze Panes command in the Window menu.

To freeze window panes:

1 Press (CTRL) + (HOME)

2 Select cell A12.
Rows 1 to 11—and no columns—need to be frozen, so the active-cell rectangle is placed in row 12, column A.

3 Choose **Window** and then **Freeze Panes.**
There are now two window panes. The upper pane is frozen; the active cell is in the lower pane.

4 Scroll down using the vertical scroll bar or ⊕
Notice that rows 1 to 11 remain visible.

5 Press (CTRL) + (HOME)
Because rows 1 to 11 are frozen, the active-cell rectangle returns to cell A12, not to cell A1. You can still position the active cell in the frozen area with the mouse or the arrow keys.

6 Choose **Window** and then **Unfreeze Panes.**

7 Set the window magnification to 70 percent.

8 Save the workbook.

9 Print the worksheet.

Although it depends on the printer, the complete worksheet probably will be printed on two pages. In the sections that follow, you will instruct Excel to print only the check register, to fit the printout on one page, and to print a header containing your name and a footer containing the date.

Specifying the Print Area

By default, Excel will print the entire worksheet. If you want to print a portion of a worksheet, you can select the area and then, in the Print dialog box, indicate that you want to print only the selection. In the following steps, you will instruct Excel to print only the register portion of the worksheet.

To specify a selection to print:

1 Select the register, A10:G21.

2 Choose **File** and then **Print**.
The Print dialog box appears.

3 In the **Print What** group, select **Selection**.

4 Select **Page Setup**.
The Page Setup dialog box appears. You can also access this dialog box from the File menu and from the Print Preview window.

 Tip The Print Area tool can be used to set the print area to the current selection. To add this tool to a toolbar, choose Toolbars from the View menu, select Customize, select the File category, and drag the tool to an on-screen toolbar.

Specifying Headers and Footers

A *header* is information that appears at the top of every page of a printout; a *footer* is information that appears at the bottom of every page. Excel divides a header or footer into three sections, left, right, and center, allowing you to decide how the information should be broken up and aligned. You can type text of your own choice into a header or a footer; Excel also has special codes, listed in Table 6.3, that will print certain commonly required items. You can type the codes in, or you can select buttons in the Header or Footer dialog boxes to have Excel insert the codes for you.

The Header and Footer list boxes contain several commonly used header and footer combinations; to customize your own header or footer, choose the appropriate command button.

Table 6.3

Button	Code	Information Printed
[#]	&[Page]	Current page number
[+]	&[Pages]	Total number of pages
[≡]	&[Tab]	Sheet-tab name
[⚙]	&[File]	File (workbook) name
[⊞]	&[Date]	Current date
[⊗]	&[Time]	Current time

The default header is the sheet-tab name, and the default footer is the current page number. In the following steps, you will specify a header containing your name, aligned to the right, and a footer containing the date, aligned to the left.

To specify a header and a footer:

1 Select the **Header/Footer** tab from the Page Setup dialog box. The Header/Footer tab appears.

2 Open the **Header** list box, scroll to the top of the list, and then select **(none)** for the header.

3 Open the **Footer** list box, scroll to the top of the list, and then select **(none)** for the footer.

4 Select **Custom Header.**

5 Click in the **Right Section** box, type your name, and then select **OK.**

6 Select **Custom Footer.**

7 Click in the **Left Section** box, click the Current Date button to insert the code for today's date, and then select **OK.**

You will now instruct Excel to fit (scale) the printout so that it fits on one page.

To scale the printout to fit on one page:

1 Select the **Page** tab in the Page Setup dialog box.

2 In the **Scaling** group, select the **Fit To** button.
Excel automatically fills in to fit the printout to one page wide by one page tall.

3 Select **OK.**

4 Select **OK** in the Print dialog box to print the worksheet.
The printout should fit on one page and contain your name in the upper-right corner and the current date in the lower-left corner.

5 Click any single cell to cancel the selection.

6 Save the workbook.

   If necessary, you can quit Excel now and continue this project later.

USING MULTIPLE WORKSHEETS

The worksheet you have just developed for balancing a checking account can, with some minor modifications, be used to balance other personal accounts. In the steps that follow, you will make two copies of the worksheet: one for use with a savings account, the other for use with a credit card account. Each worksheet—checking, savings, and credit card—will have its own sheet tab within the workbook. You will then make an account summary worksheet that consolidates information from the other three sheets in the workbook.

To copy a sheet:

1 Make sure the Checking sheet is active.

2 Position the pointer on the Checking sheet tab and hold down the mouse button.

3 Press and hold down (CTRL)
A copy-sheet cursor appears, as shown in Figure 6.32.

Figure 6.32

4 Drag the downward-pointing arrowhead so it appears between the Checking tab and the Sheet2 tab, as shown in Figure 6.33.

Figure 6.33

5 Release the mouse button, and then release (CTRL)
A new sheet, named Checking (2), appears after the original Checking worksheet. Checking (2) is active.

6 Double-click the Checking (2) sheet tab and rename it **Savings**

7 Repeating the commands you just used, copy the Savings worksheet (so it appears just before Sheet2) and rename it **Credit Card**
The order of sheet tabs should now be Checking, Savings, and Credit Card, as shown in Figure 6.34.

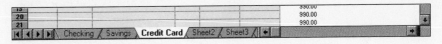

Figure 6.34

8 Save the workbook.

> ***Reminder*** To move a sheet, you drag its tab. A small arrowhead appears indicating where the sheet will be inserted among the other tabs. After you have dragged the sheet tab to the point where you want the sheet moved, you release the mouse button.

Editing Groups of Sheets

Several changes need to made to both the Savings and the Credit Card worksheets. For example, to prepare the worksheets for use, both sheets should have their initial balance forward and register areas cleared. But there are also changes that will be unique to each sheet: for example, the main title for each sheet is different.

When you want changes to affect a number of sheets at once, you can activate or select each sheet by holding down (CTRL) while clicking the sheet tab. You can also use (SHIFT) to select a group of sheet tabs by clicking on the first sheet tab in the group and holding down (SHIFT) while clicking on the last sheet tab in the group.

> **Caution** You must be extremely careful when editing groups of sheets, because changes you make to the active (visible) sheet in the group will affect all other selected sheets.

To unselect a sheet—remove it from the group of selected sheets—you can hold down (CTRL) and click the sheet's tab. To quickly unselect all the sheets in a group, you can click on any sheet tab that is not part of the group.

To group edit the Savings and Credit Card sheets:

1 Select the **Savings** sheet tab.

2 Press and hold down (CTRL) and click on the **Credit Card** sheet tab. The Savings sheet is in the foreground, but both tabs are still selected, and a [*Group*] indicator appears in the title bar.

3 Make a nonadjacent selection composed of the UserInput-styled areas: the bank statement ending balance, the initial balance forward, and the register area, as shown in Figure 6.35.

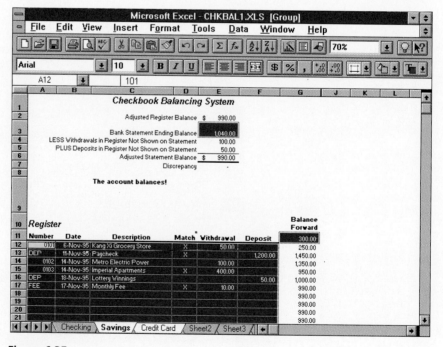

Figure 6.35

4 Press (DEL)
The selection's contents are cleared from the Savings worksheet.

5 Select the **Credit Card** sheet tab.
Notice that the selection was also cleared from the Credit Card worksheet. The Savings worksheet is still part of the selected group.

6 Select the **Checking** sheet tab.

The group selection is canceled. Notice that because the Checking sheet was not part of the group edit, it was not changed.

To modify the Savings worksheet:

1 Select the **Savings** sheet by clicking its sheet tab.

2 Select cell A1.

3 Position the pointer in the formula bar, and then double-click the word *Checkbook*, as shown in Figure 6.36.

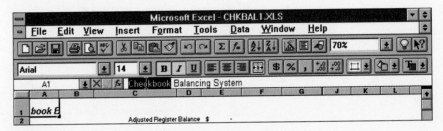

Figure 6.36

4 Type **Savings Account** to replace the word *Checkbook* in the title.

5 Press (ENTER)

6 Referring to Figure 6.37, enter a bank statement ending balance of **375** a starting balance forward of **350** and an incentive savings deposit of **25**

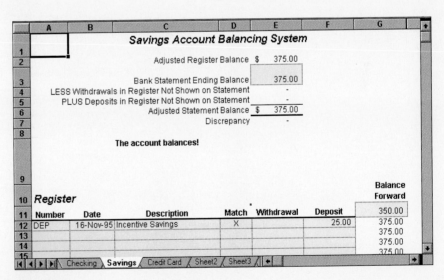

Figure 6.37

A credit card is a *liability* or *debt account*—its balance is the amount of money you owe to a lender. The larger the balance, the more money owed. The easiest way to adapt the worksheet to handle such an account is to use the withdrawals column to represent payments to the account (since numbers in this column reduce the overall balance), and to treat the deposits column as charges (since amounts in this column will increase the balance due). In the steps that follow, you will change the title of the worksheet and then use the Replace command to automatically change words in the Credit Card sheet to conform to this scheme.

To modify the Credit Card worksheet:

1 Select the **Credit Card** sheet tab.

2 Select cell A1.

3 Position the pointer in the formula bar, and then double-click the word *Checkbook*.

4 Type **Credit Card** to replace the word *Checkbook* in the title.

5 Press (ENTER) to complete the change.

6 Choose **Edit** and then **Replace**.
The Replace dialog box appears.

7 In the **Find What** box, type **Withdrawal**

8 In the **Replace with** box, type **Payment**

9 Select **Replace All**.
Notice that cells D4 and E11 were changed (the hidden cell H9 was also changed).

10 In a similar manner, use the Replace command to replace all occurrences of the word *Deposit* with *Charge*.

11 Change the text *Balance Forward* in cell G10 to **Balance Due**

12 Referring to Figure 6.38, enter a bank statement ending balance of 99570, a starting balance due of **480,** and a charge of **90** from Valerie's Velocipedes.

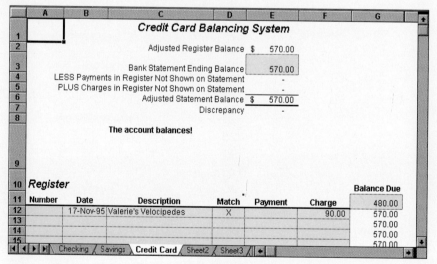

Figure 6.38

Creating a Summary Worksheet

You are now ready to create the summary worksheet, which will calculate the net worth of the accounts by adding the balances of the two asset accounts—checking and savings—and subtracting the balance of the liability account—credit card.

To create the summary worksheet:

1 Rename the Sheet2 tab to **Summary**

2 Make sure the blank Summary worksheet is active.

3 Refer to Figure 6.39 to create the skeleton of this worksheet, which should resemble the figure. Note that the worksheet in the figure is magnified 140 percent.

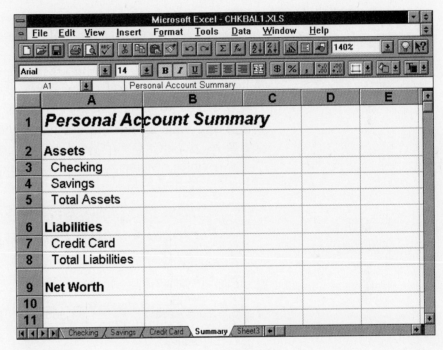

Figure 6.39

To create a formula that refers to other sheets:

1 Select cell B3 in the Summary worksheet.
You will build a formula in this cell that refers to the adjusted register balance of the Checking worksheet.

2 Type =

3 Select the **Checking** sheet tab.

4 Select the adjusted register balance amount in cell E2.

5 Press (ENTER) to complete the formula.

The completed formula in the Summary worksheet reads =Checking!E2, and its result is 990. The word *Checking* is the name of the sheet referred to by the formula, and the exclamation mark (!) serves to separate the sheet name from the cell reference E2. The cell is automatically assigned a Currency style because the cell it refers to has that format.

To create the other formulas:

1 In cell B4 of the Summary worksheet, build a formula that refers to the adjusted register balance of the Savings worksheet: type = and then select the adjusted register balance, cell E2, in the Savings worksheet.

2 In cell B5 of the Summary worksheet, use AutoSum to create a formula that computes total assets. You may need to widen column B.

3 In cell B7 of the Summary worksheet, build a formula that refers to the adjusted register balance of the Credit Card worksheet. The formula reads = 'Credit Card'!E2. The single quotation marks indicate that *Credit Card*, despite the space between the two words, is a single sheet name.

4 In cell B8, use AutoSum to create a formula that computes total liabilities (in the current version of this worksheet, only one cell contains a liability amount).

5 In cell B9, create a formula that computes net worth by subtracting total liabilities from total assets.

6 Use the **Comma Style** tool to format the middle cells B4:B8.

7 Apply thin top and medium bottom borders to cells B5 and B8.

8 Apply a double bottom border to cell B9.

The completed Summary worksheet should resemble Figure 6.40.

	A	B	C	D	E
1	**Personal Account Summary**				
2	**Assets**				
3	Checking	$ 990.00			
4	Savings	375.00			
5	Total Assets	1,365.00			
6	**Liabilities**				
7	Credit Card	570.00			
8	Total Liabilities	570.00			
9	**Net Worth**	$ 795.00			
10					
11					

Checking / Savings / Credit Card \ **Summary** / Sheet3

Figure 6.40

To trace precedents outside a sheet:

1 Open the Auditing toolbar, and dock it to the right of the vertical scroll bar.

2 Select cell B9, the net worth formula.

3 Click the **Trace Precedents** tool until all levels of precedents are shown (three times).

The screen should resemble Figure 6.41. Note that dashed tracer lines and special icons are used to indicate precedents that lie outside the current sheet.

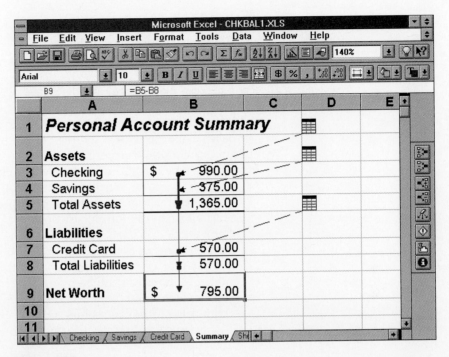

Figure 6.41

4 Remove all tracer arrows.

5 Close the Auditing toolbar.

6 Save the workbook.

THE NEXT STEP

You can extend and refine this worksheet several ways. For example, you could use range names in many of the formulas to make the formulas easier to understand. The workbook also could be adapted to handle other asset or liability accounts and produce more complex consolidations.

In the next project, you will automate the Checking worksheet using Excel's database and macro capabilities. This will make it easier to handle the check register as the number of entries increases.

This concludes Project 6. You can either exit Excel, or go on to work the Study Questions, Review Exercises, and Assignments.

SUMMARY AND EXERCISES

Summary

- Customized formats, which can preserve leading zeros and internal punctuation, are useful for entries such as serial numbers, telephone numbers, and zip codes.
- Excel can manipulate calendar dates, performing math on them and formatting them to appear in a variety of ways.
- Formulas that keep a running balance typically refer to the previous balance one row above and then adjust by adding or subtracting values appearing in the current row.
- The IF function performs a test and will give different results depending on whether the test result is true or false.
- Mixed cell references in a formula keep only the row or only the column constant when the formula is copied.
- The Function Wizard can be used to help build a function by stepping through the various arguments required by the function.
- You can hide columns from view, but they still exist, and cells within hidden columns can still be referred to by formulas.
- You can attach audio or text notes to cells, protect cells from change, or assign cells customized colors and patterns.
- You can customize styles to contain your preference of formatting attributes.
- A portion of the window can be frozen so that portion remains in view even as the worksheet is scrolled.
- A printout can contain a header and/or a footer (text at the top and/or bottom of each page) and can be scaled to be a certain size.
- Worksheets can be copied to create new, independent worksheets with their own sheet tabs. Formulas in a worksheet can refer to other worksheets in the workbook.

Key Terms and Operations

Key Terms
AutoSelect
case-sensitive
cell note
cell pattern
date arithmetic
footer
Function Wizard
header
mixed cell reference
tracking

Operations
Attach a note
Freeze/Unfreeze Panes
Hide columns
Protect a worksheet
Unlocking cells

Study Questions

Multiple Choice

1. If you clear a cell on a worksheet that is part of a selected group of sheets:
   a. Only the cell in the current sheet will be cleared.
   b. That cell in each of the grouped sheets will be cleared.
   c. That cell in the current sheet and those following (under) the current sheet will be cleared.
   d. That cell in the top sheet only will be cleared.
   e. None of the above.

2. If the format code 000 were assigned to a cell containing the number 12, how would the number appear?
   a. 000
   b. 12
   c. 12.000
   d. 0012
   e. 012

3. If cell G12 contains the formula =G11-E12+F12, and this formula is copied down one cell to G13, the newly copied formula in G13 would be:
   a. =G12-E13+F13
   b. =G11-E12+F12
   c. =G11-E13+F13
   d. =G12-E12+F12
   e. =G12-E12+F13

4. If cell A5 is empty, what would be the result of the formula =IF(ISBLANK(A5),50,100)?
   a. 50
   b. 100
   c. 0
   d. 150
   e. A5

5. In the formula =A1+A$2, the A$2 is referred to as a(n):
   a. absolute cell reference.
   b. relative cell reference.
   c. mixed cell reference.
   d. currency cell.
   e. static cell address.

6. Suppose cell A3 contains the formula =A1+A$2. If the formula were copied to B3, the copy in B3 would read:
   a. =B1+B$2
   b. =B1+A$2
   c. =B1+A$3
   d. =A1+B$2
   e. =B1+B2

7. To hide a column, you first select the column and then:
   a. Choose **Format** and then **Column**.
   b. Choose **Options** and then **Hide Column**.
   c. Choose **Edit** and then **Column Width**.
   d. Choose **Window** and then **Hide/Unhide**.
   e. Choose **Format** and then **Style**.

8. How does Excel indicate that a note is attached to a particular cell?
   a. The cell is colored green.
   b. A thick border appears around the cell.
   c. A small dot appears in the upper-right corner of the cell.
   d. The first few characters of the note appear at the top of the cell.
   e. The cell appears with a light gray background.

9. To have a cell appear with a different color or shade, choose or select:
   a. **Format** and then **Color.**
   b. **Format** and then **Patterns.**
   c. **Edit** and then **Color.**
   d. the **Color** tool.
   e. **Format** and then **Style.**

10. Information that appears at the bottom of each page of a printout is called a:
    a. running header.
    b. low title.
    c. bottom title.
    d. border.
    e. footer.

Short Answer

1. Changing a cell's color or shading is referred to as changing the cell's what?

2. Before activating protection for the entire worksheet, what should you do to the cells to which changes will be allowed?

3. What type of style uses a cell as a model or example?

4. What keys can be pressed to move from one unlocked cell to another?

5. What terms are used when referring to information that appears at the top and bottom of each page of a printout?

6. What code would be used to print the current page number in a footer?

7. Where should the active cell be positioned if you want to freeze columns A and B?

8. Which function is used to test whether a cell contains anything?

9. How many arguments does the IF function have? What are their purposes?

10. Are dates treated as numbers or as text in Excel?

For Discussion

1. Can Excel perform math on dates? If so, give an example. Describe three ways to format a date.

2. What are customized styles? What are the general steps involved in creating a customized style?

3. What are the Excel header and footer codes, and what do they mean? What options are available for positioning headers and footers on a page?

4. What is the major hazard of group-editing multiple sheets?

Review Exercises

Personal Budget

Refer to Figure 6.42 and construct a personal budget for the first six months of a year. Use AutoFill to save typing when entering the month names. Add whatever income and expense items are appropriate for your situation.

	A	B	C	D	E	F	G	H
1				Personal Budget				
2		Start	Jan	Feb	Mar	Apr	May	Jun
3	Income							
4	Salary		$1,200	$1,200	$1,200	$1,200	$1,200	$1,200
5	Expenses							
6	Rent		450	450	450	450	450	450
7	Food		250	250	250	250	250	250
8	Utilities		75	75	75	75	75	75
9	Telephone		30	30	30	30	30	30
10	Transportation		50	50	50	50	50	50
11	Entertainment		50	50	50	50	50	50
12	Other		100	100	100	100	100	100
13	Net Cash	$100	?	?	?	?	?	?
14								

Figure 6.42

Design a single net cash formula for January and copy the formula to the other net cash cells. This formula should account for any savings (or deficit) from the previous month. The Start column is used to show the amount of cash on hand at the beginning of January. This is similar to the starting balance amount in the checkbook register. The net cash formula for a particular month will take the previous month's net cash, add the current month's income, and subtract the current month's expenses. Negative amounts for net cash can be interpreted as being sums borrowed from another source, such as savings or credit card accounts. Format the worksheet and save the workbook under the name PBUDGET.

Computing a Report of Accounts Past Due

Construct a worksheet, similar to Figure 6.43, that computes the total of accounts that are greater than 30 days overdue. Use the NOW function to show today's date; format its cell to d-mmm-yy. Create a customized number format so the account numbers are punctuated as shown in the figure. You can make up your own due dates appropriate for testing.

	A	B	C	D	E
1	Report of Accounts Past Due				
2	Today's Date:	?			
3					
4	Account	Due	Amount	Past 30	
5	993-21-9147	14-Nov-95	$2,750	?	
6	994-58-6273	2-Dec-95	880	?	
7	992-45-6363	23-Oct-95	975	?	
8	998-46-4489	9-Dec-95	1,320	?	
9	Total		?	?	

Figure 6.43

The formulas in the column labeled *Past 30* perform a test: if today's date (which is computed in cell B2) minus the due date is greater than 30, then the amount is overdue and should be displayed; otherwise, 0 should be displayed. Note that an absolute cell address will be required if a single formula is to be built and copied successfully. The totals are each SUM formulas.

Format the worksheet and save the workbook under the name PAST-DUE.

Assignments

Creating a Spreadsheet of Birthdays and Ages

Construct a spreadsheet similar to Figure 6.44. Use the NOW function for today's date; format the cell as d-mmm-yy. The age column contains formulas that calculate each person's current age in years. A person's age in *days* is calculated by subtracting the birth date from today's date. Age in *years* is calculated by dividing the age in days by the number of days in a year (365.25, to adjust for leap years). Note that the result of these calculations will yield the fractional part of the age as a decimal fraction: for example, age 22.5 is 22 years 6 months, not 22 years 5 months. Format this column with the Comma style.

	A	B	C	D	E	F	G	H
1	Today's Date	?						
2	Name	Birth Date	Age	Birthday this Month?				
3	Carmen	14-Mar-68	?	?				
4	Clem	29-Oct-59	?	?				
5	Govinda	8-Nov-72	?	?				
6	Gwendolyn	1-Jul-73	?	?				
7	Jane	3-Jun-46	?	?				
8	Juan	27-May-71	?	?				
9	Mei Ling	15-Jan-74	?	?				
10	Rahula	17-Sep-74	?	?				
11	Rolf	14-Dec-70	?	?				
12	Sarvipali	21-Aug-70	?	?				
13	Xu	2-Apr-33	?	?				
14	Zhi	23-Feb-75	?	?				

Figure 6.44

The formula in the column labeled *Birthday this Month* performs a test using IF and the MONTH function: if the month of today's date is equal to the month of the birth date, then return *Yes*; otherwise, return a space.

Format the worksheet and save the workbook as BDAY.

Computing Commercial Lease Payments

The worksheet shown in Figure 6.45 shows the monthly payments due for commercial tenants in a small shopping mall. Each tenant pays the discount rate per square foot during the first year of the lease; the regular rate per square foot applies after the first year.

	A	B	C	D
1	Today's Date	?		
2				
3	Regular Rate	$16.00 / sq. ft.		
4	1st Year Discount Rate	$5.00 / sq. ft.		
5				
6	*Tenant*	*Leased Space*	*Start Date*	*Payment*
7	Clem's Fish Emporium	1,200 sq.ft.	1-Dec-94	?
8	Kang Xi Grocery Store	5,330 sq.ft.	1-Jan-95	?
9	Govinda's Gift Shop	1,450 sq.ft.	1-Oct-94	?
10	First Interdimensional Bank	3,180 sq.ft.	1-Mar-95	?
11	*Total*	11,160 sq.ft.		?
12				
13				

Figure 6.45

Construct a worksheet similar to the figure. Assign a customized numeric format for the two rate cells and create a style called SqFt, containing the appropriate numeric format, for the cells in the Leased Space column.

The formulas in the payment column check to see whether more than one year (365 days) has elapsed between the start date and today's date. The appropriate rate is multiplied by the tenant's amount of leased space.

Format the worksheet and save the workbook under the name RENT.

Balancing Your Own Checkbook

If you have a checking account, use the CHKBAL1 worksheet to reconcile it. As you use the worksheet, make note of any improvements that would make the worksheet a more effective tool. Consider how the worksheet could be adapted to reconcile other accounts, such as credit card accounts.

PROJECT 7:   USING DATABASES AND MACROS

Objectives

After completing this project, you should be able to:

▶ Describe an Excel database and its components

▶ Create a database range

▶ Use data forms to add, change, delete, and find records

▶ Use the Sort command to rearrange records

▶ Create macros using the macro recorder

▶ Create and modify customized push buttons and assign macros to them

▶ Run macros using the menu, shortcut key assignments, and custom buttons

CASE STUDY: AUTOMATING A CHECKBOOK REGISTER

In this project, you will apply two advanced features of Excel—database management and command macros—to enhance the checkbook-balancing worksheet that you built in Project 6. You will begin by considering how the checkbook register could be implemented as an Excel database. After the register is converted to function as a database, you will experiment with searching and sorting the database, and then you will construct command macros to automate the sorting.

Recognizing Databases

An Excel *database* is a collection of information organized in a list form. Everyday examples of databases abound: telephone directories, inventory lists, parts lists, customer lists, library catalogs, and so forth. Table 7.1 illustrates a typical customer-list database.

Table 7.1

LastName	FirstName	Street	City	State	Zip
Rogers	Bruce	1916 Centaur St.	New York	NY	01011
Twombly	Carol	89 Lithos Pwky.	Charlemagne	CA	92373
Gill	Eric	16 Joanna Rd. #30	Pilgrim	MA	21707
Kis	Miklos	1650 Janson Ave.	Minneapolis	MN	66192
Almeida	Jose	1926 Convention Ctr.	Mendoza	TX	73105
....	....	....	....	....	....

Each row of a database is called a *record.* A database record describes something, such as a customer, a part in an inventory, or a book. The columns of a database, called *fields,* break the record down into various aspects or categories. The fields in Table 7.1 are last name, first name, street, city, state, and zip. Each field has a *field name*, which is the formal designation of the field and in Excel appears as a column title. For example, the field name for the last name field is *LastName.*

When you design a database, it's usually best to have lots of simple, discrete fields rather than only a few complex fields. For example, a database that has a single address field containing the entire address (street address, city, state, and zip) would be harder to search and sort than a database that has separate fields for each component of an address.

What do people do with databases? Typically they *search* or *sort* the records in a database. *Searching* means finding all records that match a certain criterion, such as finding all records in the customer database that have Phoenix as the city. *Sorting* means shuffling the records into a specific order: for example, ordering all the records alphabetically based on the customer's last name.

Designing the Solution

If you consider the check register built in Project 6, you will realize that it is a kind of database. Its fields are check *Number, Date, Description, Match, Withdrawal,* and *Deposit.* The balance forward, unmatched withdrawal, and unmatched deposit columns could also be considered fields, but in this project you will confine the database to the register's first six columns.

Both searching and sorting would be useful operations to perform on a check register. You might want to find all deposits made after November 14, 1995, or you might want to sort all the register entries in alphabetical order by description. In the sections that follow, you will make some initial modifications to the check register to make it compatible with Excel's database commands.

TRANSFORMING THE CHECK REGISTER INTO A DATABASE

An Excel database is a list of records entered into an ordinary worksheet document. The first row of the database must contain field names. Ordinary text titles for columns will work for field names. Other information—such as the account reconciliation system in the Checking sheet—can be on the worksheet along with the database itself. The data records start just below the field names row. The *database range* consists of the field names row and the data records below it.

If you plan to add new records to the database, you should have some blank rows below the database to accommodate the new records. Excel databases grow downward; this growth is obstructed if something else, such as information related to another part of the worksheet, is in the way.

In the following steps, you will prepare the Checking worksheet for use as an Excel database. The cell protection system in Excel doesn't work easily with Excel databases, so to keep your task simple, you will turn off worksheet protection. Some of the other changes you will make are cosmetic and are intended to make the worksheet easier to read while you work with the new commands.

To prepare the workbook:

1 Open the workbook CHKBAL1.

2 Click the **Checking** sheet tab.

3 Unprotect the sheet, if necessary.

4 Unfreeze panes, if necessary.

5 Choose **Tools** and then **Options**, select the **View** tab, select **Gridlines** to display cell grid lines, and then select **OK**.

6 Select columns G through J; choose **Format** and then **Column**.

7 Choose **Unhide.**
Columns H and I are now visible.

8 Zoom the window to 70 percent magnification.

9 If the status bar is visible, choose **View** and then **Status Bar** to hide it.

10 Choose **File** and then **Save As**; save the workbook as CHKBAL2. The screen should resemble Figure 7.1.

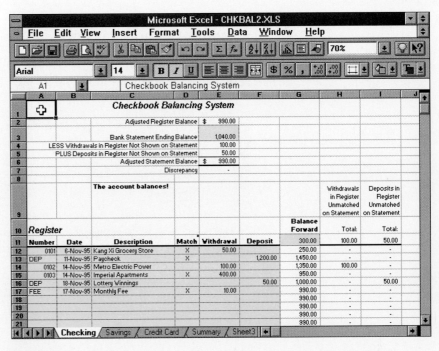

Figure 7.1

The database range will consist of the register itself, excluding the formulas for balance forward, unmatched withdrawals, and unmatched deposits. Only the records that actually contain information should be defined as being part of the database. In CHKBAL2, rows 18 through 21 have been assigned the UserInput style (within the database columns), but they do not contain information. In the following steps, you will clear these cells and then define the range A11:F17 as the database. Later, when records are added, Excel will automatically expand the defined database range to include the new records.

Using the Clear Command

The Clear command allows you to clear (erase) the contents of a cell, the note attached to a cell, the format of a cell, or all three of these. In the Clear command, Excel calls a cell's contents its *formulas*.

To clear the unused database records:

1 Select A18:F21, the blank database records.

2 Choose **Edit** and then **Clear**.

3 Select **All**.

The formulas to the right of the register must be copied down so they are present for however many records you anticipate the database will contain. You will arbitrarily set the maximum number of records allowed to 100; this means the formulas must be copied down through row 111. The SUM formulas in the unmatched columns will need to be rewritten to accommodate the new register size, and the formula that shows the adjusted register balance in cell E2 will also have to be updated so it refers to the new bottom cell of the balance forward column. In the following steps, you will use several shortcuts to handle large areas on the worksheet.

To copy the formulas downward:

1 Zoom the window to 50 percent magnification.

2 Select the formulas in the range G21:I21, as shown in Figure 7.2.

Figure 7.2

3 Drag the fill handle downward to row 111 to copy the formulas.

4 Zoom to 70 percent magnification.

5 Press (CTRL) + (HOME)

To rebuild the SUM formulas for the unmatched columns:

1 Turn off (NUM LOCK)

2 Select cell H11, which contains the total unmatched withdrawals.

3 Type **=sum(**

4 Press ⊕ and then press (CTRL) + (SHIFT) + ⊕
Excel automatically finds the bottom of the block of nonempty cells and extends the selection to that point.

5 Type **)** and press (ENTER)
The formula is =SUM(H12:H111)

6 Copy this relative reference formula to cell I11 to replace the formula that computes total unmatched deposits.

To rebuild the formula for the adjusted register balance:

1 Press (CTRL) + (HOME)

2 Select cell E2, the adjusted register balance, which contains a formula that refers to the bottom cell of the balance forward column of the register.

3 Type **=**
Now use the point mode to complete the formula.

4 Select cell G10, which contains the text *Balance Forward*.

5 Press (CTRL) + ⊕ and then press (ENTER)
The new formula reads =G111.

6 Select columns H and I, choose **Format** and then **Column.**

7 Choose **Hide.**

As in Project 6, the person using this worksheet to balance a checking account doesn't need to see these formulas.

8 Zoom to 75 percent magnification.

9 Save the workbook.

Using Tracer Arrows for Rapid Cell Movement

In Project 3, you saw how to double-click on a tracer arrow line to quickly jump back and forth between the ends of a tracer arrow. This feature is especially useful when you are analyzing the workings of a large spreadsheet such as this one.

If you first position the pointer so it becomes an arrow just touching a tracer arrow and then double-click, you will jump to one of the cells at the end of the arrow. Double-clicking again jumps to the other end of the tracer arrow.

To use the tracer arrow to position the active cell:

1 Select the adjusted register balance, cell E2.

2 Choose **Tools** and then **Auditing.**

3 Choose **Trace Precedents.**
If you don't need to use the Auditing toolbar extensively, this is a quick way to trace precedents.

4 Position the pointer so it becomes an arrow just touching the tracer arrow line.

5 Double-click the tracer line.
Cell G111, at the opposite end of the tracer arrow, is now selected.

6 Double-click the tracer line again.
Cell E2 is once again selected.

7 Choose **Tools** and then **Auditing.**

8 Choose **Remove All Arrows.**

Designating the Database Range

Most of your work so far has been to expand the size of the worksheet to accommodate more check register entries. You can now tell Excel what the database range is; once this is done, you can access some of the database management commands. The database range is the field names row and the data records below it, A11:F17. Because there are blank cells below the current last record (for the monthly fee, in A17:F17), when new records are added, Excel will expand the defined database range.

Excel can sometimes automatically identify the database range, based on the typical differences between a row of field names and the data records below this row. This feature will not work, however, if the database is not bordered by at least one blank column or row on each edge. In the case of this worksheet, you will have to explicitly identify the database range. If you name a range *Database*, Excel will presume that that range is the database range.

To designate the database range:

1 Select A11:F17, the database range, composed of the field names and the currently used data records.

2 Click in the reference area at the left end of the formula bar.

3 As shown in Figure 7.3, type **Database** and press (ENTER)

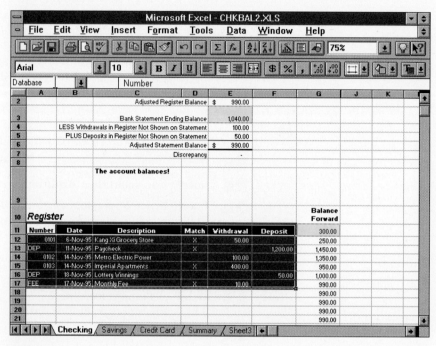

Figure 7.3

4 Click any single cell to cancel the selection.

5 Save the workbook.

Preventing the Database from Exceeding a Designated Size

You have taken a straightforward approach in creating a check register that is designed to handle a maximum of 100 records. This limit is based on how far down you copied the balance and unmatched formulas. These formulas are not part of the database itself but are critical to the proper functioning of the account balancing system. The formulas were not incorporated as part of the database to avoid complexities beyond the scope of this project. But will there be a problem if the database grows beyond row 111?

If records are entered beyond row 111, there will be no balance-forward formulas to account for the effect of these records on the account balance. And there will be no formulas to include any unmatched deposits or withdrawals in the totals used to balance the checkbook. For these reasons, the database must not be allowed to extend beyond row 111.

The solution is to put something in a cell in row 112, just below the last allowed database record. When the database runs into this, it will display a warning message, and it will not add any more records.

In the steps that follow, you will enter text in cell A112 with the purpose of blocking the database. To quickly position to cell A112, you will use the reference area. Although in this case you will type a literal cell address, most of the time the reference area is used to select defined names.

To block the database range at row 111:

1 Click in the reference area.

2 Type **A112** and press **ENTER**

3 Enter **DATABASE LIMIT** in cell A112, and make it bold.

4 Press **CTRL** + **HOME**

5 Save the workbook.

WORKING WITH DATA FORMS AND FILTERS

A *data form* is a dialog box that serves as a simple type of data-entry screen. A data form allows you to examine, edit, and move through the records of a database conveniently. Excel builds the data form based on what it finds in the field names row of the defined database (the range you named *Database* earlier in this project).

To activate the data form:

1 Choose **Data** and then **Form**.
The data entry form appears.

2 Select the title bar of the form dialog box and drag the form to the upper-right area of the screen.
This allows you to see part of the underlying worksheet. The screen should resemble Figure 7.4.

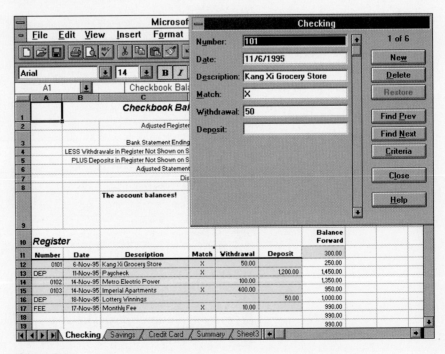

Figure 7.4

Text in the upper-right corner of the data form reads *1 of 6*. This means you are currently viewing record number 1 out of a total of 6 records in the database. The fields of the record and their values appear on the left side of the form.

The scroll arrows (or the up and down arrow keys) can be used to move from one record to another. The position of the scroll box within the scroll bar provides a visual indication of the current record's relative position in the database.

To move from one record to another in the data form:

1 Click the down scroll arrow in the data form.
You now see record 2.

2 Examine each of the remaining records.
Once you move past the last record, a blank form appears, indicating that you could type in a new record.

3 Click the up scroll arrow in the data form.
You move up one record.

In the following steps, you will add two new records, using the data form as an *interface* between the user (you) and the worksheet. As you perform these actions, observe the changes on the worksheet itself.

To add a new record:

1 Select the **New** button in the data form dialog box.
A blank form appears. Enter a new record, as shown in Figure 7.5.

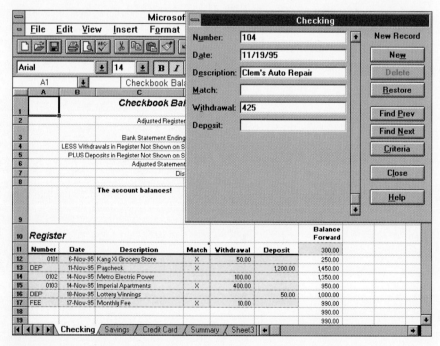

Figure 7.5

2 In the **Number** box, type **104** and then press (TAB)

3 In the **Date** box, type **11/19/95** and then press (TAB)

4 In the **Description** box, type `Clem's Auto Repair` and then press (TAB) twice to skip the **Match** field.

5 Type `425` for the **Withdrawal** amount, and then press (ENTER) to add the record to the database.

Notice that the new record appears in the worksheet. Excel has also automatically expanded the definition of the database-range name. The data form is ready for you to enter another new record.

6 Referring to Figure 7.6, enter another new record for an automated teller machine (ATM) withdrawal.

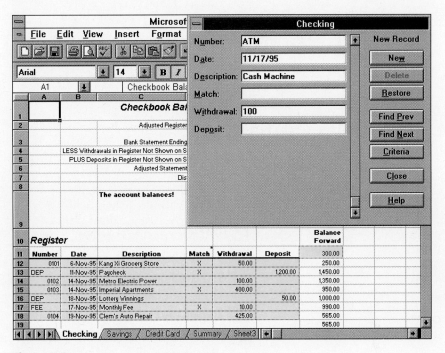

Figure 7.6

Using Selection Criteria with Data Forms

A data form can be made to display only those records that meet a particular search condition. For example, you might want to work with only records that are dated prior to 11/15/95. Or you might want to scroll through all the records that are matched in bank statements. In the steps that follow, you will construct a criterion that finds any records where the Number field contains the code *FEE*. You will also use the Delete button to delete a record.

To set search criteria:

1 Select the **Criteria** button in the data form dialog box.

The data form changes: *Criteria* appears in the upper-right corner and you do not see a record from the database. Instead, you can specify how you want each field matched in the database.

2 In the **Number** box, type `FEE`

3 Select **Find Next**.

The computer beeps and shows you a blank record. It didn't find a match, because it started its search at the bottom of the database.

4 Select **Find Prev.**
Now the form shows a record that contains *FEE* in the Number field.

5 Select **Find Prev** again.
The computer beeps—there are no more records above this one that contain *FEE* in the Number field.

6 Select **Find Next.**
There are no more records below this one that match the criteria. Suppose you wanted to delete this record.

7 Select **Delete.**
You are warned that the displayed record will be deleted permanently.

8 Select **OK** to delete the record.
Notice that the record is removed from the worksheet, and that the account no longer balances.

Using Complex Criteria

In the following steps, you will construct criteria to search for all records dated after 11/15/95, all *DEP* transactions (ordinary deposits) made after 11/15/95, and all records unmatched with bank statements (that is, records without an *X* in the Match field).

To find all records dated after 11/15/95:

1 Select **Criteria.**

2 Select **Clear** to erase the old criteria.
This does not delete any records.

3 Type **>11/15/95** for the **Date** field.

4 Select **Find Next** and **Find Prev** to confirm that the only records displayed are those whose Date field is greater than (later than) 11/15/95.

To find all DEP transactions made after 11/15/95:

1 Select **Criteria.**
The old criterion of >11/15/95 is needed again for this search, so it should not be cleared.

2 Type **DEP** for the **Number** field.
The screen should resemble Figure 7.7.

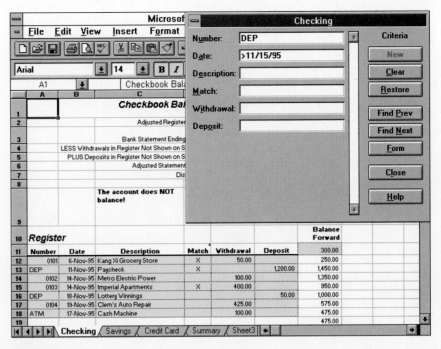

Figure 7.7

3 Using **Find Next** and **Find Prev**, confirm that just one record meets these criteria.

Filling in more than one field in the criteria screen creates an *and* relationship; in the example just completed, a record will be selected only if it contains *DEP* in the Number field *and* has a date later than 11/15/95.

To find all records unmatched with bank statements:

1 Select **Criteria**.

2 Select **Clear**.

3 Type **< >X** for the **Match** field.
The characters < > mean "not equal to."

4 Use **Find Next** and **Find Prev** to examine the selected records.

5 Select **Close** to close the dialog box.

6 Save the workbook.

Using Data Filters

Occasionally you will want to set search criteria and be able to see at once all the records that meet those criteria. Data filters are designed for this purpose. A *data filter* is a list box attached to a field; the list box is used to indicate the search conditions that apply to the field.

The AutoFilter command in the Data menu is used to place data filters on each field in the database. Initially, each filter is set to select all values for its field. Once you provide a more specific criterion in a filter, *filter mode* is activated, and any records that do not meet the search conditions are hidden from view.

In the steps that follow, you will use data filters with some of the same criteria you used with data forms in the preceding steps.

To activate the AutoFilter:

1 Choose **View** and then **Status Bar** to display the status bar.

2 Click the reference area's list-box arrow to open the Name box.

3 Click the range name **Database.**
The database range is selected.

4 Choose **Data** and then **Filter.**

5 Choose **AutoFilter.**
Notice that a small list-box arrow appears next to each field name.

6 Press (CTRL) + (HOME)

7 Zoom to 100 percent magnification.

8 Scroll the window down so row 10 is the first visible row.
The screen should resemble Figure 7.8.

	A	B	C	D	E	F	G
10	Register						Ba Fo
11	Numb	Date	Description	Matc	Withdraw:	Deposit	3
12	0101	6-Nov-95	Kang Xi Grocery Store	X	50.00		2
13	DEP	11-Nov-95	Paycheck	X		1,200.00	1,4
14	0102	14-Nov-95	Metro Electric Power		100.00		1,3
15	0103	14-Nov-95	Imperial Apartments	X	400.00		9
16	DEP	18-Nov-95	Lottery Winnings			50.00	1,0
17	0104	19-Nov-95	Clem's Auto Repair		425.00		5
18	ATM	17-Nov-95	Cash Machine		100.00		4
19							4
20							4
21							4
22							4
23							4
24							4
25							4
26							4

Checking / Savings / Credit Card / Summary / Sheet3

Ready

Figure 7.8

You will now set the filter to show only those records where the Number field contains the code *DEP.*

To filter DEP records:

1 Click the filter list-box arrow for the Number field, as shown in Figure 7.9.

	A	B	C	D	E	F	G
10	Register						Ba Fo
11	Numb	Date	Description	Matc	Withdraw:	Deposit	3
12	0101	6-Nov-95	Kang Xi Grocery Store	X	50.00		2
13	DEP	11-Nov-95	Paycheck	X		1,200.00	1,4
14	0102	14-Nov-95	Metro Electric Power		100.00		1,3
15	0103	14-Nov-95	Imperial Apartments	X	400.00		9
16	DEP	18-Nov-95	Lottery Winnings			50.00	1,0
17	0104	19-Nov-95	Clem's Auto Repair		425.00		5
18	ATM	17-Nov-95	Cash Machine		100.00		4
19							4

Figure 7.9

2 Scroll down the list and select **DEP.**
The screen should now resemble Figure 7.10.

	A	B	C	D	E	F	G
10	Register						Ba Fo
11	Numbe	Date	Description	Matc	Withdrawa	Deposit	3
13	DEP	11-Nov-95	Paycheck	X		1,200.00	1,4
16	DEP	18-Nov-95	Lottery Winnings			50.00	1,0
113							
114							
115							
116							
117							
118							
119							
120							
121							
122							
123							
124							
125							

Checking / Savings / Credit Card / Summary / Sheet3

Filter Mode

Figure 7.10

When filter mode is activated, the message *Filter Mode* appears in the status bar. Only those rows are shown whose records meet the selection criteria. The other rows still exist, but they are hidden. Notice that selected rows have blue headings and that if selection criteria are used with a field, as with Number, its filter list-box arrow is colored blue as well. (Monochrome screens will display using a different shade.)

To remove criteria for an individual filter:

1 Open the filter list box for the Number field.

2 Select **(All).**

To filter all records dated after 11/15/95:

1 Click the filter list-box arrow for the Date field.

2 Select **(Custom...).**
The Custom AutoFilter dialog box appears.

3 Open the top left list box, and then select **>,** as shown in Figure 7.11.

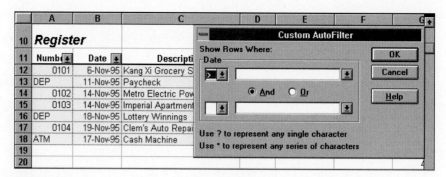

Figure 7.11

4 Click in the top right text box and type **11/15/95** as shown in Figure 7.12.
The selection criteria expressed in the dialog box are interpreted as "Show rows (records) where the Date field is greater than 11/15/95."

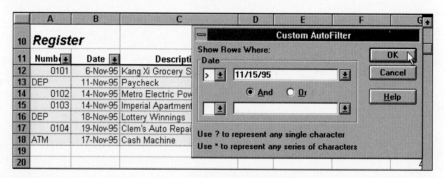

Figure 7.12

5 Select **OK** to complete the AutoFilter command.
The screen should now resemble Figure 7.13.

	A	B	C	D	E	F	G
10	**Register**						Ba Fo
11	Numb	Date	Description	Matc	Withdraw	Deposit	3
16	DEP	18-Nov-95	Lottery Winnings			50.00	1,0
17	0104	19-Nov-95	Clem's Auto Repair		425.00		5
18	ATM	17-Nov-95	Cash Machine		100.00		4
113							
114							
115							

Figure 7.13

If search criteria are specified in filters for several different fields, then the filter results are based on an *and* relationship. For example, if the filter for the Number field is again set to show only deposits, and the filter for the Date field shows only transactions made after 11/15/95, then the combined effect of the two filters will be to show only deposits made after 11/15/95.

To filter all DEP transactions dated after 11/15/95:

1 Click the filter list-box arrow for the Number field.

2 Scroll down the list and select **DEP.**

The screen should now resemble Figure 7.14. Only one record meets the combined filter criteria.

	A	B	C	D	E	F	G
10	**Register**						B F
11	Numb	Date	Description	Matc	Withdraw	Deposit	3
16	DEP	18-Nov-95	Lottery Winnings			50.00	1,0
113							
114							
115							
116							
117							

Figure 7.14

To remove criteria for all filters:

1 Choose **Data** and then **Filter.**

2 Choose **Show All.**

All rows appear.

In the next series of steps, you will create a customized filter to show only those records whose dates are between 11/7/95 and 11/18/95.

To show all records dated after 11/7/95 but before 11/18/95:

1 Click the filter list-box arrow for the Date field.

2 Select **(Custom...).**

The Custom AutoFilter dialog box appears.

3 Open the top left list box, and then select **>.**

4 Click in the top right text box and type **11/7/95**

5 Select the **And** button, if it is not already selected.

6 Open the bottom left list box, and then select **<.**

7 Click in the bottom right text box and type **11/18/95** as shown in Figure 7.15.

The selection criteria expressed in the dialog box are interpreted as "Show rows (records) where the Date field is greater than 11/7/95 and less than 11/18/95."

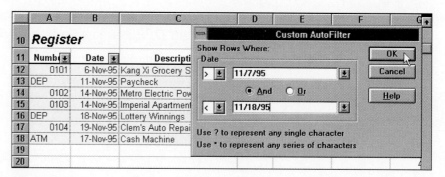

Figure 7.15

8 Select **OK** to complete the AutoFilter command.
The screen should now resemble Figure 7.16.

Figure 7.16

To turn off AutoFilter:

1 Choose **Data** and then **Filter**.

2 Choose **AutoFilter**.
The filter list box arrows should no longer be visible.

3 Press (CTRL) + (HOME)

4 Zoom to 75 percent magnification.

5 Turn off the status bar.

SORTING A DATABASE

Sorting rearranges the records in a database, putting them into a particular order according to what you specify as the *sorting key*. A key is the column or field that you want to be used as the basis for the sort. For example, the sorting key for a residential telephone directory is last name, because the records in the phone book are in ascending (alphabetical) order by last name.

A single sorting key often is not sufficient for a large database. For example, in a telephone directory, many people might have the same last name. What order should these people be listed in? The first key used is called the *primary key*, or 1st key; if another key is needed as a tiebreaker, it can be specified as a *secondary key*, or 2nd key. The 1st key for a phone book is last name, and the 2nd key is first name (a group of people with the same last name will be listed alphabetically by first name). Excel allows up to three keys, so a *tertiary key*, or 3rd key, may be specified if there are ties on both the primary and the secondary keys.

Excel's sorting command can be used on any worksheet data, not just on databases, but database sorting is certainly the most common application of the command. The *sorting range* should include all the records to be sorted; it can also include the field names, provided that they are formatted in such a way that Excel can tell the difference between them and the data records under them. If the field names are not distinguishable from data records, they will be sorted along with everything else. Though Excel can often automatically detect and select a list for sorting, in the steps that follow you will explicitly indicate the sorting range.

Tip Sorting can be a dangerous operation, because it shuffles so much data around in the worksheet. Before doing a sort, save the workbook. When you select a range of records to be sorted, make sure you extend the selection far enough to the right to include every field in the database—otherwise, the sort will break apart each record.

In the following steps, you will use the Name box to select the database range and then use the Data Sort command to complete the sort. You will sort the records by the check Number field. The 2nd key will be Date; that is, if a group of records have the same value in the Number field (for example, two records have the same DEP code), these records will be put in order by date.

To sort the database by the Number and Date fields:

1 Save the workbook.

2 Open the Name box in the reference area and select **Database**. You are not required to use a named range with sorting, although it can make sorting easier.

3 Choose **Data** and then **Sort.** The screen should resemble Figure 7.17.

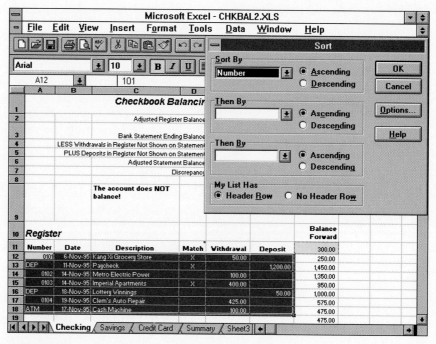

Figure 7.17

Because you want to sort first by the Number field, the first Sort By box is already correct. Notice also that the bottom of the dialog box indicates Excel has presumed that the selection to be sorted includes a field names row (called a header row).

4 Click the list-box arrow of the middle **(Then By)** box, select **Date,** and then select **OK,** as shown in Figure 7.18.

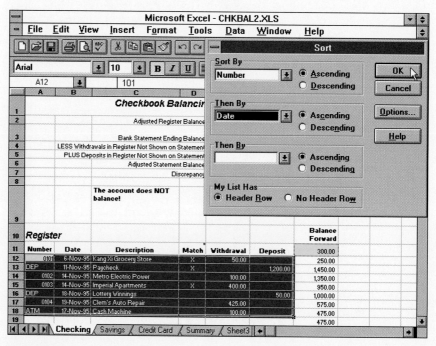

Figure 7.18

5 Press (CTRL) + (HOME)
The screen should resemble Figure 7.19.

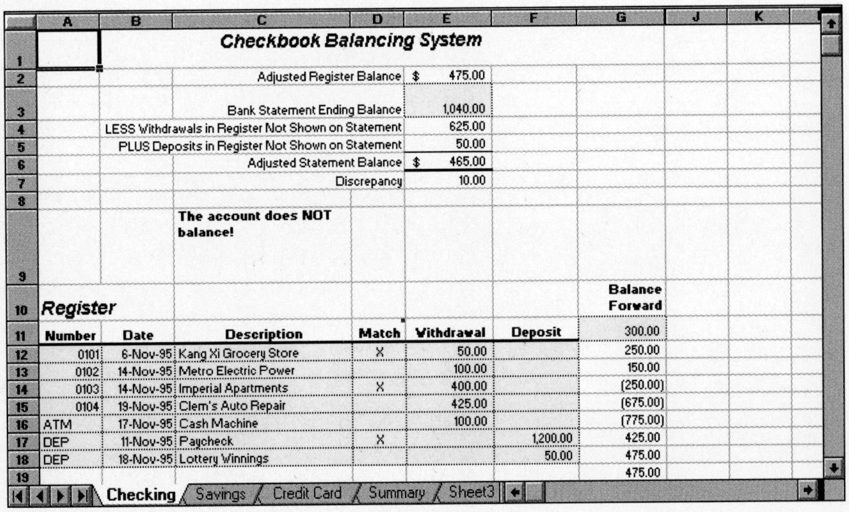

	A	B	C	D	E	F	G
1			*Checkbook Balancing System*				
2			Adjusted Register Balance	$	475.00		
3			Bank Statement Ending Balance		1,040.00		
4		LESS Withdrawals in Register Not Shown on Statement			625.00		
5		PLUS Deposits in Register Not Shown on Statement			50.00		
6			Adjusted Statement Balance	$	465.00		
7			Discrepancy		10.00		
8							
9			**The account does NOT balance!**				
10	*Register*						**Balance Forward**
11	**Number**	**Date**	**Description**	**Match**	**Withdrawal**	**Deposit**	300.00
12	0101	6-Nov-95	Kang Xi Grocery Store	X	50.00		250.00
13	0102	14-Nov-95	Metro Electric Power		100.00		150.00
14	0103	14-Nov-95	Imperial Apartments	X	400.00		(250.00)
15	0104	19-Nov-95	Clem's Auto Repair		425.00		(675.00)
16	ATM	17-Nov-95	Cash Machine		100.00		(775.00)
17	DEP	11-Nov-95	Paycheck	X		1,200.00	425.00
18	DEP	18-Nov-95	Lottery Winnings			50.00	475.00
19							475.00

Figure 7.19

The settings you made in the Sort dialog box, shown in Figure 7.18, can be understood this way: "Sort in ascending order by Number, then in ascending order by Date. My list has a header row (so don't sort the first row)."

Tip Excel's default sorting order is numbers, text, logical values, error values, and blanks.

The database is now in order based on the Number field. The last two records have the same value, DEP, in the Number field; these are put in order based on the secondary key, Date.

EXIT If necessary, you can save the workbook, quit Excel now and continue this project later.

USING COMMAND MACROS

As someone works with this checkbook register, he or she might want to sort the database in several different orders—alphabetically by description, by increasing date, by increasing number, or by match. You can simplify any repetitive task, such as using the Sort command, through the use of Excel ***command macros.*** A macro is actually a kind of computer program: a list of instructions that tells Excel to perform a sequence of commands and operations. The programming language used in Excel is called *Microsoft Visual Basic.*

When you create a macro, you give the macro a name. You can also assign a keystroke combination to the macro that will run or *execute* the macro when the user presses that combination. You can also create and assign customized buttons that can be used to run the macro. The convenience of a macro is in being able to have a series of operations performed by pressing a single key or by selecting an on-screen button.

The easiest way to create simple macros is to *record* them rather than to write them from scratch. Before you record a macro, you should think carefully about exactly what steps you want to perform while the recorder is on.

In the following steps, you will record a macro that sorts the database alphabetically by description. With Excel's macro recorder activated, you will perform the Sort command; everything you do while the recorder is on will be written into a macro. Once you have completed the sort, you will turn the recorder off and examine the macro. You can then run the macro at a later time.

To start the macro recorder:

1 Save the workbook.

2 Choose **Tools** and then **Record Macro.**

3 Choose **Record New Macro.**
The Record New Macro dialog box appears.

4 In the **Macro Name** box, type `SortByDescription`

5 Press `TAB` to select the text in the **Description** box.

6 For the macro **Description,** type `Sort check register by check Description field.`

7 Select **Options.**

8 In the **Assign To** section, select **Menu Item on Tools Menu,** and type `Sort By Desc` in the text box.

9 Select **Shortcut Key,** double-click in the **Ctrl +** text box, and type a *capital* **D.**
The edit box now reads `CTRL` + `SHIFT` +

10 Select **OK,** as shown in Figure 7.20.

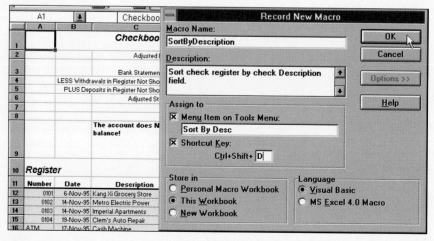

Figure 7.20

Notice that a floating toolbar containing a Stop Macro button has appeared: this button can used to stop the recorder once you are finished recording commands. Now every command you perform will be recorded. Carefully follow the next steps, which perform a sort with Description as the primary key, Date as the secondary key, and Number as the tertiary key.

To record the macro to sort by description:

1 Click in the reference area. Type **A1** and then press ⒺⓃⓉⒺⓇ
This explicitly records that you want to position to cell A1. By including occasional active-cell positioning within a macro, you can make it easier to follow later when the macro runs.

2 Open the Name box in the reference area and select **Database.**

3 Choose **Data** and then **Sort.**

4 Use the Sort dialog box to indicate that you want to sort first by description, then by date, and then by number.

5 Select **OK** to perform the sort, as shown in Figure 7.21.

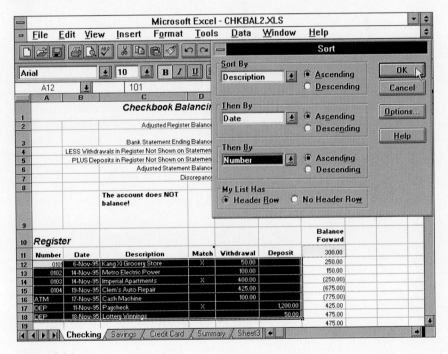

Figure 7.21

6 Click in the reference area. Type **A1** and then press ⒺⓃⓉⒺⓇ

7 Click the **Stop Macro** tool on the floating toolbar.

8 Save the workbook.

The steps you performed have been recorded into a *module sheet,* which is a document sheet designed to hold macros. Initially, a module sheet will be given the name *Module1* and will be placed after Sheet16 in the workbook. In the steps that follow, you will first delete the unneeded worksheets

(Sheet3 through Sheet16) and then activate the module sheet to examine the new macro.

To delete sheets:

1 Click on the **Sheet3** tab to select Sheet3.

2 Click the sheet-tab scrolling button to scroll to the last sheet tab.

3 Hold down (SHIFT) and click on the **Sheet16** tab.
The group of sheets from Sheet3 to Sheet16 is selected.

4 Choose **Edit** and then **Delete Sheet**.

5 Select **OK** to confirm the deletion.

6 Click the sheet-tab scrolling button to scroll to the left.
The Module1 sheet tab now appears after the Summary sheet tab.

To examine the recorded macro:

1 Select the **Module1** sheet tab.
The recorded text of the macro is now visible, along with the Visual Basic floating toolbar.

2 Save the workbook.
The screen should resemble Figure 7.22.

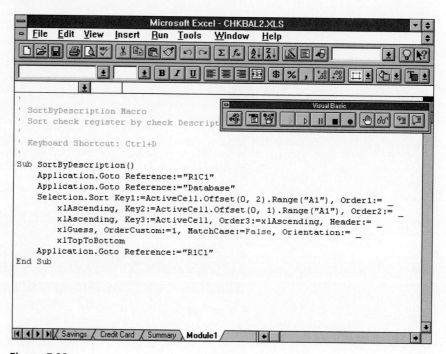

Figure 7.22

Examining a Recorded Macro

A macro describes a series of operations to be performed. Excel macros are composed mostly of statements that specify various Excel commands. In this project, you will record macros; writing macros using the statements directly is an advanced topic beyond the scope of this project.

The first several lines of the macro are each preceded by apostrophes and are colored green or appear in a different shade: these are called *comment lines*. When you run a macro, Excel will skip over comment lines. The first actual line of the recorded macro contains the text *Sub SortByDescription( )*. This means the macro's name is SortByDescription. Without understanding the details, you can still identify the portions of the macro that are concerned with selecting cells or ranges and those items that provide information regarding how to perform the sort. The end of the SortByDescription macro is marked by *End Sub*.

Running a Macro

You can run a macro by using the Macro command from the Tools menu, by pressing the macro's assigned key, by choosing the macro as a customized menu option in the Tools menu, or by creating a customized button and clicking that button.

Tip It's wise to save a workbook before running a macro, in case the macro does some damage to the worksheet.

To run the macro using the Tools menu:

1 Select the Checking worksheet.

2 Save the workbook.

3 Choose **Tools** and then **Macro.**

4 In the **Macro Name/Reference** section, select **SortByDescription.**

5 Select **Run,** as shown in Figure 7.23.

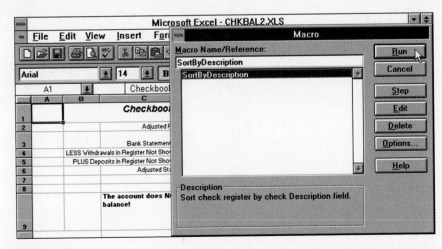

Figure 7.23

The macro runs, performing the same operations automatically that you recorded earlier. Because the database was already sorted by description, there isn't any real change to the worksheet itself.

To run the macro as a customized menu option:

1 Open the **Tools** menu.
Notice that the menu name you designated for the macro, *Sort By Desc,* is visible at the bottom of the menu.

2 Select **Sort By Desc.**
The macro runs.

To run the macro using the assigned key combination:

1 Press (CTRL) + (SHIFT) + D
The macro runs.

Creating Other Sorting Macros

What is really needed is a group of macros to sort the check register by various keys. In the following steps, you will create two more macros: one to sort by date and another to sort by Number. You will not bother to assign a key combination or menu option name to these macros, though you certainly could.

To record a macro to sort by date:

1 Save the workbook.

2 Choose **Tools** and then **Record Macro.**

3 Choose **Record New Macro.**
The Record New Macro dialog box appears.

4 In the **Macro Name** box, type `SortByDate`

5 Press (TAB) to select the text in the **Description** box.

6 For the macro **Description,** type `Sort check register by check Date field.`

7 Select **OK** to begin recording.

8 Click in the reference area. Type `A1` and then press (ENTER)

9 Open the Name box in the reference area and select **Database.**

10 Choose **Data** and then **Sort.**

11 Use the Sort dialog box to indicate that you want to sort first by date, then by number, and then by description.

12 Select **OK** to perform the sort, as shown in Figure 7.24.

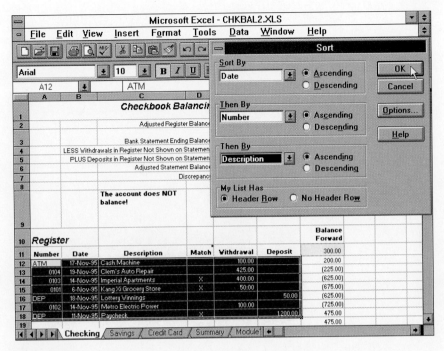

Figure 7.24

13 Click in the reference area. Type **A1** and then press (ENTER)

14 Select the **Stop Macro** tool.

15 Save the workbook.

To record a macro to sort by number:

1 Choose **Tools** and then **Record Macro.**

2 Choose **Record New Macro.**
The Record New Macro dialog box appears.

3 In the **Macro Name** box, type **SortByNumber**

4 Press (TAB) to select the text in the **Description** box.

5 For the macro **Description**, type **Sort check register by check Number field.**

6 Select **OK** to begin recording.

7 Click in the reference area. Type **A1** and then press (ENTER)

8 Open the Name box in the reference area and select **Database.**

9 Choose **Data** and then **Sort.**

10 Use the Sort dialog box to indicate that you want to sort first by number, then by date, and then by description.

11 Select **OK** to perform the sort, as shown in Figure 7.25.

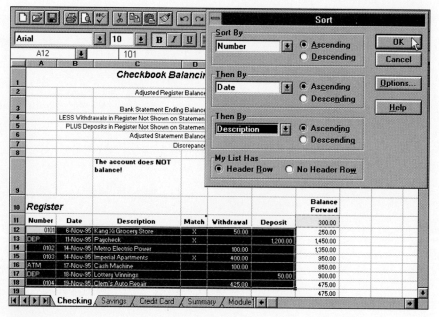

Figure 7.25

12 Click in the reference area. Type **A1** and then press ⟨ENTER⟩

13 Click the **Stop Macro** tool.

14 Save the workbook.

To examine the newly updated module sheet:

1 Switch to the module sheet.

2 Scroll down the sheet.

The three macros are very similar—the only difference should be the sort keys specified. The second two macros *could* have been created by copying and modifying the first macro, but recording is easier if you don't want to delve into the details of writing programs. In the following steps, you will try running each of the three macros.

To run the new macros:

1 Switch to the Checking worksheet.

2 Choose **Tools** and then **Options,** and turn off cell gridlines.

3 Save the workbook.

4 Choose **Tools** and then **Macro,** choose **SortByDate**, and then select **Run.**
The database should now be sorted by date.

5 Choose **Tools** and then **Macro,** choose **SortByNumber**, and then select **Run.**
The database should now be sorted by number.

Creating Customized Buttons

An alternative to using a macro key combination is to place a button (resembling a dialog-box command button) directly on the worksheet and assign a macro to the button. You can determine what the button text and format will be, as well as the button's size and location.

Creating buttons requires the Drawing toolbar. In this section, you will create three buttons—one for each macro—and place the buttons above the field names used for sorting.

To display the Drawing toolbar:

1 Increase the height of row 11 to 45 points.

2 Choose **View** and then **Toolbars.**

3 Select **Drawing** and then select **OK.**
The Drawing toolbar appears.

4 Drag the Drawing toolbar to the upper right of the worksheet area, as shown in Figure 7.26.

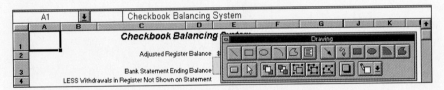

Figure 7.26

To create and assign a button:

1 Press (CTRL) + (HOME)

2 Click the **Create Button** tool on the Drawing toolbar.
The pointer changes to crosshairs.

3 Referring to Figure 7.27, drag the crosshairs to form an outline for the button above the Description column.

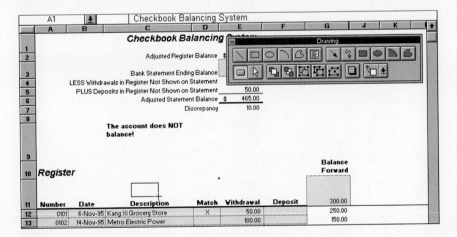

Figure 7.27

4 Release the mouse button.
An Assign to Macro dialog box appears.

5 Select **SortByDescription** and then select **OK** to assign the macro.
The button is currently selected; it has a dashed border and handles. When a button is selected, you can reposition and resize the button and change the text within it.

6 Select cell A1.

Now the button is not selected. If you position the pointer on the button and click, the macro assigned to the button runs.

7 Position the pointer on the button.

The pointer changes to a hand shape.

8 Click the button.

The macro runs, and the database is now sorted by the Description field.

If you want to reselect the button, to change its text or resize it, you can hold down (CTRL) and click the button.

To select and edit a button:

1 Position the pointer on the button.

2 Hold down (CTRL) and click.

The button is now selected.

3 Type **Sort**

The text of the button changes to *Sort*.

4 Select any cell away from the button.

The screen should resemble Figure 7.28.

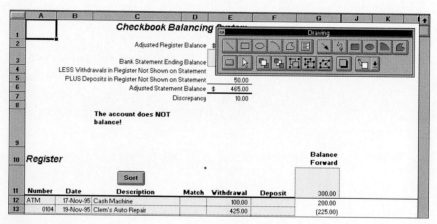

Figure 7.28

5 Use the button you created to run the macro again.

Two other Sort buttons are needed: one to place over the Number column and the other to put over the Date column. You can copy buttons; this is useful if you want to duplicate the exact size and format of a button. In the following steps, you will make two copies of the Sort button that you just created. You will then assign the other macros to the new buttons.

To copy a button:

1 Position the pointer on the customized Sort button, hold down (CTRL) and click.

2 Click the **Copy** tool on the Standard toolbar.

3 Select cell A11, and then click the **Paste** tool on the Standard toolbar.

4 Position the pointer so it is an arrow just touching any edge of the selected button. Drag the button so its outline is positioned over the Number column, as shown in Figure 7.29.

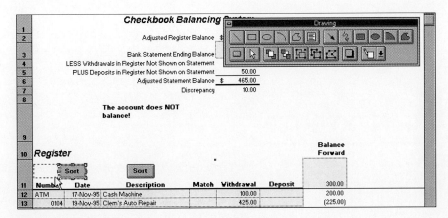

Figure 7.29

5 Release the mouse button.

6 Choose **Tools** and then **Assign Macro.**

7 Select **SortByNumber**, and then select **OK** to assign the macro.

8 Select cell B11.

9 Click the **Paste** tool on the Standard toolbar.

10 Position the button over the Date column.

11 Assign the macro SortByDate to the button.

12 Select cell A1 or any cell away from the button.

To test the customized buttons:

1 Close the Drawing toolbar.
The screen should resemble Figure 7.30.

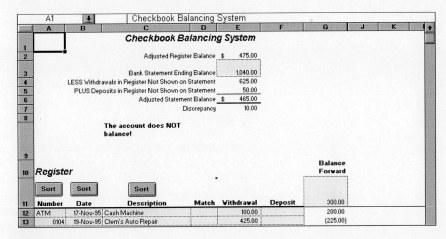

Figure 7.30

2 Try each customized sort button to make sure it works.

3 Save the workbook.

Now you can easily access the three sorting macros. If you feel that having three identical buttons (each labeled Sort) is ambiguous, you can create larger buttons with labels such as Sort By Description.

> **Tip** To delete a graphic object (such as a customized button), select the object first (with CTRL + click) and then press DEL.
> If you want a customized button to align to cell gridlines, hold down ALT while dragging the button.

THE NEXT STEP

You will occasionally create worksheets that can benefit from Excel database functions. Excel's primary value is as a spreadsheet program, however, and if your Excel databases grow large, you should consider using an application dedicated to database management.

Macros can be used to automate repetitive tasks in almost any worksheet, and as you build worksheets, you should look for opportunities to optimize them with macros. Macros should not, however, take the place of fundamental worksheet components such as well-designed formulas.

SUMMARY AND EXERCISES

Summary

- A database is a tabular list of information. Rows are called records, and columns are called fields. Each field has a field name, which in Excel is the title used to head the column.
- It is better to have more, simple fields than fewer, complicated fields.
- The Clear command can erase a cell's contents, format, note, or all of these.
- An Excel database range consists of the field names row and the data records below it. The database will grow downward provided the cells immediately below it are empty.
- Once an Excel database is defined, an automatic data form can be generated and used to add, change, delete, and search for records. The data form's Criteria option is used to specify search criteria.
- Databases can be searched so only those records that meet specific criteria are selected.
- Data filters are another method of restricting the view to only those records that meet search criteria.
- Databases can be sorted, that is the records can be put in a different order. The field used as the basis for ordering the records is called the primary key. If two records have the same value for the primary-key field, a secondary key may be used as a tiebreaker.
- The range to be sorted can include the field names row (provided it is distinguishable from the data records below it), and should extend far enough to the right to encompass all the fields of the database. You should always save before sorting.
- Command macros are a kind of computer program: they specify a sequence of operations for Excel to perform. You can record your actions and have them translated into macro form; this is easier than writing macros from scratch.
- Macros are stored in a module sheet, which is a separate document in the workbook.

- You can run a macro by using the Tools menu or by pressing the macro's assigned key combination. You should save the workbook before running a macro.
- You can create customized buttons and assign macros to them.

Key Terms and Operations

Key Terms
command macro
data filter
data form
database
database range
field
filter mode
module sheet
record (database)

search
sort
sorting key

Operations
Clear a cell
Define a database range
Record (executing) a macro
Run a macro

Study Questions

Multiple Choice

1. In an Excel database, a row of information is referred to as:
   - a. a field.
   - b. a record.
   - c. a form.
   - d. criteria.
   - e. a data list.

2. The database range consists of:
   - a. only the database records.
   - b. only the field names row.
   - c. the database records and the field names row.
   - d. the field names row and the first database record.
   - e. the first column of the database.

3. A hazard when using the Sort command is that:
   - a. It will not work on formulas.
   - b. It will scramble the list if the sort selection does not extend far enough to the right.
   - c. It will scramble the list if the sort selection does not extend far enough down.
   - d. Identical keys will cause the computer to "lock up."
   - e. You can only specify ascending sort order.

4. The interface between the database and the user is called the:
   - a. criterion range.
   - b. edit window.
   - c. information window.
   - d. input form.
   - e. data form.

5. The field or column that serves as the basis for a sort is referred to as the:
   - a. sort key.
   - b. sort criterion.
   - c. Sort Definition column.
   - d. sort button.
   - e. sort macro.

6. What is used as a tiebreaker to determine the ordering of records that have the same value for the primary sort key?
   - a. the secondary (2nd) key
   - b. the tertiary (3rd) key
   - c. the primary criterion
   - d. the secondary criterion
   - e. the fallback criterion

7. What command can be used to remove only the format of a cell (and not its contents)?
   a. Clear Formats from the Edit menu
   b. Erase from the Edit menu
   c. Clear from the Format menu
   d. Format from the Clear menu
   e. none of the above

8. What is automatically used by Excel to construct a data form?
   a. the first record of the database
   b. the criterion range
   c. the field names row
   d. the types of information stored in the last record
   e. a field names dialog box

9. What command is used to execute a previously created Excel command macro?
   a. Execute from the Options menu
   b. Execute from the Macro menu
   c. Run from the Window menu
   d. Macro from the Tools menu
   e. Macro Run from the Data menu

10. Macros are stored in what kind of document?
    a. a worksheet
    b. a workbook
    c. a module sheet
    d. a macro dialog box
    e. any of the above

Short Answer

1. The column titles in an Excel database are used to identify what database component?

2. What field(s) would be most appropriate for keeping track of people's full names?

3. The Yellow Pages uses what field as its primary key and what field as its secondary key?

4. What does an Excel database range consist of? Does this ever differ from a sorting range?

5. Can sorting be used outside the context of databases?

6. Can a recorded macro be examined and edited? If so, where is the macro stored?

7. What parts of a macro are ignored when the macro is run?

8. If a new record is added by means of a data form, will Excel adjust the definition of the database range?

9. How can you explicitly specify an Excel database range?

10. What tool is used to create customized buttons? On what toolbar is this tool found?

For Discussion

1. Why is sorting a dangerous operation? What steps can you take to minimize its hazards?

2. Explain the general steps involved in planning, recording, and executing a macro.

3. When you are designing a database, what principles should guide the specification of the database fields?

Review Exercises
Building a Macro to Sort by the Match Field

Record a macro (assign it the name *SortByMatch*) for CHKBAL2, which sorts the checkbook database by the Match field. Create a button, similar to the others already on the worksheet, to run the macro. Save the workbook before running the macro. This macro will be very similar to the macros you created in the project.

Building a Macro to Activate the Data Form

For CHKBAL2, record a macro that activates the data form in the Checking worksheet. Assign it the name *DataForm* and the key combination CTRL + SHIFT + F. After starting the macro recorder, choose Form from the Data menu. Then close the dialog box and stop the recorder. Create a button to activate this new macro and place the button in a convenient location on the worksheet. Save the updated workbook.

Assignments
Building Macros for Commonly Typed Text

One common use for short macros is to type boilerplate text, which is frequently used words or phrases. With a new workbook, create a macro assigned the name *MyName* and the key combination CTRL + SHIFT + N. Immediately after starting the macro recorder, open the Tools menu, choose Record Macro, and make sure that Use Relative References is checked. This will cause the recorder to interpret active-cell positions in a relative rather than an absolute form.

While the recorder is running, type and enter your full name in a cell, and then format the cell to appear in the Times New Roman font, with an italic font style and a size of 16 points. Then type your Social Security number in the next cell down. The lower cell should be formatted as Courier New, regular, and 12 point. Turn the macro recorder off.

Test the macro in various cells. Save the workbook under the name BLRPLT1.

Constructing a Movie Database

Listing movies is a natural and common application of databases for small computers. Make a database that lists your own top ten favorite movies or TV shows. Include fields for title, leading actor, genre, year produced, and any other aspect you want to track. Create macros for sorting the database. Save the workbook under the name MOVIE.

Constructing a Home Inventory

Design and construct a database that lists personal property. Such a database could be useful for insurance purposes. Include such fields as item description, brand, model number, quantity, date purchased, purchase price, replacement cost, and serial number. Write macros (with customized buttons) that allow the database to be sorted in several different orders. Save the workbook under the name PROPERTY.

Operations Reference

File menu	Dialog Box Tab	Description	Related Tools / Mouse Actions
New		Creates a new workbook containing (by default) 16 blank worksheets.	
Open		Opens a workbook file on disk.	
Close		Closes the current workbook.	Double-click in *workbook's* Control menu box.
Save		Saves the current workbook to disk.	
Save As		Saves the current workbook under a new name.	
Page Setup			
	Page	Adjusts the orientation (landscape/portrait) and scaling (magnification) of the printout.	
	Margins	Adjusts the margins and on-page centering of the printout.	
	Header/Footer	Specifies header and footer text.	
	Sheet	Specifies print area, print titles, printout grid lines, etc.	
Print Preview		Shows simulated printout pages on-screen.	
Print		Prints sheet(s) from workbook; also used to change printer.	
Exit		Exits (ends) the Microsoft Excel program.	Double-click in *Excel's (application) Control menu box*.

Edit menu	Dialog Box Tab	Description	Related Tools / Mouse Actions
Undo		Undoes the previous command or action (not always possible).	
Repeat		Repeats the previous command or action (not always possible).	
Cut		Removes information and places it in the clipboard.	
Copy		Copies information to the clipboard.	
Paste		Pastes information from the clipboard to a selection.	
Paste Special		Pastes formats, values, or other attributes of information from the clipboard to a selection.	
Fill		Copies information from one selection to a range of adjacent cells.	Make a selection and drag the fill handle; usually identical in effect to a combination of Copy and Paste. Hold down (CTRL) while dragging to prevent series fill.

Edit menu	Dialog Box Tab	Description	Related Tools / Mouse Actions
Clear		Erases contents and/or formats from a selection.	
Delete		Removes a selection and contracts worksheet.	
Delete Sheet		Removes an entire sheet from the workbook.	
Move or Copy Sheet		Changes order of sheets in workbook or duplicates sheets in workbook.	To move a sheet, drag its sheet tab; to copy, hold down (CTRL) and drag sheet tab.
Find		Searches for information in worksheet.	
Replace		Searches for and replaces information in worksheet.	
Go To		Positions to particular cell or named range.	Click in Name box at the left of the formula bar, and type or select address/name.

View menu	Dialog Box Tab	Description	Related Tools / Mouse Actions
Formula Bar		Displays/hides formula bar	
Status Bar		Displays/hides status bar	
Toolbars		Controls which toolbars appear; allows customization of toolbars.	Click the *right* mouse button while pointer is positioned on any toolbar's background.
Full Screen		Toggles full-screen view on/off.	
Zoom		Controls on-screen magnification of sheet.	

Insert menu	Dialog Box Tab	Description	Related Tools / Mouse Actions
Cells		Inserts a range of cells, shifting worksheet contents to make room.	
Rows		Inserts row(s) into worksheet, shifting other information down.	
Columns		Inserts column(s) into worksheet, shifting other information right.	
Worksheet		Inserts a new worksheet before current worksheet in workbook.	
Chart		Creates a chart (as new sheet or as embedded chart).	
Page Break		Forces a printout page break at current cell location.	
Function		Uses Function Wizard to step through building a function.	
Name		Creates named range or named constant.	
Note		Creates cell note.	

Format menu	Dialog Box Tab	Description	Related Tools / Mouse Actions
Cells			
	Number	Controls the appearance of values (formulas and numeric constants).	
	Alignment	Sets horizontal/vertical alignment and orientation of cell entries.	
	Font	Controls the typeface and type style of a selection.	

Border	Sets border lines for a selection.		
Patterns	Sets shading/colors of a selection.		
Protection	Controls whether cells in a selection are locked and/or hidden.		
Row	Controls height of row and whether row is hidden.	Drag bottom edge of row heading to change row height; double-click edge for "best fit."	
Column	Controls height of column and whether column is hidden.	Drag right edge of column heading to change column width; double-click edge for "best fit."	
Sheet	Sets name of sheet (on sheet tab); hides/displays sheet.	Double-click sheet tab to change sheet name.	
AutoFormat	Applies combinations of formats automatically.		
Style	Applies and defines cell styles (named sets of cell formats/attributes).		

Tools menu	Dialog Box Tab	Description	Related Tools / Mouse Actions
Spelling		Checks spelling.	
Auditing		Traces cell precedents, dependents, and errors; displays cell notes.	
Protection		Activates/deactivates sheet and workbook protection.	
Macro		Allows macros to be run or edited.	
Record Macro		Records commands into a macro.	
Options	View	Controls display of cell grid lines and various screen elements (e.g., status bar, formula bar, scroll bars).	
	Edit	Controls whether selection is changed after Enter is pressed; sets other editing features.	

Data menu	Dialog Box Tab	Description	Related Tools / Mouse Actions
Sort		Sorts information in database or other selection.	
Filter		Activates/deactivates database AutoFilter mode (to allow criteria to be used for controlling record display).	
Form		Activates database data entry form.	

Window menu	Dialog Box Tab	Description	Related Tools / Mouse Actions
Arrange		Arranges open windows.	
Freeze Panes		Freezes portion of worksheet so that portion is always visible.	

Help menu	Dialog Box Tab	Description	Related Tools / Mouse Actions
Contents		Displays table of contents for Help system.	
Search for Help On		Displays searchable, alphabetical index of all Help topics.	

Glossary

absolute cell reference A cell reference that does not change, even when the formula containing the reference is copied. Either the row, the column, or both the row and the column may be absolute. Examples: A$1, $A1, $A$1. Also called *absolute address*. Contrast with relative cell reference.

active cell The current, selected cell, as outlined by the thick border of the selection rectangle. The active cell is where the next action or command will take place. Its address is displayed in the reference area.

alignment How information (text or value) is oriented within a cell or range. Numerical values are usually right aligned, and text is either center or left aligned, though any choice of left, center, or right is possible. You can also wrap long text entries within a cell and center a title across a range of cells.

argument A piece of information provided to a function. Some functions, such as =NOW(), require no arguments; others require one or several. Multiple arguments are separated by commas, as in =IF(A3>5,1,0).

border A decorative line attached to one or more sides of a cell. A variety of line styles is available. Borders are a kind of format.

case sensitive A computer program or function within a program that distinguishes between capital and lower-case letters is said to be case sensitive. Case sensitivity can affect the outcome of sorting operations and formulas that perform logical tests.

category In charting, a category describes a certain circumstance for a variable, which means that a variable has a particular value under a certain category. The categories appear along the bottom edge (X-axis) of a chart. Each category is labeled with a category name.

cell The basic building block of an electronic spreadsheet; the intersection of a column and a row. Cells are referred to by indicating their column and row. A cell is a holding place where you can store information.

cell note Comment text attached to a cell. You can create both text and audio (sound) notes.

cell reference A cell's address, usually expressed in terms of the cell's column and row on the worksheet. For example, the cell at the intersection of column C and row 15 has the reference C15.

chart A graph that displays quantitative information visually rather than using text and figures.

chart sheet A document or sheet type in Excel, designed to hold a chart. A chart sheet can be linked to worksheets.

chart type The kind of graph or chart. Excel has 14 major chart types, such as pie chart, line chart, and column chart.

circular reference A formula which directly or indirectly refers to itself. Circular references are almost always mistakes. Example: the formula =0.08*C15 if contained in cell C15 would be a circular reference.

column The vertical subdivision of a worksheet; columns are labeled with letters of the alphabet.

command macro A kind of computer program written specifically to run within Excel. Simple macros consist of recorded Excel commands. Macros are stored in module sheets.

constant A number or text entry which does not change; information typed in literally rather than a formula.

copy To duplicate some or all of the contents of a cell or range.

customized number format A user-defined cell format designed to display specialized number entries in a particular form. Common examples include formats for serial numbers, telephone numbers, Social Security numbers, zip codes, and part numbers.

data filter A method of using logical selection criteria to restrict which records of a database are displayed on-screen. Records (rows) that do not match the criteria are hidden from view.

data form A dialog box designed to make entry of database records easier. The various fields of the database become text boxes within the dialog box.

data marker The graphic symbol used to plot information on a chart. Data markers include lines, bars, and other symbols.

data series A set of related data values or observations used in constructing charts. The gross national product for each of the years 1970 through 1990 is an example of a data series.

database An organized table or list of information. The rows of the database are called records and the columns are called fields.

date arithmetic Use of calendar dates in mathematical calculations. For example, Excel dates can be subtracted from one another to determine the number of days between the two dates.

date format A number format appropriate for the display of a calendar date.

defined name A user-created name that refers to a constant, a cell, or a range of cells. Defined names can make formulas and macros easier to read and understand. Also called *range names*.

dependent cells Cell (containing a formula) that depends on a particular cell for information.

embedded chart A chart contained within a worksheet. Contrast with chart sheet.

execute To run a program or macro; to cause the program or macro to perform the instructions that comprise it.

explode In pie charts, to emphasize a particular pie slice by pulling it out from the pie.

field Within a database record, a field is a specific category of information. For example, a personnel record will contain fields for Social Security number, first name, last name, street address, and so forth.

font A typeface; a kind of letterform. In Excel, each font has a name (such as Arial), a size (such as 12 point), and a style (such as italic). Font styles should not be confused with cell styles. Effects such as underlining and color can also apply to a font.

footer Information appearing on the bottom of each page of a printout.

format   The appearance of information within a cell. Font, alignment, and number format are among the more important aspects of a cell's format. **formula**   A kind of cell entry that performs a calculation. All formulas begin with an equal sign. Normally, the result of the formula (as opposed to the formula itself) appears within the worksheet. Formulas can automatically change their result if there are changes in the cells upon which they depend, and formulas are the main reason that electronic spreadsheets are so useful.

function   A built-in mathematical operation in Excel. There are hundreds of functions with many uses. Perhaps the most common function is SUM, which totals the values in a range of cells. Example: =SUM(A3:A7) sums the range of cells from A3 to A7.

header   Information appearing at the top of each page of a printout.

information window   A special window designed to provide additional information about the active cell in a worksheet. Information windows can be used to monitor such things as cell formats, protection, dependents, and precedents.

key   In database sorting, a key is a field used to determine the ordering of records. The primary, or 1st, key determines the major sorting order; records tied on their primary keys also can be ordered using a 2nd and 3rd key. In a telephone book, the 1st key is last name and the 2nd key is first name.

legend   On a chart, a legend shows how different colors and data markers correspond to the data series used to make the chart.

linked text   On a chart sheet, linked text is derived from a worksheet cell. If the original text changes in the worksheet, the linked text in the chart changes as well.

locked cell   A cell whose contents cannot be edited or replaced. A formula in a locked cell can change its result, however.

mixed cell reference   A cell reference in which only the column reference or only the row reference is fixed. Examples: A$1, $A1.

module (module sheet)
A sheet designed to contain Excel macros. Also called a macro sheet.

move   To remove information from one location and place it in another. Unlike copying, moving "picks up" the contents of a cell or range and places those contents elsewhere.

nonadjacent selection   A compound selection of multiple ranges. A nonadjacent selection need not form a rectangle or be composed of a single selected area.

number (number constant)   Numbers are constant numeric values (such as 3 or -1.9) and are a basic kind of cell entry.

pattern   The shading and coloring of a cell. A kind of format. **point (measurement unit)**   The basic unit of typographic measurement; a point is 1/72 inch. Used in describing the size of printed characters.

point (point mode)   A method of building formulas that reduces the need to keep track of literal cell references and instead allows you to use the mouse or arrow keys to "point" to the cells or ranges that will be referred to in the formula.

precedent cell   Cell upon which formulas in other cells depend. A change in a precedent cell can cause the result of a dependent formula to change.

priority   The relative "binding strength" of an Excel arithmetic operator. The priority of operators in a formula determines the order in which operations are performed. For example, because multiplication has higher priority than addition, the formula $=2+2*10$ has the result 22, not 40.

protection   Preventing the contents of cells in a worksheet from being modified. Protection is often used to ensure that formulas are not accidentally destroyed by the users of a worksheet.

range   A rectangular block of cells, identified by any two of its diagonal corner cells. A range can be as small as one cell or as large as the entire worksheet. Example: the rectangle of cells whose upper-left corner is A3 and whose lower-right corner is D5 is called A3:D5.

record (database)   A row of information in a database. A record is composed of fields.

relative cell reference   Within a formula, a cell reference that can change if the formula is copied. This is the default (standard) kind of cell reference in Excel formulas and is most often what will work best if a formula is copied. Contrast with absolute cell reference.

row   The horizontal subdivision of a worksheet. Rows are labeled with numbers.

selection   A group of cells that have been marked to be affected by a command or other action. Selection is usually done by dragging with the mouse, though several other methods are available.

sort   To rearrange information according to some ordering rule. Usually sorting is applied to Excel databases. See also key.

style (cell style)   A group of formats identified by a name. Several predefined but modifiable cell styles are available; you can also create your own cell styles.

text (text constant)   Data, usually consisting of words, that serves to identify parts of the worksheet or to store non-numeric information.

unlocked cell   A cell for which changes are allowed. Contrast with locked cell.

value   A number constant or a formula that produces a numeric result. Values can participate in arithmetic calculations.

workbook   The basic file type in Excel. Workbooks can contain sheets of various kinds: worksheets, chart sheets, and modules (module sheets).

worksheet (spreadsheet)   A table consisting of rows and columns of information, ideal for setting up calculations for a wide variety of applications. Originally implemented on green columnar paper, worksheets can now be manipulated with programs such as Excel.

wrap   To break a long line of text into two or more lines.

X-axis   The horizontal axis (usually the bottom edge) of a chart. The X-axis is often broken into the various chart categories.

Y-axis   The vertical axis (usually the left edge) of a chart. The Y-axis is often a numerical scale.

zoom   To magnify or reduce the view of a worksheet or chart.

Index

charts, 151–152
chart titles, 154–155
worksheets, 33–34
ISBLANK function 177–178.
See also Functions
Italics, 116, 117

Legends, 133, 140–141
Line charts, 132. *See also* Charts
Linkage, chart-worksheet,
143–144
Locking cells, 190–191
Lowercase, in formulas, 177

Macros
buttons for, 237–239
examining, 232–233
overview, 229–230
recording, 230–232, 234–
236
running, 233–234, 236
stopping, 231
storing, 6, 231–232
MAX function, 50. *See also*
Functions
Maximize button, 8
Memory, 30
Menu bar, 4, 6
MIN function, 50. *See also*
Functions
Minimize button, 5
Mixed cell references, 178–180
Module sheets, 231–232
=MONTH(A1) function, 169.
See also Functions
Mouse
ENTER with, 12–13
pointer shapes, 9–10
SHIFT with, 11
using with Excel, 3
Moving
cells, 42–43, 48
worksheets, 197
Multiplication, in formulas, 29

Names
for constants, 103–105
in formulas, 104–105
for macros, 229, 230, 233
for ranges, 123–124
for workbooks, 30
for worksheets, 34
Normal style, 76, 82
Notes, for cells, 189–190
=NOW() function, 169. *See also*
Functions
Numbers. *See also* Constants
entering, 25–26, 100–102
"magic" numbers, 102–103
numeric formats, 94–95,
113–116, 167–168
sorting by, 227–229, 235–
236
values, 24
Number sign (#), in too-narrow
columns, 25

Opening workbooks, 32, 35
Operators, arithmetic, 28–29
Orientation, print, 122–123
Outlines, 119–122, 136, 191

Page numbers and page count,
195
Palettes, 135–136

Panes, freezing, 194
Parentheses, for functions, 49
Paste command, 48
Patterns, cell, 191–192
Percent, in formulas, 29
PGDN and PGUP keys, 7, 8
Pie charts. *See also* Charts
building, 147–148
changing type, 150
exploding slices, 149–150
modifying, 148–149
uses for, 132, 147
Plus sign, 9, 29
PMT function, 50. *See also*
Functions
Pointer, mouse, 9–10
Point mode, 26
Points, measurement in, 72, 116
Precedents, 61, 62–64, 215
Printing
basic procedure, 73
charts, 144, 155–156
without gridlines, 73–76,
122
headers and footers, 195–
196
orientation, 122–123
portions of worksheet, 194–
195
preview, 142, 144
scaling printouts, 122, 196
Priority of operations, 28–29
Protecting cells, 190–191, 193–
194

RAM, 30
Ranges. *See also* Cells
clearing, 68
database, 212, 213, 215–216
defined, 10
functions for, 50
inserting, 65–66
naming, 123–124
selecting, 10–11, 12–13,
182–183
Recalculating worksheets, 28
Recording macros, 230–232,
234–236
Records, 211. *See also* Databases;
Data forms
Relative cell references, 49
Restore button, 4
Rows
headings, 5
height, 72
role in worksheets, 7
selecting, 11–12
titles, 43, 100
Running macros, 233–234, 236

Saving
basic procedure, 31–32
frequency of, 30
before modifying worksheet,
61
before running macro, 233
before sorting, 227
under another name, 32, 72–
73
Scaling, 122, 196
Scrolling, 5, 6–7, 8
Searching
databases
basic procedure, 219–220

with complex criteria,
220–221
data filters in, 221–226
defined, 211
for Help topics, 17–18
Selecting
cell ranges, 10–11, 12–13
columns or rows, 11–12
data entry via, 45–46
macro buttons, 238–239
nonadjacent selections, 12–
13
with quick selection, 182
single cells, 10
with tracking, 182, 183
worksheets, 13–14
Selection criteria (database),
219–221. *See also* Data filters
Series fill, 97–98, 97–98
Sheet tabs, 5, 6, 34–35, 195
SHIFT, 7, 11, 197–198
Sizing
charts, 142–143
databases, 216–217
windows, 4–6, 8
worksheets, 95–97, 122
Sorting databases
basic procedure, 226–229
default sort order, 229
defined, 211
macros for. *See* Macros
Sound, in cell notes, 189
Spelling, checking, 43–44
Spreadsheet programs, 2
Spreadsheets. *See* Worksheets
Standard Toolbar, 4
Starting Excel, 3
Status bar, 4, 6
Strings, 177
Styles. *See also* Formatting
changing, 76–77
custom cell styles, 192–193
examining, with information
windows, 81–82
numeric formatting and,
113–114, 170
overview, 76
Subtraction, in formulas, 29
SUM function, 50–52, 67. *See
also* Functions

TAB, 45, 193
Tab scrolling buttons, 6–7
Text. *See also* Constants; Footers;
Headers; Headings; Legends;
Titles
aligning, 71, 98–99, 118, 122
converting range to, 95
entering, 24
joining, in formulas, 29
spell-checking, 43–44
3-D charts. *See* Column charts,
3-D
Tiling windows, 80
Time, 195
TipWizard, 19
Title bar, 4
Titles
chart, 133, 140–141, 154–
155
column, 44–45, 97–99, 118
main, 42, 116–117
row, 43, 100

subtitles, 94–95, 117
Toolbars. *See also specific feature
or function*
overview, 4, 6
customizing, 83–85
hiding and placing, 14–16
returning to default settings,
85
ToolTip (mouse pointer), 10
Tracing precedents and
dependents, 61, 62–64, 215
Tracking, 182–183

Underlined text, 116
Undo command, 48
Unlocking cells, 190–191
Uppercase, in formulas, 177

Value command, 81

=WEEKDAY(A1) function,
169. *See also* Functions
Windows
application windows, 4
arranging, 80
freezing panes, 194
information windows. *See
Information windows*
switching between, 79
Workbook window, 4–6
Workbooks. *See also* Worksheets
overview, 6
closing, 32
names, in header or footer,
195
opening, 32, 35
saving. *See* Saving
working with multiple, 35
Workboook window, 4–
6. *See also* Windows
Worksheets. *See also*
Workbooks; Workbook
window
changing among, 6–7
changing view, 96–97, 106–
107
components, 7. *See also
specific component*
copying, 196–197
deleting, 232
formatting. *See* Formatting
inserting, 33–34
linked to charts, 143–144
naming, 34
navigating, 7
overview, 1–2
printing. *See* Printing
protecting, 191
rearranging, 34–35
recalculating, 28
relation of charts to, 134
scrolling, 8
selecting, 13–14
sizing, 95–97, 122
spell-checking, 43–44
transforming into databases,
212–216
working with groups, 197–
200

X-axis, 133

Y-axis, 133
=YEAR(A1) function, 169. *See
also* Functions

Zoom Control, 96–97